SECOND LINE RESCUE

SECOND LINE
RESCUE

Improvised Responses to Katrina and Rita

Edited by

Barry Jean Ancelet,
Marcia Gaudet,
and Carl Lindahl

University Press of Mississippi / Jackson

www.upress.state.ms.us

The University Press of Mississippi is a member
of the Association of American University Presses.

First printing 2013
∞
Library of Congress Cataloging-in-Publication Data

Second line rescue : improvised responses to Katrina and Rita
/ edited by Barry Jean Ancelet, Marcia Gaudet, Carl Lindahl.
    p. cm.
  Includes bibliographical references and index.
  ISBN 978-1-61703-796-2 (hardback) — ISBN 978-1-61703-797-9
(ebook) 1. Hurricane Katrina, 2005. 2. Hurricane Rita, 2005.
3. Disaster relief—Gulf Coast (U.S.) 4. Disaster victims—Gulf
Coast (U.S.) 5. Hurricanes—Gulf Coast (U.S.)—Social aspects .
I. Ancelet, Barry Jean. II. Gaudet, Marcia G. III. Lindahl, Carl.
  HV6362005.G85 S43 2013
  363.34'9220976090511—dc23   2012040174

British Library Cataloging-in-Publication Data available

Dedicated to all Gulf Coast citizens who
tended to their stricken neighbors with courage,
resourcefulness, compassion, and generosity.

In their honor, all royalties for this book will be donated
to the New Orleans Area Habitat for Humanity and the
Louisiana Coastal Protection and Restoration Authority.

Contents

PART TWO
Vernacular Self-Rescue: "Victims" Save One Another and Themselves

ERNEST J. GAINES

Preface

Where Have You Gone, New Orleans?

[From *National Geographic*, August 2006, 54–57.
Used with permission of Ernest J. Gaines.]

Editors' Note: Louisiana writer Ernest J. Gaines and his wife, Dianne, pro-vided a safe haven in their home in Oscar, Louisiana, (about 105 miles northwest of New Orleans and 25 miles northwest of Baton Rouge), for four-teen family members from New Orleans. Dianne's son, daughter-in-law, and granddaughter arrived the day before the hurricane and other family members shortly after. Her ninety-five-year-old uncle had been evacuated by boat from a high-rise building and taken to Baton Rouge where they found him at the LSU Pete Maravich Assembly Center. The Gaineses had a weekend home in New Orleans—Dianne's family home in Mid-City, built in 1903 and renovated by Dianne and her sister a few years earlier. It was a few blocks from Dooky Chase Restaurant and walking distance from the French Quarter. After Katrina, the house was flooded and two feet of water remained in the house for two to three weeks. The house had to be gutted and everything in it was lost.

Yes, New Orleans will bounce back. Taxis and buses and limousines will leave hotels and casinos, cutting in and out of traffic to deliver passengers to Louis Armstrong International Airport. They will pass by homes and apartments and offices and neighborhood grocery stores and neighborhood bars that had been, now gone but for the debris.

Yes, New Orleans will bounce back, because the taxis and buses and limousines will bring people back from Louis Armstrong airport to hotels and casinos, passing by the debris of Katrina. New Orleans will come back because the debris of homes and lives will eventually be cleared away from the streets, and the people in the taxis and buses, and especially those in limousines, will look out the window and forget what had been. Yes, after clearing all the debris of clothing and toys and furniture—refrigerators and TV sets and armoires and chifforobes (bought from Sears, Roebuck in the forties) and dressers and washstands and old pianos—and handbags and tricycles and broken dishes and dolls with one arm and no head and old laceless boxing gloves—after all this has been cleared away, New Orleans will come back.

New Orleans will come back after the old sidewalks and potholes in the streets have been repaired. Yes, New Orleans will come back after bulldozers have knocked down homes in the Ninth Ward and cleared away all remnants of the people who lived there. New Orleans will come back when streetcars run up and down St. Charles Street, and tourists won't be afraid of getting off anywhere. New Orleans will come back when infrastructure is back in place on streets like Gentilly, when trees and flowers like azaleas and camellias and magnolias are blooming again on Esplanade. New Orleans will come back when you can go to Dooky Chase and order your favorite Creole meal, and later visit Snug Harbor, where the bartender knows exactly how you like your martini. Yes, for some New Orleans will come back.

There will be times when you can cross Bourbon Street in front of traffic, knowing all the time they won't dare hit you because this is the Big Easy, and you can do anything you like. You can walk down Royal Street and look into antique shops, dreaming but never buying. Or you can go to Café du Monde for beignets and café au lait. There will be musicians out on the sidewalk—they may not be the same ones as before Katrina, but there will be music. And there will be the old carriages, driven by old men, with tired old mules, and you can go for a ride in the French Quarter or along the French Market.

Yes, New Orleans will come back after politicians have argued over what part of the city should be rebuilt, and what part of the city should not be rebuilt at all. There will be town meetings, and there will be private citizens screaming at politicians, but in the end New Orleans will be rebuilt. Let us not worry, there will always be New Orleans.

But I imagine stories of loss, and I wonder.

The Joseph sisters—so we will call them, for this is only a story—used to walk two miles to church every Sunday in starched white dresses and white hats and white gloves. They walked Indian style on the narrow, broken sidewalk, the older sister in front, the younger one a pace or two behind. Every Sunday they would go to the nine o'clock service. They would come back a couple of hours later, take off their neat white dresses, hats, and gloves, and put on everyday wearing clothes and sit out on the porch. But Katrina changed all that. The older sister drowned when six feet of water came into the house. The other sister was rescued and taken away. Some said she was taken to Houston, some said Detroit. Others said they believed she went to Atlanta, but they weren't sure.

Or imagine a man standing among the crowd on Canal Street watching the Mardi Gras floats go by. There were thousands of people, but the man remembered one voice, a little boy who called out to the floats: "Throw me something, mister, throw me something, throw me something, mister, throw me something." There were thousands and thousands of screaming voices, but the man remembered that one voice. Each time one of the revelers on the floats would throw something—a doubloon, a string of beads, a plastic horn, or a plastic whistle—someone else would get to the prize before the boy did. Then the man had the luck to catch a red plastic horn, but when he looked for the boy, the boy was not there. Who was that little boy? Where did he go? Why did he leave before he got his treasure? The man heard another voice behind him, a woman's, saying, "You gon' keep that little horn, mister? I got some beads for my little girl, but nothing for my little boy. He sure would like that little red horn."

That was years before Katrina. Two months after the storm, imagine this same man driving down South Claiborne Avenue, where he noticed a little red plastic horn on a pile of debris. He wondered if it could possibly be the same one he had given to the woman. No, no, it could not be. The people on the floats must have thrown thousands of those things since then. But he still wondered. What had happened to the woman? What had happened to her children? Were they alive, scattered all over the country, or were they dead?

There were other stories—true stories—just like these.

New Orleans, New Orleans, New Orleans, you will come back. But will you be my New Orleans, or the little boy's New Orleans, or the woman's New Orleans, or the Joseph sisters' New Orleans? I doubt it. Katrina and the politicians have made you a different New Orleans forever.

BARRY JEAN ANCELET, MARCIA GAUDET, AND CARL LINDAHL

Introduction

Second Line Rescue: Improvised Responses to
Katrina and Rita

There is, of course, the conundrum of custom in New Orleans. The ability not
merely to adapt but to improvise is itself inherent in all our notions of tradition.
Here, improvisation *is* the tradition. And we have all of us always known as much.
—**Brenda Marie Osbey**

Each second line is a living monument to the force and integrity of community.
—**Helen A. Regis**

This is not another book about what went wrong in the aftermath of Hurricanes Katrina and Rita. Rather, it is a book about what went right in
spite of it all. It is a book about improvised solutions in the spirit of the
New Orleans African American tradition of second lining. Traditionally,
the jazz musicians and mourners at funerals who were the official part of
a procession were the "first line," and the people who followed along or
beside the official processions were called the "second line." People join
in unofficially to strut, dance, and improvise their way along the route in
New Orleans jazz funerals, Mardi Gras parades, wedding marches, and
other processional events. In the city known for its parades and its music,
a second line parade—led by a brass band followed by people carrying
umbrellas and waving white handkerchiefs—can also be an event in itself,
wending its way unofficially through the streets.

Unlike many of the official responders, the vernacular rescuers represented here avoided getting stuck in the institutional traffic jam—in
the words of General Russel Honoré, they were not "stuck on stupid."
They improvised ways around the paralysis produced by a breakdown in

communications and infrastructure and the fears produced by erroneous or questionable reporting. It is no accident that residents of New Orleans, wherever they were, eventually looked to their ability to improvise a com- munity-affirming second line procession as a critically important indica- tion of social and cultural survival in the following years. This strategy of improvisation had helped them to survive, and the second line can serve as a living symbol of that survival. Even in other places along the Gulf Coast where the New Orleans tradition is not practiced, the improvisation and social solidarity that it represents are at the heart of their own rescue and recovery stories.

The essays, personal narratives, media reports, and field studies pre- sented here all have to do with vernacular responses that illustrate the difference between disastrously inept institutional responses and the practical, effective responses that emerge from the people themselves. Individuals and close-knit communities find solutions that come roaring forth to solve problems when institutions fail to address them adequately or even worse, paralyze any action to improvise solutions on the ground, and actually prevent things from getting done. Such was the situation in the aftermath of Hurricanes Katrina and Rita, which devastated the Loui- siana coast in August and September 2005.

The vernacular responses and solutions recorded in this book are rooted in south Louisiana's cultural historical background. It is no acci- dent that those who improvise in jazz, blues, second lines, Cajun waltzes, and zydeco two-steps also improvise to get people off their roofs. In addi- tion, the Mardi Gras, with its longstanding tradition of the carnivalesque, is all about subverting ineffective authority to accomplish what must be done—and south Louisiana culture is expert at carnivalesque approaches which were pressed into service in the absence of solutions from the official world. Typically, carnivalesque play inverts, subverts, and mocks authority in order to eventually reconfirm the status quo. In this case, the real work of rescue made instinctive, ingenious use of the strategies of play, as well as those of social cooperation to actually do what needed to be done.

Along with the stifling government response, the sensationalized media coverage added to the problem by creating panic often based on unfounded and unsubstantiated rumors. The reporting of unverified shootings and rapes as well as images of looting without any attempts at contextualization added to the problem. Tulane University professor Gaurav Desai expressed the frustration of many in Louisiana when he referred to the news coverage following Katrina as "the rhetorical Third Worlding of New Orleans and Louisiana" by the national media (6).

The pieces in this collection, about people who were directly involved in the events, give a remarkably different perspective on them. This inside perspective, until now, has been scattered in e-mails and other sources. We think it is important to gather them together to honor this alternate view of the events surrounding Katrina and Rita.

The first part of this collection deals with Gulf Coast rescuers from without: those who, safe in their own homes and neighborhoods, marshaled their resources to help their storm-stricken fellows. Many of these were first responders, those official and unofficial rescuers who went into flooded New Orleans and other Gulf Coast communities initially to get people out. This rescue mode evolved into the role of "second responders," those people who continued to improvise solutions to ongoing problems caused by evacuation and subsequent displacement. The pieces represent an eclectic collection of vernacular responders and the various ways in which responses were recorded. It includes some analysis and scholarly approaches, but it also includes direct responses and first-hand field reports from those in the midst of the crisis.

In many cases—especially where governmental institutions thwarted vernacular aid from outside—the "victims" themselves were the first responders. The second part of the book features the words of hurricane survivors displaced from New Orleans and other Gulf Coast communities to Houston, Texas. In 2006 and 2007, they recorded their storm stories for fellow survivors, in humble tones that always understated their personal heroism while extolling the courage and resourcefulness of the family members, friends, and strangers with whom they weathered the storm. Some of these survivors were trapped in their homes when Hurricane Katrina hit; others had evacuated beforehand. Both groups suffered devastating loss and displacement, and both relied upon the inner strengths of their community culture to survive, adapt, and then refashion their lives in a foreign environment.

As much as the stories of the "outside" and "inside" responders may seem to differ at first glance, all of the stories recorded here bespeak a shared history of close-knit community bonds and survival skills sharpened by hard times.

While there are some photographs of the events presented here, there are not many simply because both self-rescuers and outside rescuers were focused primarily on the pressing issues of the moment. This book is not intended as a photo documentary of these events. In the midst of the disaster, the focus was on surviving the present, not documenting it. The photos included provide coincidental illustration of some of the activity that a few responders encountered. Most of the images that capture the actual events resulted from photography just as vernacular as the rescue efforts they depict. In a way, the fact that these rescuers did not produce more photographs is an indication that they were focused on the right thing.

Note: As we were reading the copy-edited manuscript for this book, Hurricane Isaac hit the Louisiana and Mississippi coasts, reaching New Orleans on August 29, 2012, the seventh anniversary of Hurricane Katrina. Though Isaac did not have the force of Katrina, it was clear that significant things had been learned from the Katrina experience. Preparations were in place, the reinforced levees held in the New Orleans area, the media did a much better job, and there was recognition of the importance of vernacular rescuers in parishes where the levees, unfortunately, could not hold back the floodwaters. In Plaquemines Parish, a father and son team (both named Jesse Shaffer) rescued one hundred twenty neighbors with their boats.

SOURCES CITED

Desai, Gaurav. 2005. Member to Member: In the Aftermath of Hurricane Katrina. *MLA Newsletter* (Winter): 5–6.

Osbey, Brenda Marie. 2008. One More Last Chance: Ritual and the Jazz Funeral. In *Louisiana Culture from the Colonial Era to Katrina*, ed. John Lowe, 286. Baton Rouge: Louisiana State University Press, 2008.

Regis, Helen A. 1999. Second Lines, Minstrelsy, and the Contested Landscapes of New Orleans Afro-Creole Festivals. *American Anthropology* 14: 472–504, 482.

PART 1

Vernacular Responders

In the Eye of the Storms and Afterward

BARRY JEAN ANCELET

Storm Stories

The Social and Cultural Implications of Katrina and Rita

Monday morning as Hurricane Katrina made landfall in St. Bernard and Plaquemines Parishes, my family and I watched the grim reports on television. Storm-chasing reporters gave us a direct view of nature's wrath, making the barely balmy weather we saw from our own windows from our home just outside Lafayette, about 120 miles west, seem surreal. As the day progressed, initial reports concerning New Orleans seemed relatively promising. The storm had drifted slightly to the east. The city was battered but the levees had apparently held. Only later did the grim news emerge that three levees had breached and the city was rapidly flooding. Only later did the even grimmer news emerge that the lack of emergency response was further deteriorating an already horrible situation. Those who had managed to evacuate were pouring into shelters and homes throughout south Louisiana and beyond.

Nearly everyone I know scrambled to help in any number of ways. We responded instinctively in ways that have been filtered through perspectives we have developed over several centuries. Thousands of people immediately culled their closets to provide clothing and bedding for the seven thousand evacuees in Lafayette's Cajundome and dozens of other improvised shelters until the Red Cross supplies began to arrive. People who love to cook for large gatherings showed up to cook. Every remotely mobile makeshift cooking contraption was mobilized to barbecue and boil and grill and fry food until the MREs began to arrive. Schoolteachers and artists went in to read and work with the children there. My wife and I sorted and distributed donated clothing for several days. My own two eldest sons Jean and François had just started at LSU Medical School in New Orleans. They had evacuated Sunday and were with us; both joined the relief effort on Tuesday and went back into the city. Jean had worked for Acadian Ambulance before leaving for school; he called and rejoined them. François joined a flotilla of small boats that headed to New Orleans to help rescue the stranded. After he returned to Lafayette, he served for a couple of weeks as a regular medical support volunteer at the Cajundome.

A few weeks later, Louisiana was hit again by another catastrophic storm, Hurricane Rita. Much of Cameron Parish was destroyed. The one intact building there was the same courthouse that survived Hurricane Audrey that had hit almost the exact same spot in 1957. Vermilion Parish south of LA 14 was swamped by a late storm surge that came after the eye had made landfall farther to the west. The cattle, cane, and fishing industries there were devastated. Most of Calcasieu and parts of Jeff Davis Parishes were severely damaged by the winds and torrential rains. Nearly six months later, many places were still without power. The issues of cultural and social continuity in these places have attracted less attention from the national media than the more familiar New Orleans (though several reporters and news researchers naïvely asked me if these storms will mean the end of Cajun culture), but they are no less important to consider.

As a folklorist, I found myself wondering what we could do in response to such situations. Obviously, we can help people and institutions to consider and understand the cultural and social implications of such catastrophic events, in the short term as well as the long term. So colleagues from the area, including Marcia Gaudet, John Laudun, Ray Brassieur, Susan Roach, and Maida Owens, started to think about it and talk about it. Nick Spitzer relocated temporarily to Lafayette and contributed greatly to the local and national discourse. Carl Lindahl was in contact from Houston, where he volunteered at the Astrodome, and as always, inspired us with his unfailingly moral and socially conscious concerns, working with displaced survivors there and teaching them to document their own stories.

As folklorists, we know that even a seemingly tiny rip in the transmission of tradition can contribute to the irretrievable loss of that tradition (c.f. Mire 1990). This is what some of these areas have faced in the aftermath of the storms. New Orleans, a cultural engine that has generated so much of the popular culture we enjoy throughout America and the world today, from jazz to the blues to rock to funk, from Creole cottages to Creole cuisine to Creole art, will undoubtedly be rebuilt in some version, but everyone is wondering how the massive displacement of an entire city population will affect that city's cultural and social continuity.

New Orleans has experienced a number of calamities that have threatened its existence. It burned twice during its early days, and twice nearly half the population died of yellow fever. It has survived countless hurricanes back to a time long before they had names like Betsy and Camille and Katrina. It has survived floods, like the ones in 1927 and 1940 and 1980. It has survived corruption of epidemic proportions among its politicians and police officers. The culture and social structure of the city have proved to be miraculously resilient throughout history, rebuilding and evolving in ways that the most clever folklorists, ethnomusicologists, and cultural anthropologists could never have anticipated. This is happening again. Some form of creolized culture is emerging from the sludge and wrecked buildings. Two bars in the French Quarter, which did not flood, returned to continuous operation as soon as the winds died down.

There have been other massive migrations (forced and unforced) that have affected the culture and social structure of this nation. The fact that there are people of so many races and ethnicities on this continent is the result of the long-term immigration of Europeans, Africans, and Asians. After the Revolutionary War, the descendants of those who first established the original thirteen colonies headed west across the Appalachians, often brutally displacing the Native Americans who lived there (Jackson [1881] 1995). After the Louisiana Purchase and the War of 1812, new waves of people poured into the middle of the country. The Indian Removal Act of 1830 was used to force untold numbers of Native Americans from their homelands to strange lands across the continent, including the Cherokee who were sent down the infamous Trail of Tears to Oklahoma. After the Civil War, untold numbers of former slaves headed north, while many in the rest of the country headed west. After the Great Flood of 1927, southerners again headed north. During the Great Depression, people from the dust bowls and the South once again headed out in all directions. After World War II, rural folks headed into cities. Each time, those who were migrating brought with them aspects of their culture. They influenced and were influenced by their new contexts in ways that eventually came to be part of the ever-evolving cultural scene. For example, places like Chicago and New York became important centers for new versions of imported blues and jazz, Detroit eventually produced Motown, and Bakersfield and Austin became the homes of fascinating country music alternatives. More specifically to Louisiana, Cajuns and Creoles flocked to southeast Texas and Houston and the Bay Area of California in the early part of the twentieth century, establishing dancehalls and restaurants that featured music and food from South Louisiana with new twists and twangs. During the oil bust of the 1980s, Cajuns and Creoles sought employment and shelter in urban centers such as Atlanta and Denver, where they also continued to celebrate their music and food.

The current displacement of people from New Orleans will produce new cultural combinations that we cannot even imagine yet. There are Yats (named for the native New Orleanian question, "Where y'at?") and Ninth Warders who have been evacuated to places such as Phoenix, Salt Lake City, and Cape Cod. How long they stay there will be anyone's guess. Some insisted on returning as parts of New Orleans have been dried out, cleaned up, and rebuilt. Others may prefer to stay to take advantage of what may be a vast improvement in job and housing opportunities. Real-life counterparts of Ignatius Reilly (antihero of Toole's *A Confederacy of Dunces*), forced out of their familiar neighborhoods for the first time ever, are finding that the world has interests they never knew. Meanwhile, some of the meanest streets of New Orleans, the projects and poorest neighborhoods most adversely affected by the storm and subsequent flooding are being bulldozed and cleared for a new start, or abandoned. Initial reports suggested that an aerial view of New Orleans would eventually look more like it did a century ago with the city huddled toward the bend in the river and on its natural ridges; nevertheless, many are resettling some neighborhoods that were flooded. The Superdome was renovated to serve both the city and tourism again. These new spaces are refilling with new growth. And that growth is guided by forces that are constantly being improvised. Given the city's track record, there is a good chance that this improvisation will produce results that are surprising and surprisingly effective. But there will undoubtedly be national and international forces and interests playing into the mix as well. Many continue to wonder aloud if New Orleans will ever be the same. The question is, the same as what? New Orleans culture has always been improvised and creolized in ways that are as wonderfully unanticipatable as jazz riffs. The cultural process will likely continue even if the cultural products it produces change. On a tragic-comic note, one wonders if Fats Domino will wince each time he sings "Let the Four Winds Blow" and one wonders if patrons of Pat O'Brien's will be able to enjoy their signature drink, the Hurricane, without thinking of Katrina.

In the places where displaced New Orleanians have landed with enough critical mass, they may manage to maintain a significant degree of cultural continuity. There have been other examples of this phenomenon. Consider an example from a neighboring society: according to historian Carl Brasseaux, roughly 50 percent of the French peasants who eventually became the Acadians came from a twenty-mile radius around Loudun in northern Poitou province (Brasseaux 1987). This demographic fact, which was determined after an exhaustive examination of early colonial records, helps to explain the intensely resilient cultural and social identity of the Acadians. When the British exiled them from Nova Scotia in 1755, it was with the expressed intent of dispersing them among the British colonies so that they might be absorbed and acculturated. This did not happen. Instead of eliminating the Acadian identity, the exile galvanized it. Those Acadians who arrived in Louisiana between 1764 and 1788 were expected to dissolve into French Creole society. This did not happen. They preserved their cultural and social specificity well past the French and Spanish periods. Under pressure from the fierce nationalism that accompanied World War I, they were expected to melt in the American pot. This did not happen. Cajuns found ways to negotiate the mainstream and continue to celebrate their traditions and language. Those living in the southwestern parishes recently affected by Rita were there because they returned and rebuilt after Audrey.

Something like this is likely among the New Orleanians who are currently adrift in America. Instead of no New Orleans, we may end up with many little New Orleans. The likes of the Nevilles and the Meters and Dr. John and Fats Domino and the Wild Tchoupitoulas will not go gentle into that good night. The inevitable funerals are followed by jazz parades. But what makes New Orleans culture what it is comes from the often untidy but wildly fecund creolization process that has occurred there based on the city's blend of ethnicities and races. Hopefully, representatives from all parts of that magical mix will be able to gear it up again. (A recent poll suggested that as many as 40 percent may never return, but polls are probably as useful and accurate in this endeavor as in political campaigns.) It is also important, as Nick Spitzer pointed out in an *All Things Considered* interview on September 9, 2005, that the off-Bourbon scene in the neighborhoods must be considered as well. Much of what makes New

Orleans sound and look and taste the ways it does comes from that eclectic local scene. The big operations have a lot of momentum behind them.
The French Quarter, which did not flood, was up and running within a
few weeks after the storm. The Café du Monde reopened with much press
attention and fanfare by mid-October 2005. The Fairgrounds, a continu-
ously operating thoroughbred racetrack since 1872, regrouped. The Saints
played in LSU's Tiger Stadium in Baton Rouge in 2005; they were back in
the Superdome in 2006, and eventually won the 2010 Super Bowl, reener-
gizing the city in the process. The New Orleans Jazz and Heritage Festival
geared itself back up in time for its April 2006 dates, with superstars such
as Bob Dylan pitching in to celebrate the survival of New Orleans music.
But what about the neighborhood bars and clubs all over town?

In the case of Mardi Gras, most of the biggest institutionally organized
parades geared back up in time for the 2006 season despite considerable
criticism from certain segments of the society. (On the one hand, critics
wondered about the appropriateness of throwing a party in the midst of
the devastation. On the other hand, Mardi Gras has always been about
community affirmation, and so it may have been a most appropriate way
to express the desire and commitment of many to return and revive the
city.) The more improvisational neighborhood krewes and the Mardi Gras
Indians took to the streets as well to perform some version of their annual
community affirming rituals.

The people who had the easiest time returning to the city were the
ones with money and resources. As the place was dried up and cleaned
up and the infrastructure went back up, many returned to rebuild. But at
the other end of the socioeconomic spectrum, those who were eventually
evacuated too far away after way too long from places like the Civic Center
and the Dome have had as hard a time returning as they did getting out,
for the same economic reasons. According to a recent poll, as many as 40
percent have expressed a desire to remain where they are now, having discovered educational, economic, and social opportunities that they could
not have previously imagined. New Orleans is reviving, but if a significant
part of the cultural mix is missing, it cannot and will not be the same. The
storm did not only rip off the roofs of buildings in the city. It also ripped
the cover off of the poorest parts of town, exposing the hopeless cycle of
crushing poverty there for the entire nation and the world to see. There
is no getting that cat back into the bag. The problem can no longer be
ignored. In the aftermath, the cover has also been ripped off of the longstanding history of police brutality and corruption in New Orleans. While
there were certainly many NOPD officers who acted heroically despite a

lack of communications and resources during and after the storm, others were caught looting businesses and abusing victims. In one case, police officers apparently stole and sold over two hundred cars from a local lot. In now-infamous footage, network news organizations caught police officers brutally beating an elderly man and attacking a reporter in the Quarter. The new police chief's insistence that the attack was not racially motivated was disingenuous or misinformed. Those who know New Orleans know that these things are unfortunately not unusual in this city that has been plagued with civil rights abuses by the police at least as far back as the 1891 lynching of Italian Americans in the New Orleans jail by Irish American supporters of the recently slain police chief David Hennessy. More recently, the Algiers case, the Len Davis case, and many others have kept civil rights attorneys, including my friend Mary Howell, quite busy in the Big Easy for decades. The difference in this case, of course, was the presence of dozens of journalists and news crews who were recording and reporting on what was going on. As we sort out these difficulties among those who make it back, things could even change for the better. But these events will be part of the story as well.

Folklorists must also remind everyone that New Orleans was not alone in the Katrina tragedy. The Mississippi and Alabama gulf coasts have their own complex and fragile cultural, social, and ecological systems that are still adversely affected. Jefferson and St. Tammany Parishes west and north of the city were devastated. Much of Plaquemines and St. Bernard Parishes below New Orleans remains virtually uninhabitable. The traditional culture of loggers, shrimpers, commercial fishermen, oystermen, cane and citrus farmers, oil field workers, and countless other occupations is jeopardized by a significant loss of context, as is the traditional culture, not only of Creoles and Cajuns, but also of Isleños, Yugoslavs, Vietnamese, Cambodians, and many other groups. And then came Rita, disrupting the lives of everyone in southwestern Louisiana, including many of the same traditional occupations, along with cattlemen and rice farmers. Towns such as Delcambre and Erath were without many basic services for several months as a result of the storms. In Intracoastal City, oil-related businesses are still struggling to come back. Commercial shrimpers and crabbers, lacking the outside resources of big oil, are having a harder time. And all of this was compounded, of course, by the BP oil spill of 2010.

Another thing folklorists can do is listen to the stories, record them, and try to derive from a collection of them the story of these events in ways that may not otherwise be considered. An important part of these disasters and the response to them will be found in countless stories from victims and volunteers. While working in the Astrodome, Carl Lindahl noticed that the people there needed to tell someone the story of what had happened to them. I noticed that various volunteers from the Lafayette area also needed to tell their stories of frustration and success. Historians and folklorists at my university, including public history graduate student Jason Foster and retired English professor Ann Dobie, gathered oral histories to document as much of this process as possible so that there will be a record of it for future consideration. Dobie eventually gathered her research in a book, *Fifty-eight Days in the Cajundome Shelter.* Faculty members and students of Tulane, UNO, Southern NO, Loyola, Delgado, and Xavier, where the entire fall semester of 2005 was canceled, undoubtedly have their own stories to tell and collect.

As I considered collecting the storm stories I was hearing, I found myself instinctively attracted to the stories that were being told by rescuers and others who had tried in various ways to help. Their stories were consistently about getting around institutional inertia. They represented the power of vernacular responses and of creolized solutions. I have long been interested in heroic action. When faced with a challenging situation, one either does the right thing or not, and forever afterward, that will always be what that person will have done or not done. Otherwise ordinary people can sometimes instinctively react in extraordinary ways to solve problems. Conversely, people who are in positions of power and authority can sometimes act badly or simply fail to act. The heroes in these storm stories had many characteristics of the counterculture's trickster hero, long admired by Cajuns and Creoles alike.

The effects of Katrina and Rita were terrible. But nature is what it is; these storms had no more evil intent than the Lisbon earthquakes of 1755, which generated much discussion about "natural evil" among the French *philosophes* of the eighteenth century. Contrary to the suggestions of some televangelists, this storm did not represent the wrath of God (Wise 2005), as Comedy Central's faux newsman Stephen Colbert suggested with his tongue firmly in cheek. There is also little anyone in government could have done to prevent the damage of such intense winds and tidal surges, though the quality of the levees is a different issue. The real problem in this case was the human response following the natural disaster. As events unfolded, it became clear that the institutional response to this catastrophe was woefully inadequate and inept. Governmental agencies at the state and federal levels seemed incapable of generating any momentum or traction in the relief effort (Thomas 2005). Indeed, spokespersons at various levels seemed incapable of understanding or articulating what should be done. FEMA director Brown and Homeland Security secretary Michael Chertoff remained confused in interview after interview following the storm, despite President Bush's assertion that they were doing "a fine job." (Someone suggested to me that we might have been better served by a LeBlanc than a Brown.) Many died not as a result of the storm but as a result of neglect in its aftermath. Two institutional exceptions mentioned by many who were affected, as well as those who participated in the improvised rescue efforts, were Louisiana Wildlife and Fisheries and the Coast Guard, both of whom quietly but effectively reached and rescued thousands.

As Rita approached, the evacuation rate among storm-wary residents of Cameron, Calcasieu, and Vermilion Parishes was right at 100 percent, as much due to the still vivid memory of Audrey in 1957 as to the more recent effects of Katrina. There was widespread devastation from winds and storm surge, but virtually no casualties. And the high water there was salty but not polluted and receded in a timely fashion, allowing the mostly rural residents to return to deal with their own ruined homesteads and businesses in ways and with resources that were remarkably different from those of their urban counterparts.

A cultural response that tried to do some good surged instinctively from the communities within and around the city. There were undoubtedly some looters who were only out for their own gain, the ones the media focused on who were carrying off television sets and new tennis shoes. During his rescue effort, UL graduate student Jason Foster even found some young men joy riding in stolen post office trucks instead of using them to haul their neighbors out of the flooded city. But there were many others who recognized the desperation of the situation and took matters into their own hands to help the members of the families and their communities, commandeering and redistributing available resources, as they put it, especially food, water, and medical supplies. People from nearby areas headed to the city with any resources they could put their hands on. Many Cajuns and Creoles, for example, improvised rescue efforts. We did this for reasons that come from far back in our history.

The French settlers who became the Acadians learned quickly in their new frontier context to depend only on their own efforts (Brasseaux 1987). They were apparently the first European settlers in the New World to vote, filling what was essentially a power vacuum produced by a lack of *seigneurs* and governmental authorities. They arrived in what is now Nova Scotia between 1632 and 1642 and already by the 1650 census several heads of household ran the census takers off telling them the information they were seeking was none of their business. With their colony punted back and forth between England and France until 1713, they learned to ignore what colonial authority there was, continuing to trade with New France while under English rule and with New England while under French rule. The Cajuns, heirs of this fierce sense of independence, have continued to depend on their own self-sufficient strategies for survival in Louisiana (Brasseaux 1992; Ancelet 1991). Black Creoles also have a history based on improvising solutions. A tight social co-op system has enabled them to survive by networking the community's resources.

Cooperative *boucheries* provided fresh meat regularly to community members before refrigeration. *Ramasseries* gathered community members to bring in a sick neighbor's crop. Barns and houses were often raised by a gathering of neighbors and family members. Benefit dances gathered contributions for those in need. It is with this sense of social cooperation that we have responded to previous disasters, including Audrey, Betsy, Hilda, Juan, Ivan, and Lili. In 1992, Andrew roared through southern Florida destroying among other places the town of Homestead. Essentially a retirement community, many residents there did not have a wide social safety net of nearby family members and were dependent on the emergency services provided by the various levels of government. When the storm entered the Gulf, restrengthened, and hit Morgan City, Franklin, and New Iberia, emergency response teams were on hand anticipating the worst. Although many were grateful for the assistance, Red Cross teams and others found that many others declined help, explaining that their families were already on hand to help rebuild.

In the wake of both storms, people from south Louisiana instinctively reacted the same way we always have, driven by a longstanding survival strategy based on the vernacular power of social cooperatives. To be fair, this can-do vernacular power strategy is also characteristic of what is best about America in general. The frontier taught us all the value of working together to improvise solutions. What did not work in this case was the institutional response, which seemed to be paralyzed into inaction by several factors, including apparent ineptitude and a complete breakdown in communications. This institutional inertia made improvised rescue efforts much more difficult than necessary. For example, after Katrina, it was clear from news reports that people were surrounded by water and needed to be rescued. There is a standing armada of small, flat-bottomed fishing boats in Cajun country, where the real measure of success is not the number of cars one owns but the number of trailers. (A person with a boat trailer, a horse trailer, and a cooking contraption trailer is greatly admired.) Tuesday after the storm, when it was clear that the levees had broken and thousands of people were stranded, and that institutional resources were failing to arrive, a call went out in the Lafayette area for small boat owners to gather at the Acadiana Mall and to convoy to New Orleans to help in the rescue operation. They were told to show up in pairs, preferably with at least one paramedic or other first responder per boat, with lights and ample supplies of gas, water, and food. When they arrived at the I-10/610 split, they ran into utter chaos, driven primarily, it seems, by a lack of communication (Thomas 2005). Clearly no one was in charge, but those who were there, including Red Cross and military personnel, city and state police, all told the Cajun flotilla volunteers that they could not go into the water. Reasons varied: it was too dangerous, people were shooting, they might be looters, their boats were too big. Many of the boaters were turned back. A few persisted; those that eventually reached the water did so because their owners succeeded in tricking their way in. Their stories are remarkable.

KRVS public radio station manager David Spizale and his son Matthew managed to get into the water as well with the help of a guy dressed in apparent military fatigues with the name Quibodeaux over his pocket. As the volunteers were trying to negotiate their way past the police, Red Cross, and FEMA authorities, Quibodeaux appeared seemingly out of nowhere and started barking out orders to make immediate and efficient use of all available manpower. Everyone assumed he was in charge and things got moving. After the boats were in water, he disappeared. No one knew who he was or what authority, if any, he represented. He was seen later jogging down the interstate, apparently to some other location where resources were clogged. Dave is from New Orleans and had family there and so knew his way around the city. He and Matt headed for his old neighborhood near the lake and UNO. He found it surreal to be heading down familiar streets along Canal Boulevard in a boat with his depth finder showing eight feet, finding his way by reading the street signs a foot above the water level. They rescued over two dozen people before they were made to come out themselves.

My son François and his friend Marshall made it into the water by bypassing the authorities after a series of missteps caused by a breakdown in communication. When they arrived at the I-10/610 split, they were sent to the next exit on 10 at West End Boulevard. There, they met a lone state trooper who routinely turned everyone back around, insisting that the only orders he had were that no civilians were allowed in. They returned to the split, and were told to return home. Frustrated but undaunted,

they crossed the median between the split with their four-wheel-drive
Jeep Cherokee and launched their boat on the outbound ramp before the
authorities could prevent them. They were joined by four other guys in
two flat-bottom boats and a football player from Rayne High School in
an airboat. They found themselves blocked from the area where people
were stranded by a railroad track (that they would have avoided if they
had launched at West End). They all helped each other to portage the flat-
bottoms across, but the airboat was another matter. With its Chevy 350
engine, it was far too heavy to pull over. The football player told them not
to worry about him, but they remained curious. Then they heard a chainsaw from the other side of the tracks and saw three pines fall. He apparently lined them up to improvise a ramp. They heard him rev up and then
saw him come flying over the top. When he reached the water on the other
side, they asked him how he would get back across later, since there were
no trees in that side. He said, "When this boat comes out, the water will be
low enough to go under the bridge." Apparently he meant to stay a while.

These guys did not go off half-cocked. Their sense of preparedness
goes beyond even the Boy Scouts. They know that you don't go out there
fragile. They had stocked lots of water, extra gas, snack food, Q beam lights
. . . They are veterans of many duck hunts at places like Wax Lake Out-
let where conditions are as rough as they get. In fact, François compared
the two experiences. "It was like hunting the Wax without the right stuff.
Every step you take, you get stuck deep in the mud. You work to get that
foot loose and the next step is stuck again. You can see where you want to
go, but every step takes forever and all your strength. Then we realized we
could just drive by the authorities. After that, everything got easier. It was
like hunting the Wax with a pirogue. We'd see the flashing blue and red
lights or someone with a red cross on his chest and the only question was
right or left to get around them. It was the only way we could get anything
done." They brought over four hundred people out, carrying six with them
in their boat and pulling ten more in a flat-bottom they found floating in
the flooded waters and commandeered. They repeatedly refused orders
to come out. A crawfisherman from Kaplan working with them tested the
waters with a paddle as he approached the ramp and dropped his passengers off when they were close enough to wade in so that authorities would
not pull his boat out.

The reception that François described among the people they were
rescuing was dramatically different from what was being reported in
the media. He told of approaching about forty African American people on an overpass surrounded by eight to ten feet of water on all sides.

Understandably wary, some of the stranded called out to ask who these guys in the boats were and what their intentions were. Creole scholar Deborah Clifton pointed out to me that the apprehension of African Americans to get into a boat run by white people taking them to an undetermined destination had understandable historical undercurrents. Someone in the boats responded, "We're volunteer search and rescue. We've come to take you to safety if you want to go." At that point, a woman began shouting, "Thank you, Jesus, for sending your sons to help us." There were too many of the stranded people for the number of boats and the rescuers were a little concerned about the possibility of losing control of the situation as they approached. Instead, they found these folks organized and polite, the men helping the women and children into the boats first and offering to wait for the next run. François and his fellow rescuers were finally forced to come out when they ran out of gas and FEMA, Red Cross, and law enforcement officials refused to refill their tanks.

Other members of my family volunteered at the Cajundome in Lafayette. François, a first-year medical student, volunteered in the makeshift triage unit there, taking vital signs and histories among the evacuees who needed medical attention. My wife, Caroline, was put to work distributing donated clothes and supplies. My daughter Clélie worked at the information desk making announcements. They both also read to children and organized a writing project that took some of the children on an outing in Lafayette's Girard Park. Caroline has a knack for spotting interesting people and interesting situations. She met a grandmother who was providing daycare for twenty-three of her grandchildren when the storm hit. They were all evacuated to Lafayette, but had no idea where the parents of the children were for several days. Caroline and Clélie visited them regularly and did their laundry for a couple of weeks. They also listened to the grandmother as she told her story and wondered about how she would care for such a large number of charges. Eventually the parents arrived and relieved the stress.

I spent most of my time as volunteer at the Cajundome unloading and processing the mountains of donations that were being dropped off at the rear loading dock. There were a few local Red Cross officials overseeing the general operation, but our effort was organized by a guy from Ville Platte who simply filled the power vacuum to do what had to be done. Under his able, improvised supervision we created a merchandise distribution system out of thin air. In addition to carloads of used clothing and shoes, people brought consumable necessities of all sorts, including everything from diapers and sanitary napkins to bottled water and toothpaste. Some

large-scale donations arrived on pallets. All we had to cut these large bundles were our own pocketknives. After nearly a week on the dock, the
semester started. I decided I would put in a few hours there before going
home on the first day of classes. When I arrived, I was directed to the front
door. The national folks had showed up and established a perimeter. It was
now necessary to obtain pictured identification to enter the dome. I was
told this would take about forty minutes. I was then told that I could not
enter the facility with my pocketknife. I tried to explain that I had spent
the last few days cutting bundles with that very same knife, but I was told
that it was a security issue. I decided that if I was considered a security
risk with my pocketknife, I was no longer needed, and I left in a huff. As I
began to drive away, I reconsidered the situation. I realized that I was only
hurting those who needed help the most. So I drove around to the back
of the dome, taking advantage of the porous perimeter, parked near the
docks, and went back to work for a few hours fully armed.

After Rita, our local television stations ran a crawl, again requesting
small boats to help evacuate flooded areas in southern Vermilion Parish. The crawl had barely finished running across the screen when François was outside hitching up our boat to head out again. I yelled to him
from the porch as he was leaving that I bet he would encounter a different reception. He nodded knowingly. Later that day, after pulling people
and pets out of Bayou Tigue south of Delcambre, he returned to report a
completely different scene. As the boaters arrived at the spot where LA 14
went underwater south of Abbeville, they were given specific destinations
and rescue sites by sheriff's deputies running the makeshift staging area.
In this case, local officials were not paralyzed by fear of looters and shoot-
ers driven by a media in a feeding frenzy, or by a lack of communication,
and they knew how to use homemade help and exactly where to send it.
The flooded highway that was considered a barrier in New Orleans was
considered a launching ramp in Vermilion Parish.

In an article in *The Nation*, Mike Davis and Anthony Fontenot
described the vernacular efforts of "the folks of Ville Platte, a poor Cajun
and black Creole community with a median income less than half that of
the rest of the nation [who] have opened their doors over the past three
weeks to more than 5,000 of the displaced people they call 'company' (the
words 'refugee' and 'evacuee' are considered too impersonal, even impolite)" (Davis and Fontenot 2005).

They went on to point out that "Ville Platte's homemade rescue
and relief effort—organized around the popular slogan 'If not us, then
who?'—stood in striking contrast to the incompetence of higher levels of

government" (Davis and Fontenot 2005). The authors quoted a woman named Jennifer who articulated perfectly the underlying philosophy behind this homemade relief effort: "'Listen, my committee is my telephone. I call folks and they respond. Food, clothing, cots, medicine—it's all provided. Even poor people down here have some extra deer meat in the freezer or an old quilt or an extra bed. And all of us know how to spontaneously cooperate. My God, we're always organizing christenings or family gatherings. So why do we need a lot of formal leadership?' In a nation currently without competent leadership, this may be a reasonable, even deeply profound, question" (Davis and Fontenot 2005).

There were many stories of frustration from Katrina. Jefferson Parish president Aaron Broussard wept in a televised interview over the loss of a deputy's mother who died five days after the storm still waiting to be rescued. One of the worst horrors was the widely reported St. Rita's nursing home incident where thirty patients died before rescuers could arrive to evacuate them. The national media both exposed important stories and contributed to the catastrophic mess. Overwhelmed with endless interviews, many officials found it difficult to address the problems at hand. This prompted part of New Orleans mayor Nagin's rant calling for a moratorium on press conferences. More important, the endless repetition of two-minute loops of looters, the reports of women and children being raped in the Convention Center (which later proved to be false), and dubious reports of people shooting at rescue helicopters paralyzed operations in New Orleans. News crews in helicopters showing live shots of people on their roofs waving SOS signs and white shirts asked on the air, "Why is no one coming to get these people?" I found myself asking out loud, "Why don't you stop what you're doing and get them yourselves? You're there." There were some examples of news people getting involved. There was footage of one local journalist from Channel 26, the ABC affiliate in New Orleans, doing a report from the Interstate 10-610 split who stopped what he was doing and ran to the rescue of a man who had driven his car into the deep water covering the highway. Local stations, such as WWNO, improvised detailed coverage that provided important information in local terms for local folks about what was happening in specific neighborhoods and areas. Some reporters who made it to the Superdome shared water and food. But as Cliff Deal, a member of the Louisiana Museum task force that went in to assess the damage to the city's dozens of historical and cultural collections, told me, "The national news outfits reporting from the areas near the dome and the convention center about the horrible conditions there all had lights, food, water, shelter and makeup."

He described the surreal feeling he got driving along Carondelet Street at speeds up to fifty miles per hour to avoid getting carjacked and coming upon what looked like the concert in the jungle scene from *Apocalypse Now* on Canal Street.

My wife's cousin, Tim Supple, reported a similar experience. He and his brother Robert loaded a truck and a trailer full of food, water, and other supplies and headed to New Orleans. They had heard the stories of looting and chaos and were braced for the worst, carrying a pistol and a shotgun just in case. Anticipating that they would be unable to reach the city via I-10, they took old U.S. 90. Near Chalmette, they encountered a convoy of medical volunteers from Arkansas who were looking for the "town" of St. Bernard. (It is a parish.) They directed the volunteers to Chalmette and joined the convoy up to that point. Tim reported that they were all packing weapons as well. When they moved out, they were told to hold their weapons at the ready in visible positions to deter any possible hijack attempts. However, they met with no resistance while looking for people to help. Instead they saw people walking along the roads waving, some obviously needing help. The group stuck to their plan to get to St. Bernard. At that point, the Supple brothers broke off and went across the Crescent City Connection bridge. They eventually drove right up to the Superdome. They asked police officers there if they thought it might cause trouble if they handed out their supplies. The officers said no, so they did. Tim and Robert both described the crowd as polite, patient, and appreciative, contrary to the impression given by media reports. Given that they had reached these places, Cliff Deal and the Supples reported wondering why rescuers could not. At the same time, as the press eventually reported, trucks filled with FEMA ice and provisions were driving aimlessly around the country waiting for specific instructions concerning what to do with their cargos. The difference between institutional and vernacular efforts was obvious.

For Rita, the networks positioned themselves primarily in Galveston and Houston anticipating the worst there, according to weather forecasts. When the storm veered right to head toward the Louisiana state line, they found themselves boxed out. Lafayette's local ABC and CBS affiliates, as well as Lake Charles's local NBC affiliate, were forced to improvise local solutions. When the storm knocked out main power at all three stations, they managed to stay on the air using generators and even linking with local radio stations to broadcast consolidated news reports. Unable to send out reporters to the devastated and flooded areas, they used local residents as reporters, airing their e-mail, telephone, and text messages.

These reports made for some of the most compelling television news I have ever seen. They were also immediately useful for thousands of evacuees who were desperate for any information on their neighborhoods and towns. The nature of these locally generated stories was remarkably different from the network news stories. They were unsensational and focused on pragmatic, community-based issues, such as how neighborhoods and towns were affected and what resources were available, where and from whom.

Contemporary stories reminded many of similar situations from earlier storms. As the news media reported that the only building left intact in all of Cameron Parish after Rita was the courthouse, nearly everyone of a certain age remembered that it was the same courthouse that was the only building left intact in the parish after Audrey in 1957 as well. They remembered the similar images of ruined cane crops and the dead cattle and the piles of boats on the road and the buildings found miles from where they had been. They also remembered the more than five hundred drowned residents from Audrey. They remembered so well, in fact, that everyone evacuated this time. Some stories had light moments. One man who had returned to check on his home reached his family by cell phone to tell them he had good news and bad news. The good news was that the house seemed structurally sound. The bad news was that it wasn't on their property anymore. One tugboat operator actually rode out the storm in his boat near Intracoastal City. The next day, he was in contact with the local television stations, text messaging and e-mailing via satellite phone reports and digital images of the destruction. A local television anchor commenting on the photographs asked him where he was. He told him that he was in Intracoastal City. The anchor said, "So you can see all of this from the canal?" "No," he answered, "I'm *in* Intracoastal City."

Seventy-five-year-old Moisy Baudoin sat with his wife, Louella, in the driveway in front of their flooded home in Delcambre telling me about the water coming over the railroad tracks during Rita. He was insistent that this was something no one remembered ever seeing before, including his eighty-seven-year-old boss Lane LeBlanc. He did remember taking his small flat-bottom boat out south of the tracks as a young man during Audrey to rescue his neighbors who were on their roofs to escape the rising water. There wasn't the media coverage or the satellite reports or the Doplar radars we have today, he explained. People didn't know what was happening. He remembered some asking as he approached their flooded homes, "How high is the water going to go?" He remembered answering, "I don't know, but I'm here for you if you want to come." He remembered that the water eventually receded as quickly as it had risen, leaving his boat aground alongside the road.

Moisy and Louella seemed dazed when we arrived. The water had receded but the floor of their home was covered with sludge. We offered to start cleaning up a bit, but they said there was no water pressure. There was also no electricity and they would soon lose all the food in their five well-stocked freezers. Anticipating this common post-hurricane problem, we had brought along every ice chest we owned and we started unloading the freezers to transfer the food to space we would commandeer in the freezers of friends and family back home. François found a large squeegee and began pushing mud out of the house. This simple gesture seemed to reactivate the Baudoins and the clean up started. The next day, he had found a tile setter and arranged for new floors to be installed. We also brought a few boxes full of their waterlogged family photo albums to see if anything could be salvaged. (People who have lost everything in fires or floods often insist that the pictures are what they regret losing the most.) My mother and father, Maude and Elmo Ancelet, worked for several weeks meticulously blotting them and drying them in front of the air conditioner on their porch. They salvaged well over two-thirds of the photographs, to everyone's amazement, and returned them to the grateful Baudoins.

A few weeks after Rita, Moisy took me on a tour of south Vermilion, where we saw numerous houses that had been washed off their foundations, rammed into tree lines or electrical poles or fences or ditches. The brick home of one of his friends in south Delcambre had been seriously damaged. The entire south wall had been washed out. When we arrived, we found the owner repacking the bearings on his rice cart. He had already got his school bus and two tractors running again. He showed us the insurance settlement check he had just received. It was for $1,640. He declared, as he put it back into his shirt pocket, that he was not sure whether he should frame it, flush it, or cash it.

As I spoke to Tim Supple about the apparent need and ability to improvise solutions among all those who had apparently had to trick their way into New Orleans to provide rescue and assistance, he said it reminded him of a family story about what his father and a neighbor from Franklin had done during Audrey in 1957. They flagged down the passenger train in town and told the conductor to wait there until they rounded up the people from town, mostly black, who could not get out on their own to put them on the train. The conductor said he couldn't do that. Mr. Kyle, the neighbor, told him he could and would. The conductor asked what he would do if he didn't wait. Mr. Kyle said, "Well, I'll shoot you and drive the train out myself." The conductor thought again about the situation and agreed it was the right thing to do. He asked where he should take the evacuees. Mr. Kyle's answer was a gem of understated, vernacular logic, "I would head north. There's a hurricane coming in the gulf." The conductor waited and hundreds were evacuated to safety somewhere near Alexandria, thanks to the willingness and ability of all three men to think, rethink, and act on the fly, to improvise solutions that weren't in the handbook.

The strain of displacement also produced an instant rash of urban legends fueled by the rumor mill. In Lafayette and Baton Rouge, both of which nearly doubled in population with the arrival of evacuees after Katrina, unfounded stories about carjackings, robberies, and rapes sprouted like weeds all over town. These stories were of course based on the perception of some that that's the way New Orleans folks, especially the black and poor evacuees who were there, would likely act. Local drivers began to notice out-of-town dealership insignia on the cars that were clogging the streets. Anyone who cut you off driving like a maniac must be from New Orleans. After Rita, Lake Charles experienced similar stress-driven rumor-mongering. Cooler heads eventually prevailed as officials in all three cities, including Lafayette City–Parish president Joey Durel, Lake Charles mayor Randy Roach, and the news staff at Baton Rouge's WAFB-TV reacted proactively, going on the air to dispel the rumors and ask for calm and consideration in these trying times.

There were other remarkable stories of hope and human dignity. Robert LeBlanc from Houma made it into the flooded city in his boat to help rescue the stranded after Katrina and sent a message about his experiences in an e-mail to friends. His stories confirm many of those I have collected. (See Robert LeBlanc's e-mail in this collection.) So do the stories of Glen Miguez, a volunteer rescuer in south Vermilion Parish during Hurricane Rita. (See the interview with Glen Miguez in this collection.) Sharon Suire and her husband, Elie, also had a remarkable tale of survival based on luck and improvised ingenuity. They went to check on her parents who had elected to remain in their home at Jean-Marie boat landing south of Delcambre. Despite the sheriff's request that all residents evacuate, they decided to stay with them rather than leaving them alone. When the tidal surge came in, they found themselves trapped in the house. Sharon Suire recounts their experience:

There were winds about 80, 82 miles an hour, 86 miles an hour. And then all of a sudden, it got real quiet. Then all of a sudden, I heard like a tidal wave coming in slow, water coming in, and it was into the house.

The wind died down, and then it was very quiet, and I could hear the water, you know, hitting against the house underneath and it was coming up in the bedroom. So I got up and I told my Dad, I said, "The water's coming into the house." I said, "Daddy, do you have any life jackets?" I had my headlight on. He said, "Yes, let's go in the back bedroom." They had four life jackets.

By the time we were able to put all our life jackets on—it was my dad, my mom, my husband, and myself—by the time we finished putting the life jackets on and we zipped them, in the house, we had water to our waists. And from eight o'clock until five a.m. in the morning, we were floating in the house, up to the ceiling. When daybreak came, we could see to go outside. We swam with the life jackets, and we went in the oak tree.

And we tried to open the doors. We couldn't. There was so much water pressure. So I don't know if it was God's will or what, but the front door just opened to let us out. And it was daybreak. We could see. We got into the tree, the oak tree in front of the house, and we stayed there. We could hear the helicopters. They knew we had stayed. And we stayed there in the oak tree for nine and a half hours. The reason I know this, I had a watch, a waterproof watch. And then they rescued us. And from there, they took us to the hospital in Lafayette. (Sharon Suire 2012)

While many institutions were paralyzed by a number of factors, including a lack of communication and an inability to think outside the manual, there were also a few institutions that overcame bureaucracy and panic to get things done. The U.S. Coast Guard and Louisiana's Department of Wildlife and Fisheries were praised by the local news media and governmental officials alike for their ability to improvise effective use of their own resources, such as boats and communications, in the aftermath of the storm and levee failure. Wildlife and Fisheries personnel also recognized the value and potential of available community resources, working with volunteers to evacuate numerous stranded citizens. And they did what they did without much fanfare, flying under the radar of most media stories, which had a tendency to focus on reports of looting and shooting rather than rescue and resilience. There were also a few exceptions among the media, mostly local, who were able to keep their eyes on the ball, while others were blinded by the catastrophe. Some news crews even put their cameras and microphones down for a minute to join immediate, improvised rescue efforts.

Acadian Ambulance, a large, private regional company serving most of south Louisiana and beyond along the Gulf Coast, was another of the rare institutions that proved to be remarkably effective in spite of the adverse conditions. Acadian crews coming in to evacuate nursing homes and other facilities initially reported having difficulty talking their way through the troubled perimeter of the city. Yet they persisted and improvised solutions on the fly. Drivers and paramedics reported feeling overwhelmed at the enormity of the task and frustrated by the lack of coordination and the breakdown in communications. Some wept. Yet they insisted on returning to try over and over again, many after only three or four hours of sleep, according to Acadian vice president Jerry Romero. In a corporate video documentary (2005), members of Acadian's management team, as well as paramedics, medical staff, drivers, and pilots examined their own efforts, as well as the very nature of the corporate culture that may have enabled them to accomplish all that they did. Company CEO Richard Zuschlag put it succinctly, "We had to throw all the rules out the window."

The ability and willingness of both management and staff at Acadian to improvise solutions turned obstacles into opportunities. One employee referred to the effort as "orchestrated chaos." They set up a triage center at the I-10 Causeway exit, converting the cloverleaf ramps into four improvised helipads, in order to expedite the process of transferring patients out of New Orleans and on to hospitals in nearby communities (Judice 2011, 11). They cobbled together communications, according to Acadian employee Clay Henry, "whether it was by cellular or by high band VHF radio." Jerry Romero evaluated this process:

> We sort of used some Cajun ingenuity for [communications] also, because we didn't have . . . Our backup plans didn't work. Our backup systems didn't work, so a couple of things. We immediately got some satellite phones. I don't know who we got them from, but one of our logistics people got on the phone and somehow got some satellite phones. So we sent them out and our people in New Orleans started using satellite phones to talk with us. And also, Iberia Parish sheriff Sid Hebert has a mobile command post, a radio command post, and he deployed it to Gretna, to our station on the other side of the river . . . And we used that as a dispatch center for a few days . . . That helped us limp by for a few days. It wasn't in the plan. We had an unbelievable amount of people calling to offer help, and the more this became a story, the more calls we got. They'd call us. We had ambulance services, individuals, groups of doctors . . . And I was in the position [of determining] what do I do with all of these offers? Where do I tell them to go? There's no organization. Where do I tell these people where to go? (Romero 2011)

Dispatch supervisor Mike Sonnier turned the top of the Tulane Hospital parking garage into a helipad by having Tulane personnel cut down the metal light poles on top (Judice 2001, 17). Flight paramedic Marc Creswell and his team improvised a similar landing site at Meadowcrest, a hospital in New Orleans East by cutting down trees in a parking lot, with the help of a borrowed chainsaw (Judice 2011, 21). Marc Creswell and his team of paramedics came up with the idea of converting Kentwood water boxes into carriers for infant patients by ripping out the middle portions and then stuffing blankets into them (Judice 2011, 32). Another team converted latex gloves into makeshift baby bottles, as described by an EMT in the Acadian corporate documentary (2005): "As people were coming up to us, not able to feed their babies because they didn't have their bottles, we got together as a group and discussed how we could remedy this situation, and came up with the idea of using a glove and putting a hole in the finger of the glove so that way they could use the glove to feed their children" (2005). Another EMT identified and commandeered available transportation resources:

> Our fleet manager, our fleet vice president, Bill Vidacovich, he is an unbelievable can-do kind of person. He's originally from New Orleans, but he's been in Lafayette for thirty-five years. He borrowed an amphibious vehicle to get to the Superdome. He had some of his mechanics and they just went there to help. He borrowed an eighteen-wheeler. The eighteen-wheelers at a certain point could get to New Orleans Charity, because the water was high enough so that cars and pickup trucks couldn't get through, but an eighteen-wheeler could get through. He flagged one down. It was an empty eighteen-wheeler. And he said, "Can you help us evacuate patients?" So he got the eighteen-wheeler. They drove over to New Orleans Charity and they were putting patients and family members and nurses and doctors in the back of the eighteen-wheeler and taking them out. (Romero 2011)

Another story illustrating the improvisational character of the paramedics involved the difficult issue of pets:

> One story, [a paramedic says,] "I was at I-10 and the Causeway and I had this sick lady on the stretcher and another sick person on the bench seat. We needed to go, we needed to go, and she says, 'I'm not going without my pet.'" I think it was a dog. And they said, "We have a policy. We don't take pets in the ambulance." She said, "Well, take me out of the ambulance. I'm not going without my pet." So he said, "What do I do with this?" He didn't call anybody

to ask for permission. He couldn't have gotten through anyway. He just said, "Put your dog in here. We need to go." Turns out, we had several of those [situations], those who brought pets with them. (Romero 2011)

As the Acadian documentary's narrator put it: "Acadian improvised ways to work with volunteers and government resources as well, including the military, to accomplish the immediate goal of evacuating patients, without regard to credit." Dr. Ross Judice, then medical director at Acadian, also generously spread the credit around:

Although I am extremely proud of my Acadian colleagues, there were count-less others who helped with equal dedication. Some of those include the Coast Guard, the National Guard, FEMA, hospitals, EMS, medical profes-sionals, civilian helicopter companies, churches, civic organizations, local businesses and local fire & police departments. Then there were the friends, neighbors and average folks who helped by cooking meals for our medics, bringing us clean clothes, offering their boats, tools and manpower and assisting us in a hundred different ways. (Judice 2011, 5)

And the improvisational effort was evident throughout south Louisi-ana. In Lafayette, the Cajundome was turned into a shelter. Finding many in need of medical attention there, local doctors improvised a full-blown clinic, complete with a pharmacy:

The Cajundome was never part of an evacuation plan. It's never a pre-storm shelter. I think they may have opened it up afterward. It became an after-the-storm shelter. And at some point, there were some doctors that decided, "There's a lot of sick people here." And they created a clinic at the Cajundome, and it was amazing. It was open for about, seems like two weeks. I think the Red Cross ended up shutting it down. I walked over there. We had people and ambulances available to help. I went over there, and they actually had it set up where they had registration, they had labs, they had private room areas with curtains. They had [it divided up.] This is where our diabetics are, this is where our pregnant women are . . . . This was at the Cajundome and the Convention Center [in Lafayette]. The Convention Center had the special needs patients, the ones that needed hospital beds or something. That was never in the plan. It was some local doctors, Dr. Andy Blaylock and the eye doctor, Dr. Azar. And they had all these volunteer doctors, and a pharmacy. They set up a pharmacy . . . at the Cajundome. (Romero 2011)

At Acadian's Lafayette headquarters, which had become action central, there was more community support: "All the restaurants were donating food. They were coming and saying, 'Where do you want food?' We had people out here in this parking lot cooking. We didn't have to go out and buy any food. They were cooking three meals a day out in the parking lot. Restaurants were either delivering, or [regular guys] with their cookers out here on the trailers barbecuing and cooking whatever" (Romero 2011).

In staffer Erroll Babineaux's analysis of the situation, one sees the improvisation as the heart of the effort: "That is not something that you can dictate to employees, that is in the heart of the Acadian employee, that they're going to go in and do their job" (2005). When asked how Acadian Ambulance employees, from top to bottom, were able to accomplish what they did, Jerry Romero settled on two essential reasons. First, he said, "It has something to do with who we are. Our people have historically had a can-do approach to solving problems" (Romero 2011). And second, he explained that this kind of employee improvisation is not only tolerated, but appreciated. To illustrate, he told the story of a more recent event in which an Acadian EMT arrived on the scene of an accident on the Atchafalaya Basin causeway to find that an injured person had been thrown off the bridge and into the water some twenty feet below.

> Like jumping off the I-10 bridge over the Atchafalaya Basin. You know, that's against policy. But we had a guy that . . . You know, there was a wreck and a patient was in the water, and what are you going to do? He got a rope and two by-standers had already jumped in the water to try to make sure the guy didn't drown, but there was a patient with a neck injury or back injury in the water, so he got a rope and he tied onto the bridge and he rappelled down with a spine board and took care of the patient until a boat could come and they put him on the boat. There are things like that that our safety department frowns on. (Romero 2011)

Romero explained that such effort is not in any manuals, and that it is even frowned upon by their safety advisors. But the patient's life was saved without injury to the spine. When I asked about the results of the event for the EMT, Romero said that he was not reprimanded, but rewarded for his effort. He went on to suggest that this tolerance and appreciation for effective improvisation at the heart of Acadian's corporate culture contributed directly to their ability to deal with the chaos of Katrina: "We always train our medics and our managers, if you make the best decision based on patient care, then you're probably going to be okay. When it comes to decisions in a rescue or a hurricane situation, and I can't call my boss, what do I do? You think about what's the best thing for the patient. And I think that's what a lot of these individuals did, and they did the right thing" (Romero 2011). Dr. Judice put it succinctly: "Government operate[d] in silos and by the rules. Private citizens and companies reinvented the rules . . . Only by ignoring their rules were we able to evacuate as many people as we did . . . Innovation provided in real time saved the day" (Judice 2011, 110–11).

The effects of these hurricanes are complex. There will be long-term effects that we will only discover as they evolve. Some may ultimately turn out to be positive, such as the vastly improved disaster plans at all levels, including the Louisiana Emergency Management Units (LEMU): "What resulted from that is LEMU, Louisiana Emergency Medical Unit, which is run by Dr. Andy Blaylock. There is now a series of trailers, five trailers that are mobile clinics than [can be] deployed. Because of that experience, they decided—and they got some state funding for it—[to create] some local clinics that they'll deploy out to disaster sites, for the people that need clinics and not emergency care" (Romero 2011).

On the other hand, there will be problems we have not imagined yet and there will be opportunities hiding in some of those problems. But those who think they know Katrina and Rita are sadly mistaken. We've only just met. The state budget will continue to be adversely affected for years. Hard-hit places like the Ninth Ward, Shell Beach, Pointe à la Hache, Holly Beach, and Cameron years later still show evidence of the destruction caused by the storms. Despite President Bush's promise to provide "one of the largest reconstruction efforts the world has ever seen" (quoted in Davis 2006), government support stalled, leaving much of the affected areas still in the dark and in ruins long after. Rebuilding efforts have been frustrated by a number of factors, including difficult and problematic insurance settlements and the need to revamp building codes and reconsider risk zones before deciding how and even if to proceed. One of the major sticking points is in FEMA's revisions of floodplain maps. Some recovery efforts are caught in endless loops: school districts are waiting on neighborhoods who are waiting on city councils who are waiting on merchants who are waiting on school districts. Issues important to local residents can sometimes fly under the radar of outside observers, including the press. More than five years after Rita, the towns of Erath and Delcambre had few operating grocery stores and no pharmacies, forcing residents to drive to New Iberia or Abbeville for basic provisions. Some places have slowly emerged from the chaos based on local efforts, but in order for local will power to prevail, it must be supported by institutional power, including electrical power. Residents of Chalmette have tackled the restoration of their community block by block. Residents of Erath at one point met to consider moving the entire south end of town north of the railroad tracks. Many residents refused and have opted to have their houses raised instead, in some cases as much as eight to ten feet. Other fishermen have geared back up again as boats were removed from where many were left in piles onshore and replaced into the waterways. Some fishermen, already under duress before the storms, decided to call it quits; many of their boats were abandoned and still lie where the floodwaters deposited them. Some farmers and ranchers worked hard to restore their operations, rebuilding barns and sheds and oiling machinery and learning how to leach fields to reduce salt levels. Rice and cane fields are back in production and cattle are once again grazing on marshland and open prairies. Others decided that it was time to consider other occupations or retire. An effective barometer of the popular and economic effects of the storms is the prevailing $25+ price tag on five-pound orders of boiled crawfish. Meanwhile, the institutional confusion and ineptitude continues, perhaps best symbolized in the stories about the thousands of mobile homes that were stranded for years, some ironically in places like Hope, Arkansas.

There are many stories like these that need to be told and heard so that the world will know what really happened in New Orleans and in south Louisiana. We all need to listen to them and to understand and make known their value. Neither the media nor the government bureaucracies got it right. These stories about the value and effect of vernacular power and creolized solutions are essential to achieve a full understanding of what happened during and after the Gulf storms of 2005.

SOURCES CITED

Ancelet, Barry Jean, Jay Edwards, and Glen Pitre. 1991. *Cajun Country.* Jackson: University Press of Mississippi.
Ancelet, Jacques François. 2005. Personal interview.
Ancelet, Jean Charles-Edouard. 2005. Personal interview.
Anything I Catch: The Handfishing Story, d. Patrick Mire. 1990. Attakapas Productions.
Baudoin, Moisy. 2005. Personal interview.
Begnaud, Kenneth. 2005. Personal interview.
Bourne, Jr., Joel K. 2004. Gone with the Water. *National Geographic* (October).
Brasseaux, Carl A. 1987. *The Founding of New Acadia.* Baton Rouge: Louisiana State University Press.

———. 1992. *From Acadian to Cajun.* Jackson: University Press of Mississippi.

Davis, Mike. 2006. Who Is Killing New Orleans? *The Nation* (April 10).

Davis, Mike, and Anthony Fontenot. 2005. Hurricane Gumbo. *The Nation* (November 7).

Deal, Cliff. 2005. Personal interview.

Dobie, Ann B. 2008. *Fifty-eight Days in the Cajundome Shelter.* New Orleans: Pelican Press.

Dormon, James H. 1983. *The People Called Cajuns: An Introduction to an Ethnohistory.* Lafayette: University of Southwestern Louisiana, Center for Louisiana Studies.

Howell, Mary. 2005. Personal interview.

Jackson, Helen Hunt. 1881. *A Century of Dishonor: A Sketch of the United States Government's Dealings with Some of the Indian Tribes.* New York: Harper & Brothers (Norman: University of Oklahoma Press, 1995).

Judice, Dr. Ross. 2011. *The Katrina Diaries: First Hand Accounts from Medics and Miracle Workers.* Ross Judice (eBook).

LeBlanc, Robert. 2005. Personal interview.

Romero, Jerry. 2005. Personal interview.

———. 2011. Personal interview.

Spizale, David. 2005. Personal interview.

Suire, Sharon, and Elie Suire. 2012. Personal interview.

Supple, Tim. 2005. Personal interview.

Thomas, Evan, et al. 2005. How Bush Blew It: Bureaucratic timidity. Bad phone lines. And a failure of imagination. Why the government was so slow to respond to catastrophe. *Newsweek* (September 12).

Wise, Tim. 2005. A God With Whom I am Not Familiar. www.counterpunch.com, September 5.

ROBERT LEBLANC

My Hurricane Story

The Positive Stories Must Get Out

Editors' Note: This message was e-mailed to friends by Robert LeBlanc, who was involved in the rescue effort in New Orleans. It quickly went locally viral and was eventually posted on a NOLA Web site. It was forwarded to coauthor Barry Jean Ancelet by Amanda LaFleur, with the comment:

> *Just when I was beginning to despair over the disheartening stories of the violence hindering rescue efforts in New Orleans, I found this post on the NOLA Web site, so I wanted to share it with you. Read until the end. It's worth it.*

Name: Robert LeBlanc
Subject: My Hurricane Story—The Positive Stories Must Get Out
Story: Please help me to get this story out. We need to get the truth out and these people helped.

Jeff Rau, a family and now personal friend to whom I will forever be linked, and I were volunteering with a boat and pulling people out of the water on Wednesday. I have a first-hand experience of what we encountered. In my opinion, almost everything being portrayed in the media is a complete bastardization of what is really happening. The result is that good people are dying and losing family members. These people need help and need to get out. We can sort out all of the social and political issues later, but human beings with any sense of compassion would agree that the travesty that is going on here in New Orleans needs to end and people's lives need to be saved and families need to be put back together. Now.

I will tell you that I would probably disagree with most of the people that still need to be saved on political, social, and cultural values. However, it must be noted that these people love their friends and families like I do, desire to live like I do, and care for their respective communities (I was amazed at the sight of seemingly young and poor black people caring for sickly and seemingly well-to-do white people and tourists still needing evacuation from New Orleans' downtown area while the news media were reporting that the exact opposite was occuring) the same way I care for mine.

Seven people in particular who stood out during our rescue and whose stories deserve to be told:

1.) We were in motor boats all day ferrying people back and forth approximately a mile and a half each way (from Carrollton Ave down Airline Hwy to the Causeway overpass). Early in the day, we witnessed a black man in a boat with no motor paddling with a piece of lumber. He rescued people in the boat and paddled them to safety, at least an hour and a half each way. He then, amidst all of the boats with motors, turned around and paddled back out across the mile and a half stretch to do his part in getting more people out. He seemingly refused to give up or occupy any of the motored boat resources because he did not want to slow us down in our efforts. I saw him at about 5:00 p.m., paddling away from the rescue point back out into the neighborhoods just two hours before nightfall. I am sure that his trip took at least an hour and a half each trip, and he was going back to get more people knowing that he'd run out of daylight and conditions would become extremely dangerous if his boat took on water or he got lost. He did all of this with a two-by-four.

2.) One of the groups that we rescued were 50 people standing on the bridge that crosses over Airline Hwy just before getting to Carrollton Ave going toward downtown. Most of these people had been there, with no food, water, or anyplace to go since Monday morning (we got to them Wed afternoon) and surrounded by 10 feet of water in every direction. There was one guy who had been there since the beginning, organizing people and helping more people to get to the bridge safely as more water flowed into the city on Wednesday morning due to the levee breach. He did not leave the bridge until everyone got off safely, even deferring to people who had gotten to the bridge Wed morning and, although inconvenienced by loss of power and weather damage, did have the luxury of some food and some water as late as Tuesday evening. This guy waited on the bridge until dusk, and was one of the last boats out that night. He could have easily not made it out that night and been stranded on the bridge alone. He knew this while he continued to defer to other people.

3.) The third story may be the most compelling. I will not mince words. This was in a really rough neighborhood and we came across five seemingly unsavory characters. One had scars from what seemed to be gunshot wounds. We found these guys at a two-story recreational complex, one of the only two-story buildings in the neighborhood. They had broken into the center and tried to rustle as many people as possible from the neighborhood into the center. These guys stayed outside in the center all day, getting everyone out of the rec center onto boats. We approached them at approximately 6:30 p.m., obviously one of the last trips of the day, and they sent us further into the neighborhood to get more people out of homes and off rooftops instead of getting on themselves. This at the risk of their not getting out and having to stay in the water for an undetermined amount of time (you have to understand the uncertainty that all of the people in these accounts faced without having any info on the rescue efforts, how far or deep the flooding was, or where to go if they did want to swim or walk out). These five guys were on the last boat out of the neighborhood at sundown. They were incredibly grateful, mentioned numerous times 'God is going to bless y'all for this.' When we got them to the dock, they offered us an Allen Iverson jersey off of one of their backs as a gesture of gratitude, which was literally probably the most valuable possession among them all. Obviously, we declined, but I remain tremendously impacted by this gesture.

I don't know what to do with all of this, but I think we need to get these stories out. Some of what is being portrayed among the media is happening and is terrible, but it is among a very small group of people, not the majority. They make it seem like all of New Orleans has somehow taken the atmosphere of the mobs in Mogadishu portrayed in the book and movie "Black Hawk Down," which is making volunteers (including us) more hesitant and rescue attempts more difficult. As a result, people are dying. My family has been volunteering at the shelters here in Houma and can count on one hand the number of people among thousands who have not said "Thank You." or "God Bless You." Their lives shattered and families torn apart, gracious just to have us serve them beans and rice.

If anything, these seven people's stories deserve to be told, so that people across the world will know what they really did in the midst of this devastation. So that it will not be assumed that they were looting hospitals, they were shooting at helicopters, and they were setting buildings on fire. It must be known that they, like many other people that we encountered, sacrificed themselves during all of this to help other people in more dire straits than their own.

It is also important to know that this account is coming from someone who is politically conservative, believes in capitalism and free enterprise, and is traditionally against many of the opinions and stances of activists like Michael Moore and other liberals on most of the hot-topic political issues of the day. Believe me, I am not the political activist. This transcends politics. This is about humanity and helping mankind. We need to get these people out. Save their lives. We can sort out all of the political and social issues later. People need to know the truth of what is going on at the ground level so that they know that New Orleans and the people stranded there are, despite being panicked and desperate, gracious people and they deserve the chance to live. They need all of our help, as well.

This is an accurate account of things. Jeffery Rau would probably tell the same exact stories.

Thanks,

Robert LeBlanc

FRANÇOIS ANCELET

Dear Lynda
Man Helping Man

Editors' Note: Jacques François Ancelet, son of coauthor Barry Jean Ance-let, was a first-year student at the Louisiana State University Medical School in New Orleans when Katrina hit the coast. He and his brother Jean, also a first-year medical school student, evacuated to the home of their parents, along with a dozen of their classmates from various parts of the country. When they saw the announcement the morning after that help was needed in New Orleans, they all began to improvise what they would do. When author and cartoonist Lynda Barry, a family friend, heard about the students' efforts, she sent a contribution to help support them. François's thank you note to her articulated and illuminated what they had encountered firsthand.

Dear Lynda,

I want to thank you for your support of the relief efforts here in Lafayette. As you know, Jean and I have been working long days between here at home and in New Orleans. While entertaining my fellow classmates and

evacuees well away from the danger in Lafayette the night of the hurricane, I heard a passer by mention that they needed boats in New Orleans.
Unlike the response of the public officials, the response of the medical
school classes of 2008 and 2009 was swift and forceful. I called a friend
and had him prepare the boat while another friend and I gathered emergency supplies well into the night. By early morning, we had relief efforts
waiting at every major shelter in the area and a couple boats on the way
to New Orleans.

As Marshall and I arrived in New Orleans, we came face to face with
a very powerful sight. Any lack of motivation, any lack of energy dissolved
immediately. We saw at least 500 soaking wet evacuees lining up at buses
headed out of the city and one woman was kissing the asphalt on the interstate. After dropping off food and water to these people, we continued
down Interstate 10 and met a literal sea of water. After continuous days
and nights of working and with better than 400 live extractions, we pulled
the boat from the water, making room for another wave of rescue workers.
Immediately after we got on the road home, we received an influx of phone
calls from friends and classmates calling for help from the shelters. Here
we are, first- and second-year medical students actually getting hands on
experience and doing things that just last week were years to come.

One of the things that I find the most noteworthy about this entire
ordeal is the lack of official leadership, support, and financial aid. You can
clearly see it in the news but it is even more evident here on the ground.
On several occasions while in the boat, I caught myself questioning my
presence in the water. The conclusion that I came to was that someone
had to be there and that apparently, the other eight boats with me were
just as crazy. One thing that I can assure you of is that what happened on
the water and in the shelters immediately following the hurricane was in
no way an official endeavor. It was quite simply, the finest form of man
helping man that I have ever seen. In the people trapped in houses, on
cars, and in trees, you could see the purest form of need and in the rescue
workers, a dedication to helping them. Not to sound sappy but a crawfish
farmer from Kaplan told me that the most tragic aspect of this situation
was the indifference of the government in favor of red tape and protocol.
He said that his "protocol was to get these people out and I don't need to
ask my daddy for permission."

This started as a letter to thank you for your support and became a
description of the situation here. I guess that my disgust in the "official"
response, and my pride in the response of ordinary people drive me to
want to tell the true story. Maybe I'll write a book or a really pissed off

letter to some big name newspaper. Anyway, your donation is and will be greatly appreciated by all those that it touches. It is that kind of support that has allowed these people to survive. I'll write more later to let you know where the money went. Continue to spread the news up north and keep in touch. Thanks again.

François

GLEN MIGUEZ AND BARRY JEAN ANCELET

An Interview with Glen Miguez

Glen Miguez lives in Delcambre, a small town 20 miles south of Lafayette and 115 miles west of New Orleans. As Rita approached, he had hitched his sixteen-foot flat-bottom boat to his truck and was evacuating Delcambre with his family. When he encountered the tidal surge pouring over LA 14, he realized that he would not be able to make it to higher ground, so he turned around and headed back to town. When he arrived at the ridge near the bridge, the mayor asked if he could help to rescue some of those who were stranded in their flooded homes. He unloaded his family, launched his boat, and spent the entire day picking people up and taking them to safety. His is one of many similar stories of the vernacular rescuers who pitched in during the storm and its aftermath, saving people, pets, cattle, and horses.

BARRY JEAN ANCELET (BA): So, tell me about what happened. How were you involved?

GLEN MIGUEZ (GM): We moved, me, my wife, and my daughter, we had moved to Delcambre, at her mama's house, by the school. And that morning, about six o'clock, I told my wife, I said, "Let's take the boat and my truck." I had a white four-wheel drive, big truck. I said, "Let's go see how far we can make it," you know, as usual. You know, get off this road, it's low. I knew that. So we got about to the red light in Delcambre, at the bank. We turned right, and about a quarter of a mile, the tidal wave just came. I told my wife and my son-in-law, I said, "We can't make it. I'll have to turn around." I turned around, and I looked toward Highway 14, at the red light, they had all kinds of flashing lights there, cops and all kind of stuff. So I said, "Let's go see what's going on." So the mayor of town was there. He said, "Where are you going?" I said, "I was going to my house, but I can't make it." He said, "Man, we need your boat and a bunch of little boats to pick up people, start picking up." I said, "Well, OK." So I picked up one girl. She was at the red light. Denise Dooley. She had the shrimp shop in Delcambre. Her mom and them were across on the north side of Highway 14. So I just backed my boat off 14, right on the water.

BA: You used it as a boat launch?

GM: As a boat launch. And my son-in-law went get his boat, and came and helped us. Bud. Craig LeBlanc. He went get his boat and I did all the north as much as I could pick up. And then I crossed my boat over the tracks and he said, "Y'all start working the south side. Back and forth, every house." We had a cop with us all the time. And we kept going back and forth picking people. Most of them were on their porches, stuff like that, waiting for a ride. They didn't want to get in the water. We'd pick them up and go at the bridge by the LeBlanc Oil, and the current was so strong over the railroad tracks that we couldn't go straight. It would have taken us like a waterfall over the tracks.

So there were four or five people. We would just stop our boat and we'd take fuel, water, and we'd take off again. And we did that until about 9:30, pick up people like that, 9:30, then all the other little boats started coming. So the mayor said, "Y'all start doing this end of town, out in the country." I knew Mr. Boyoncé, right here. Big, big house. Him and his dad, Peter Boyoncé. He and his dad never leave for a hurricane. And I knew he was in that house. So I told that cop, I said, "Listen, let's go." Because I know, the old man was ninety-one years old, at the time. So I got there. I hit on the roof. Nothing. I said, "Somebody might have gone in the attic." You know. So I got in. We went under the carport and we hit. They didn't come out. So I said, "Well, somebody might have picked them up, or they left, you know." By that time, I turned in front of his house, he was hollering, "I'm over here. I'm over here. Me and daddy." I said, "How are y'all?

Are y'all all right?" He said, "Yeah, Daddy's on top of the snack bar sitting on a chair." And he had arthritis, poor old soul. So, the cop stayed right there by my boat to hold on to the post. I guess we had about a foot of space before the roof. So I had my life jacket on, I grabbed a life jacket. I went to meet the old man. And we put him a life jacket. And we pulled him out. We couldn't put him in the boat. He was old, too old, and hurting with arthritis. So his son said, "I got a truck and my car somewhere in the front yard." Didn't know where they were at. Under water. So I started walking. I hit them. So I made the cop bring my boat there. Put the old man on the car to load him in my boat. He was cold, poor soul. He was freezing, shaking so bad. I said, "You're getting hypothermic." So I had my slicker coat and I covered him good. And I told the little fellow, "We're going to just roll." And I went wide open, straight across, passed over barbed wire and never hit a fence. And I went through town wide open. I said, "The damage is done. I mean, sorry. We've got to go."

So we dropped him off, and kept picking up, picking up. And the neighbor over here, they stayed at their house, too. But they got on top of an icebox and floated across the pasture right here. Her and her husband. They saw us, but we couldn't see them. They had so much debris all over the place. She said, "I saw when y'all passed. I thought y'all would have come and get us." I said, "I didn't see y'all." So when we made the round, I passed like that, I went like that, came back to the house. Nothing. So we came back like that, and I got about half way, we turned. I cut across on Country Drive. And we picked up three other people right there, brought them in.

And then, a cop from New Iberia said, "I've got nine of my family behind Erath." And I said, "Well, I don't know where." He said, "Well, can I go with you?" I said, "Yeah." So we took off in my little boat. Cut across the field. Went to pick them up. And they were all in the house. All safe. They had water, I guess about six inches in the house. They wanted to go to Erath. I wasn't supposed to come that far, but I said, "I'm going to go." And so I went bring them to Erath at the railroad tracks. Came back. Picked up two other people. They had seen me. I said, "I can't pick y'all up now, but I'll send somebody to pick y'all up, or I'll pass back this afternoon, pick y'all up. I picked those two people up. Came back to Delcambre. I went drop them off. I came back. They had one lady that had cancer. She didn't want to leave. So we kept playing with her, playing with her. She didn't want to leave, so her daughter said, "Well, I'll stay." I said, "Once we leave, they won't let us come back." It was getting dark, five o'clock. The mayor said, "That's all. We don't want to put y'all in danger."

BA: Because there was no electricity.

GM: No electricity, nothing. Rain, rained hard. Hard, hard, hard. All during the day, we had to stop behind houses and let the wind slow down a little bit. Then it would pass.

Then the airboats would pass. So, the back way on 330 from Delcambre, got about half way. He must have hit a mailbox or something. Flipped his airboat. We had to pick them up, bring them back to town, and come back.

And on the Viking Bridge, right here, they had six people waiting on the bridge. It was high right there. So we picked them up, brought them back. Lonny Dubois and them. Brought them to Delcambre. But once we got to Delcambre, we didn't know where people were going. The National Guard would pick them up, and bring them to a school in New Iberia, I think. That's where they would go, bring them to a school. That was it, all day long.

BA: It sounds like you knew most of the people you were picking up.

GM: Yeah, I was born and raised in Delcambre. But we didn't go passed the bridge right here, the canal.

BA: Not only did you know the people, but you knew who had stayed.

GM: Yeah, and I knew the road, where to pass and not to pass, you know, stuff like that. But at one time, we had to stop. We had stopped at the ballpark in town. We tied on a big post, the light post. And the posts were rocking like that. I said, "Man, we're not in a good place." So I told the cop, "We're going to let go and we're going to go behind this house right here, and wait a while." You couldn't see right in front of you. It was raining so hard. About ten o'clock, that happened. But after it slowed down, we took off again. I had two bilge pumps and I'd leave them running all the time. All the time, all the time.

BA: What kind of boat were you driving?

GM: That little flat right there, outside. Sixteen-foot flat with a 40 Yamaha. I still got it.

BA: Kind of interesting that a guy in a sixteen-foot flat-bottom with a Yamaha 40 was picking up a guy who flipped his airboat.

GM: Yeah. He had to have hit a mailbox, and it rolled it over.

BA: Who was the cop with you? Was he local?

GM: Yeah, Brady Segura.

BA: A sheriff's deputy?

GM: No, Delcambre police. Yeah, he got in with us and two or three from New Iberia. Cops. Everybody had a cop. They were kind of worried, like New Orleans. But that was totally different. Them people, they wanted to get out and go. They weren't worried about stealing or nothing like that.

I didn't know it, but the next day, I came over here. The Sunday, me and my son-in-law came. I had a camp in the Chêne Canal, and we came over here. I could see my house, the roof on my house. I said, "There's nothing wrong with it. I got under the carport. They must have had about four feet of water still on the Sunday. I said, "There's something wrong." I kept feeling for the steps. I had three steps to come up in to my house. I said, "Well, I can't find the steps." I found it odd, so we go up to the door. Man, it was like somebody had gotten mad at us and just knocked everything. It floated. A total loss. It had floated about ten feet, I guess, against some hedges I had. It hung up on the hedges. It floated about ten feet. And then it stopped right there and when it went back down, the piers went through and through the floor. I had about eight feet of water, at least seven feet. My dishes on the second shelf in my cabinet had water in them.

BA: What about cows and horses?

GM: Yeah, we lost quite a bit of cows, bunch of horses. I had a brahma bull. I knew I was about the only one who had brahma bulls. Two people. And right by the cemetery, we had gone back to Delcambre, I saw a brahma lying down dead in the ditch. I said, "Can't be my bull way over here." So the next day, we went. I said, "Let's flip him over." We flipped him over. It was our brand. But what we did, I had some cable cutters. Every time we'd see some cows. Them cows would go like in a corner, and they'd hit the fence. They wouldn't swim over. So we'd cut the wires and let them climb on to Highway 330. They stayed on the road. Got them out of the water.

BA: So you saved a few cows too?

GM: Quite a few. Quite a few cows, yeah. Horses, they found high ground right here. We left them alone. And then there was no feed, no water. They couldn't drink that salt water. So we finally got enough drums and put fresh water. The little hay we found, we saved. We had just baled hay, but it all floated away.

BA: Who was keeping you supplied during that time?

GM: The town of Delcambre. They had water, a little bit of water, and gas. I had two twelve-gallon tanks. I could have run all day long on that. But they didn't want us to get stranded. So he gave us an extra five. And we did with that. The National Guard came in. I don't know what time they came in. And they told the mayor, we had overreacted. We shouldn't have done that. He said, "I couldn't have waited for y'all. Those people were stranded." He said, "My boys, when y'all got here, we had everybody out. And, for instance, right there by the ballpark, they got one of y'all's trucks head first in the ditch. Y'all didn't know the road. Y'all just drove it right in." A big, big, big truck. Head first in the ditch. We had to bring them boys back. They didn't know the area like we did. It was raining so hard, the air-boats were flooding out. The rain was hitting on their carburetors. They'd shut down. So they'd just tie their boats and we'd take off. We'd pick them up and bring them back.

From 6:30 in the morning till about five o'clock, we did not stop. We kept on going, back and forth, back and forth, back and forth. We'd slow down for the rain, and then take off again.

BA: Did y'all stop for the dark?
GM: Yeah. About five o'clock, the mayor said, "That's enough. I don't want to put y'all in it. Then we'd have to start looking for y'all." So we shut it down. It was getting cool, too. Wet and cold.

BA: How many people do you figure you got out?
GM: Oh . . . my boat, probably in the fifties, probably. My first one on this end, I picked up, because I knew he had stayed. The black fellow. And he said, "I knew you'd have come back for me."

BA: What was the reaction of the people you were picking up?
GM: They were scared. More than anything else, they were scared. If I would have flipped my boat, I guess, or we don't know. But I'd put them sitting down, and they wouldn't face the front. They'd all face me, and we'd just take off. And Brady's a big fellow. When I picked up them seven people in Erath, that little girl was crying, crying, and crying. Young little girl. I said, "We're going to bring you back to safety." So I told Brady, I said, "You might have to stay over here, and I'll pick you up on the way back." So we started putting everybody in my boat. We had about two inches of water before it would come in. I said, "Brady, you can't come." He said, "Well, I'll stay. Go bring them and pick me up. We'll pick up them other people. And we'll come back home."

BA: Did you run into anybody who was any trouble?
GM: No, not one person. They knew me and when they saw the boat, they knew they had to get in the boat and I'd bring them to safety. Everybody.

We had trouble for [Hurricane] Ike. Two people. They didn't want to come. I said, "If you want to come, I'll take you, but if you don't want to come, well . . ." But for Rita, everybody jumped in. They wanted to get out.

If you know the area, it's a lot easier. We worked back and forth, back and forth. From road to road, back and forth, back and forth. We'd holler. And we had a hammer. We'd hit on the house. If nobody would come, we'd keep on going. Most of the people were on their porches, waiting.

Where the water was coming over the tracks, it was like a waterfall. I'm not kidding you. It was shocking. The people who would get out of the boat, most of the time, they'd fall. The current would get them dizzy. Walking on the blacktop, it would get them dizzy, so they'd fall. People were picking them up, and putting them in that big truck, National Guard truck. I didn't see a lot of them people again until two weeks after, a lot of them. We didn't know where they had gone. They wouldn't let nobody in, because they were worried about people stealing.

BA: Did anybody you had picked up contact you?
GM: Yeah. Everybody. They were saying, "You're a hero." I'm not a hero. I was just doing what I had to do. You know what I mean? Not a hero. They said, "You didn't have to do that." I know I didn't have to, but somebody had to do it. It was there to do. And I'd do it again. I hope I don't have to, but I'd do it again.

MIKE DAVIS AND ANTHONY FONTENOT

Hurricane Gumbo

[Originally published in the November 7, 2005, issue of *The Nation*.]

Evangeline Parish, Louisiana

Nothing is moving in Evangeline Parish except for the sky. Black rain bands, the precursors of Hurricane Rita's fury, scud by at disconcerting velocity. Wind gusts uproot ancient oaks and topple a decrepit billboard advertising an extinct brand of chewing tobacco. The rice fields are flooding and the roads are barricaded with tree debris.

Millions of desperate Texans and southern Louisianans are still gridlocked on interstate highways headed north from Rita's path, but here in Ville Platte, a town of 11,000 in the heart of Acadiana (French-speaking southern Louisiana), the traditional response to an impending hurricane is not to evacuate but to gather together and cook.

Dolores Fontenot, matriarch of a clan that ordinarily mobilizes forty members for Sunday dinner (the "immediate family") and 800 for a wedding (the "extended family"), is supervising the preparation of a colossal

44

crab gumbo. Its rich aroma is sensory reassurance against the increasingly sinister machine-gunning of the rain on her home's boarded-up windows.

Although every major utility from Baton Rouge to Galveston has crashed, a noisy generator in the carport keeps lights flickering inside as little kids chase one another and older men converse worriedly about the fate of their boats and hunting camps. There are disturbing reports about the waters rising around Pecan Island, Holly Beach and Abbeville.

In addition to Fontenot kin, the table is also set for three eminent immunologists from Latin America, whose laboratories at the Tulane and LSU medical centers in New Orleans were flooded by Katrina, destroying several years of invaluable cancer research. The doctors, two from Medellín, Colombia, and one from Mexico City, joke that Ville Platte has become the "Cajun Ark."

It is a surprisingly apt analogy. The folks of Ville Platte, a poor Cajun and black Creole community with a median income less than half that of the rest of the nation, have opened their doors over the past three weeks to more than 5,000 of the displaced people they call "company" (the words "refugee" and "evacuee" are considered too impersonal, even impolite). Local fishermen and hunters, moreover, were among the first volunteers to take boats into New Orleans to rescue desperate residents from their flooded homes.

Ville Platte's homemade rescue and relief effort—organized around the popular slogan "If not us, then who?"—stands in striking contrast to the incompetence of higher levels of government as well as to the hostility of other, wealthier towns, including some white suburbs of New Orleans, toward influxes of evacuees, especially poor people of color. Indeed, Evangeline Parish as a whole has become a surprising island of interracial solidarity and self-organization in a state better known for incorrigible racism and corruption.

What makes Ville Platte and some of its neighboring communities so exceptional?

Part of the answer, we discovered, has been the subtle growth of a regional "nationalism" that has drawn southern Louisiana's root cultures—African American, black Creole, Cajun and French Indian—closer together in response to the grim and ever-growing threats of environmental and cultural extinction. There is a shared, painful recognition that the land is rapidly sinking and dying, as much from the onslaught of corporate globalization as from climate wrath.

If one wanted to be fashionably academic, Ville Platte's big-hearted-ness might be construed as a conscious response to the "postcolonial" crisis of Acadiana. In plainer language, it is an act of love in a time of danger: a radical but traditionalist gesture that defies most of the simplistic antinomies—liberal versus conservative, red state versus blue state, freedom of choice versus family values, and so on—that the media use to categorize contemporary American life.

But before arguing theory, it is first necessary to introduce some of the ordinary heroes sitting around Dolores Fontenot's generous dinner table as Rita shakes the earth outside.

The Cajun Navy

Edna Fontenot passes around bottles of beer—Corona in honor of the Latin American guests. He is a lean, gentle-spirited man in his late 40s with an impressive résumé of mechanical skills and survival expertise.

"You know, we were all watching New Orleans on television and we realized that somebody's got to help all these people, because nothing was happening. Nothing. Then there was a call [by the Louisiana Department of Wildlife and Fisheries] for small boats. So I said, I'm going. I knew I could do something. I lived in New Orleans and know how to get around on water."

Edna drove to nearby Lafayette (Acadiana's informal capital city) then convoyed with scores of other boat owners to Old Metairie, across from the broken 17th Street Canal that had emptied the waters of Lake Pontchartrain into central New Orleans.

"There was no FEMA, just a big ol' bunch of Cajun guys in their boats. We tried to coordinate best we could, but it was still chaos. It was steaming hot and there was a smell of death. The people on the rooftops and overpasses were desperate. They had been there for several days in the sun with no food, no water. They were dehydrated, blistered and sick . . . giving up, you know, ready to die."

Edna stayed for two days until floating debris broke his propeller. Although FEMA has recently taken credit for the majority of rescues, Edna scoffs at its claims. Apart from the Coast Guard, he saw only the Wildlife and Fisheries' "Cajun Navy" in action. "That was it. Just us volunteers." He feels guilty that he couldn't afford to fix his boat and return. "I had some good times in that damn city," he says softly, "and, you know, I have more black friends there than white."

City of the Dead

While Edna was saving the living, his brother-in-law, a police detective from another city, was engaged in the grueling, macabre work of retrieving bodies. "Vincent" (his real name can't be used) went out each night in a Fisheries boat with a scuba diver and an M-16-toting National Guard escort.

"I wore a [hazmat] space suit and piloted the boat. I was chosen because I'm trained in forensics, and since I am a Cajun the higher powers assumed I was a water baby. We worked at night because of the heat and to avoid the goddamn news helicopters that hover like vultures during the daytime. We didn't want some poor son of a bitch seeing his grandma covered with ants or crabs on the 6 o'clock news."

Ants and crabs? "Hey, this is Louisiana. The minute New Orleans flooded it became swamp again. The ecosystem returns. Ants float and they build big colonies on floating bodies the same as they would upon a cypress log. And the crabs eat carrion. We'd pulled the crabs off, but the goddamn ants were a real problem."

Vincent described the exhausting, gruesome work of hauling bloated bodies aboard the boat and then zipping them into body bags. (FEMA neglected water, food rations and medicine, but did fly thousands of body bags into Louis Armstrong Airport.) Although Vincent was supposed to tag the bags, few victims had any identification. Some didn't have faces.

One of us asks about the demographics of death.

We pulled seventy-seven bodies out of the water. Half were little kids. It was tough—no one died with their eyes closed, and all had fought like hell, some slowly drowning in their attics.

I deal with crime scenes and human remains all the time and usually keep a professional distance. You have to, if you want to continue to do your job. But sometimes a case really gets to you. We found the corpse of a woman clutching a young baby. Mother or sister, I don't know. I couldn't pry the infant out of the woman's grasp without breaking her fingers. After finally separating them, the baby left a perfect outline imprinted across the lady's chest. That will really haunt me. And so will the goddamn cries of the people we left behind.

We were under strict orders to remove only bodies. But there were still lots of people on the roofs or leaning out the windows of their houses. They were crazy with fear and thirst. They screamed, begged and cursed us. But we had a boatload of bodies, some probably infectious. So we saved the dead and left the living.

Vincent believes that the "sniper activity" so luridly reported in the media was from stranded people who were outraged when boats and helicopters ignored them.

Madonna and Child

Danny Guidry, a paramedic married to a Fontenot cousin, has a story with a happier ending. Along with his partner and driver, he was sent with dozens of ambulances and rescue units from the Cajun parishes to the edge of New Orleans.

As victims were brought in by volunteers in boats or by the Coast Guard in their big Black Hawk helicopters, Danny classified them according to the severity of their condition and took the most critical cases to Baton Rouge, one and a half hours away through the pandemonium of emergency traffic.

Since southern Louisiana's only full-fledged trauma center was in a rapidly flooding hospital in New Orleans, most of the injured or sick evacuees were dropped at a triage center in a Baton Rouge sports stadium where a single nurse, just 24 years old, was in charge of sorting out cases and sending the most serious to already overwhelmed local hospitals.

"By my third trip," Danny explained, "I was working on automatic pilot. You just shut yourself off from the pain and turmoil around you and concentrate on doing your job as carefully and quickly as possible." But, like Vincent, he found one case extraordinary.

> She was a young lady, thirty-three weeks pregnant, in premature labor. She had been in a hospital ready for a caesarean section when the evacuation of the city was announced. Her physician stopped the labor and sent her home, presuming, I guess, that she had access to a car, which she didn't. Her husband went out to look for food, then the levee broke. When we picked her up, the husband had been missing for several days. To make matters more complicated, she was cradling a 9-month-old baby that she had rescued from a crack-addict neighbor. Both she and the infant were heat stressed, and my sixth sense told me she might not make it to Baton Rouge.
>
> It was the longest run of my career. Her IV was bad and I was running out of fluid. She was getting paler, and her blood pressure was falling dangerously. My orders were to take her to the central triage center, but I told my partner to punch it and head straight to the nearest hospital.

Out of professional protocol I never divulge personal information to a victim. But this case really moved me, so I gave this young woman my phone number and urged her, Please call when you are out of labor. In fact, I kept phoning the hospital to monitor her progress. She had a healthy baby and eventually found her husband. Meanwhile, the infant she had saved was reunited with its mother. Having come this far with this girl, I just couldn't walk away, so my wife and I invited her and her husband to Ville Platte. We found them a little house and she's getting ready to go to college in Lafayette. I helped board up their windows this afternoon.

"Just Friends"

In between Rita's windy tantrums, we made a quick run down to the Civic Center Shelter, where volunteers welcomed new "company" from the hurricane-threatened Louisiana-Texas border area.

The shelter is supported only by local resources but provides ample beds, toys, television, Internet access, superb Cajun-Creole cooking and hospitality to evacuees staying only for a few nights or waiting to be rehoused on a medium-term basis with local residents.

The center's founders include Edna's "Kosher Cajun" cousin Mark Krasnoff (his dad was from Brooklyn) and Jennifer Vidrine, who has become its full-time coordinator. Everyone had told us that Jennifer has the most gorgeous smile in Louisiana. Although she hadn't slept in two days, her smile indeed brightened the entire shelter.

An LSU graduate with a recent fellowship at Harvard's prestigious Kennedy School, Jennifer has had every opportunity to conquer the world, but she wouldn't think of leaving Ville Platte. She talks about the first week after Katrina.

"There were just thousands of tired, scared people on the roads of Evangeline Parish. Not just in cars: Some were walking, carrying everything they still owned in a backpack. Some were crying; they had a look of hopelessness. It was like *The Grapes of Wrath*. Most knew nothing about Ville Platte, but were amazed when we invited them into our homes."

It sounds too good to be true: Acadiana, despite deep cross-racial kinships of culture, religion and blood, was once a bastion of Jim Crow. Just a few years ago an effort by Ville Platte authorities to redistrict the town to dilute the black vote was struck down as a violation of the Voting Rights Act. So we ask Jennifer, who's both "French" and African American, if the relief effort isn't discreetly color-coded, with a preference for suburban white refugees.

She's unflappable. "No, not at all. We embrace everyone with the same love. And the whole community supports this project: black, white, Catholic, Baptist. Perhaps one-third of all private homes have taken in out-of-town folks. And it doesn't matter where our 'company' comes from: the Ninth Ward [black] or Chalmette [white]. That's just the way we are. We're all raised to take care of neighbors and give kindness to strangers. This is what makes this little town special and why I love it so much."

Jennifer praises local schoolteachers and the City Council. But when we ask about the contribution of the national relief organizations and the federal government, she points to the banner over the shelter's entrance: NO RED CROSS, NO SALVATION ARMY OR FEDERAL FUNDS . . . JUST FRIENDS.

"I started trying to contact the Red Cross immediately. I phoned them for thirteen days straight. I was told 'no personnel are available.' [According to the *Wall Street Journal*, the Red Cross, which raised $1 billion in the name of aiding Katrina victims, had 163,000 volunteers available.] Finally, they promised to come, but then canceled at the last minute. FEMA is just the same. We have yet to see the federal government in person." Indeed, before Rita closed the roads, we saw no evidence of a federal presence, although we ran across several SUVs with Halliburton logos.

Ville Platte, whose black majority has an annual per capita income of only $5,300, has thus managed to help thousands of strangers without a single cent of Red Cross or federal aid. We remain incredulous: What superior organizational principle or charismatic leadership is responsible for such an achievement?

Jennifer is bemused. "Listen, my committee is my telephone. I call folks and they respond. Food, clothing, cots, medicine—it's all provided. Even poor people down here have some extra deer meat in the freezer or an old quilt or an extra bed. And all of us know how to spontaneously cooperate. My God, we're always organizing christenings or family gatherings. So why do we need a lot of formal leadership?" In a nation currently without competent leadership, this may be a reasonable, even deeply profound, question.

The People's Republic of the Bayous?

So what does it all mean?

Mark Krasnoff thinks Ville Platte is the shape of things to come: southern Louisiana getting its interracial act together to take on its colonizers and rulers. A small, wiry man with the build of a dancer or gymnast, he is an actor (most recently in a prophetic FX network TV drama, *Oil Storm*, about a category 6 hurricane hitting the Gulf Coast) and a stunning bilingual raconteur. He is also the Che Guevara-cum-Huey Long of Evangeline Parish. His beat-up pickup wears the bumper sticker LOUISIANA: THIRD WORLD AND PROUD OF IT.

> Look, Louisiana is the same as any exploited oil-rich country—like a Nigeria or Venezuela. For generations the big oil and gas companies have pumped billions out of our bayous and offshore waters, and all we get back is coastal erosion, pollution, cancer and poverty. And now bloated bodies and dead towns.
>
> People in the rest of America need to understand there are no "natural" disasters in Louisiana. This is one of the richest lands in the world—everything from sugar and crawfish to oil and sulfur—but we're neck-to-neck with Mississippi as the poorest state. Sure, Washington builds impressive levees to safeguard river commerce and the shipping industry, but do you honestly think they give a shit about blacks, Indians and coonasses [pejorative for Cajuns]? Poor people's levees, if they even existed, were about as good as our schools [among the worst in the nation]. Katrina just followed the outlines of inequality.

Mark is incandescent. "The very soul of Louisiana is now at stake." He enumerates the working-class cultures threatened with extinction: the "second line" black neighborhoods of New Orleans, the French Indians in Houma, the Isleño (Canary Islander) and Vietnamese fishermen in Plaquemines, Cajun communities all along the Gulf Coast. "If our 'leaders' have their way this whole goddamn region will become either a toxic graveyard or a big museum where jazz, zydeco, and Cajun music will still be played for tourists but the cultures that gave them life are defunct or dispersed."

Mark's worst fears, of course, are rapidly becoming facts on the ground. Bush's Housing Secretary, Alphonso Jackson, told the *Houston Chronicle* on September 30, "I think it would be a mistake to rebuild the Ninth Ward." He predicted that New Orleans' black population, 67 percent before Katrina, would shrink to 35 to 40 percent. "New Orleans is not going to be as black as it was for a long time, if ever again," he said.

This was undoubtedly music to the ears of Republican master strategist Karl Rove, who knows that the loss of 10,000 or 15,000 active black Democratic voters could alter the balance of power in Louisiana and transform overnight a pink state into a red state. The GOP could gain another senator as well as the governorship.

Mark's preferred solution is secession: "Let us keep our oil and gas revenues and we can preserve our way of life as well. We don't really belong to the same cultural system anyway. You prize money, competition and individual success; we value family, community and celebration. Give us independence and we'll restore the wetlands, rebuild the Ninth Ward and move the capital to Evangeline Parish. If you wish, you can ship the Statue of Liberty to Ville Platte and we'll add a new inscription: Send us your tired and huddled masses and we'll feed them hurricane gumbo."

We all laugh, but everyone understands it is gallows humor. Ordinary people across Louisiana and the Gulf Coast are beginning to understand what it's like to be Palestinians or Iraqis at the receiving end of Washington's hypocritical promises and disastrous governmental and military actions.

Katrina and Rita have stripped Louisiana naked: Exposed to a brutal light are government neglect, corporate rapine and blatant ethnic cleansing. Equally revealed, however, is the bayou country's ancient moral bedrock of populist revolt, cultural resistance and New Testament generosity. But when in the entire bloody course of history has the kindness of strangers ever defeated the conspiracy of money and power?

JOCELYN H. DONLON AND JON G. DONLON

Government Gives Tradition the Go-Ahead

The Atchafalaya Welcome Center's Role in Hurricane Katrina Recovery

[This article was originally published in the *Louisiana Folklore Miscellany*, Volume 16–17 in 2008.]

The assault of Katrina and Rita—if not the biggest, longest, or most deadly catastrophic event in world history—is undeniably the catastrophic event of our lifetime—one which we will spend the rest of our lives trying to understand and recover from. There is no need to catalog the numerous horrifying stories of government failure that followed the wholesale loss of life, the widespread destruction of housing, and the loss of income for many. We have all, by now, heard countless accounts of the failure of government to meet the needs of hurricane victims and to cooperate with civic-minded citizens and businesses. And we have all—at least we're assuming all—felt the indignity associated with such failure.

But in our fieldwork to document hurricane stories, we found a case that made us feel unashamed. This article is to unabashedly celebrate a local example of cooperation between government and citizens which worked not just well, but exceptionally well: The staff at the Butte La Rose Atchafalaya Welcome Center responded to victims of Hurricane Katrina with not only basic necessities but also with grace, generosity, and an organic hospitality embedded in local tradition and shared community values.

When the staff of the Atchafalaya Welcome Center got "the call" and the credit card from Angele Davis, secretary of tourism, on the Wednesday after Katrina made landfall, the welcome center began to play quick host to thousands of our tired, our hungry, our own huddled masses yearning to eat and to be clean again.

In her work with the State of Louisiana Office of Homeland Security and Emergency Preparedness Emergency Operations Center, otherwise known as "Command Center," Angele Davis had identified the Atchafalaya Welcome Center as well as the state welcome center in Alexandria as being on the path of the exit buses transiting evacuees from New Orleans. Davis's role, as she described it, was to secure transportation for first responders, relief workers, and evacuees. She also worked with DOTD to provide logistical assistance in mapping bus routes as they exited the Superdome and Convention Center. Following Davis's directive, the Atchafalaya center did indeed become a very welcome island of brief respite for hurricane victims who were evacuated from the Superdome and the Convention Center. Over the course of three days, the staff and community volunteers fed, clothed, and literally rehumanized more than 100,000 people.

The Atchafalaya Welcome Center is the flagship for a once-planned series of heavily enhanced "portal" rest stops (needless to say, these plans have been delayed by the hurricanes). From its inception, the Atchafalaya Welcome Center has been a community facility. Residents participated in government meetings to help design it, their handiwork is on exhibit there, and they have been an active part of its success by volunteering for events. Because they were already familiar with the welcome center as a community site, they knew exactly where to go when help was needed.

We have had some history with this welcome center. Five years ago, we prepared a cultural inventory of resources to be used in the exhibit area; we sat in on meetings to consult on design and interpretation; we have written educational materials for the Atchafalaya Basin Program tied to a fieldtrip to the welcome center; and we have generally been advocates for its effectiveness. Grounded in our Basin fieldwork, we delivered a paper a few years ago at the Louisiana Folklore Society meeting describing *Atchafalaya Basin Houseboat Communities*. In it, we explained that "traditional campboat communities in the Atchafalaya Basin developed their own culture and way of life, as well as passing along, generation by generation, a lavish body of technical information about their specialized skills. Fathers, uncles, mothers, aunts, and friends taught young people their way of life."

In the instance of the welcome center, it's not necessarily technical minutia of commercial fishing being transmitted from generation to generation, but the shared values and traditions of community and family that were brought to bear. From within the folk group of Acadiana, in general, and of St. Martin Parish, in particular, people came together to serve as hosts without having to be taught how. To outsiders traumatized by the storm, they extended their sense of community to create a human connection, however short term it was. We will describe the relief effort and explain how reliance on local community norms created an exemplary achievement in the wake of Hurricane Katrina, traits that remain powerful assets with which to model preferred outcomes in the future.

The title of this article suggests that the people at the Atchafalaya Welcome Center waited for "the call" from Command Center in order to begin responding to hurricane victims. But that's not entirely accurate. If we were to rename the paper today, it might read something like, "Government Gives Tradition the Go-Ahead for Efforts Already Begun." Angele Davis told us, "The first call I made was around 9:00 at night, and I said, 'You need to get ready for 6:00 tomorrow morning.'" But before Cyndi Bruner-Wilkerson, director of the welcome center, got Davis's call, she was already working with the local network of civic leaders to respond to evacuees traveling in their personal vehicles.

Dona Degatur Richard, director of the St. Martin Parish Tourism Commission, Tina Begnaud, director of Breaux Bridge's Chamber of Commerce, and Lieutenant Nick Breaux with the sheriff's department in St. Martin Parish had, even before Katrina, begun to see a need for welcome centers to serve as disaster response facilities with Hurricane Ivan. As Dona Richard puts it:

> It started with Ivan, really. Last year, for the evacuation with Hurricane Ivan, that morning when the staff got here, the parking lot was full. It was people that didn't have money for a hotel. The shelters hadn't opened up. Red Cross hadn't opened up. We're below I-10, so they'll probably never open up a Red Cross shelter in St. Martin Parish. Cyndi and I and Marel had talked about how we needed to find a way to feed these people. Cause the people that were here last year—you knew they didn't have money to eat.

The most revealing lines in this narrative are "We're below I-10, so they'll probably never open up a Red Cross shelter in St. Martin Parish" and "We needed to find a way to feed these people." Together these lines indicate the local ingenuity grounded in a sense of place that, time and again, has characterized our fieldwork in the Basin. Dona recognizes their being situated in a low-lying area, not likely a site for a shelter; and it is the challenges of this low-lying area that have produced generations of people who have thrived through their own ingenuity. When Dona said, "We needed to find a way to feed these people," she was echoing the generations of residents who found a way to survive in this land of make-do. And she was extending the values of community, sharing to those outside her immediate circle. The relief workers seemed to respond to the people coming through in much the same way that we respond to friends in grief: we bring them food and we give them a tissue or, in this case, a wet wipe.

The collective ingenuity and traditions of sharing informed the Atchafalaya Welcome Center's effort from the outset. On the Tuesday morning following Katrina's landfall, Cyndi began to play the hand she and the others had been dealt. She said:

> We actually saw the first passenger car post-evacuees from New Orleans (because the levee broke we now know) early Tuesday morning. We saw people who had barely anything because they fled. People in their own vehicles with pets, children . . . We also saw the military. It wasn't just people westbound; it was eastbound into New Orleans. Convoys. So we had some stored bottle water, so we started pulling the water out and icing it down and Liney [the groundskeeper] left to go pick up some ice. Someone arrived with cold cuts and cheese. I don't know how that happened. [she says to Dona] Did y'all make those phone calls? And they brought bread. So we started throwing sandwiches together to feed the soldiers, who were so appreciative. So they had MREs which they started sharing with us, when they found out we couldn't find our trailer truckload full. They said, "We have 120; we'll give you 40."

And, thus, this organic, home-grown community effort informally began, despite the government's initial failure to deliver the expected MREs. The welcome center became an official, full-fledge state-sanctioned disaster response center on Wednesday, with Angele Davis's call from Command Center, and lasted through the following Sunday, round the clock. In Davis's words, "Many of the people had been without food, clothing, water, for so long that we didn't want to just put them on a bus and send them on multiple-hour trips without giving them the opportunity to get food and get cleaned up." She worked with FEMA and the Office of Homeland Security to get seventy port-o-lets on the ground, to attempt to get MREs there, and to deliver water, lots of water. As Cyndi said, "We had seven trailer truckloads of water . . . we had little bitty bottles, we had big bottles, we had gallon jugs, we had every kind of water the government could send us."

Because the people running the relief effort are also members of a local community, they knew immediately whom to contact. Early on, Cyndi contacted Frank Gerami, the owner of Party Central in Lafayette, who set up a twenty-by-forty-foot tent with tables and cooling fans. Dona contacted Byron Blanchard, with the Crawfish Festival Association, who provided refrigerators for the kitchen, so that the mountains of home-cooked food delivered by residents could be preserved. But her own words tell a more complete story of community connections:

> [Mark Bernard with the Crawfish Festival Association] happened to be off that week on vacation, and he had tried going with a boat to New Orleans, and he couldn't . . . they didn't need him. . . . So I had called him for something else, cause he and I are good friends. So he ended up spending all of his time here. The Crawfish Festival is a very civic-minded organization, so they ended up coming here, too, and those were the people to go to. If you need something, you go to them.

The people at the welcome center knew, already, who to go to for help. But the effort worked because the community—individuals, businesses, civic organizations—also knew to come without being asked. The staff oversaw three to four hundred volunteers, including children. As Cyndi said:

> We had ten- and eleven-year-old children who were energetic. And their parents were so pleased. Because their task was to take large boxes of baby wipes . . . people just love getting a little small bag of baby wipes that they could clean themselves and get the sweat or the dirt off . . . so the children were taking little Ziplocs and boxes of wipes and making little mini wipe-bags. . . . We also had people who donated toys and things. And they would put little groups of things together, sheets of paper and crayons and things, and they would fold it all up and give the children coming through two or three crayons . . .

Their willingness to engage the children in the volunteer effort goes a long way in explaining how community traditions and values have been transmitted through the generations.

An understanding of the needs of children and infants was central to the response effort. Paula Leon, a local volunteer, was one of many to help with "the babies." When the "baby section" eventually moved to the porch outside, she was put in charge of it. She told horrific stories of babies showing up in nothing but a Winn Dixie shopping bag, cut with two arm-holes. Of babies in shredded blankets. Of babies separated from mothers. Of babies dangling listlessly in the arms of strangers. On the sprawling porch of the welcome center, Paula established a "baby section," where she could clean and reclothe babies, and wrap them in a newly donated blanket, while the adults with them were able to eat the food provided by the community.

While the government was willing to provide MREs, the community knew that an MRE wasn't enough. People showed up to cook jambalaya on the grounds, they delivered loaves of bread and sandwich meat, and our favorite food story is about the okra donated by "John" at the Wal-Mart in Breaux Bridge; this story is told mostly by Tina Begnaud, with the Breaux Bridge Chamber of Commerce:

> You know when St. Bernard came through, it was about 8:00, I guess. We had just finished feeding three Greyhound buses, and I was in the kitchen (they didn't really like me in the kitchen, I wasn't in charge of KP), but, well, Ms. Betty would get so nervous that she wouldn't have enough food. And it was like, "Ms. Betty, it's gonna be fine. Don't worry about it. It's all gonna fall into place." I said, "Y'all don't like me to cook, I'm going outside." So I go out on the porch and I'm drinking me a little bottle of water, because we had so much water, that's all they would let us drink! I'm smoking a cigarette, and I go, "Oh my God . . ."
> DONA: That's not really what you said . . .
> TINA: . . . I did, "Oh no!" There were seventeen buses—school buses—coming off the interstate. I came running in, "MS BETTYYYYYY!!!" I said, "Ms. Betty, what we gonna do. There's seventeen school buses!" She said, "You better be lying to me!" I said, "No, I swear!" You know, they wouldn't believe everything I would tell them. So someone had smothered some okra . . .
> NICK SAYS: Wal-Mart sent 2 5-gallon containers of smothered okra.
> TINA CONTINUES: We put it on the stove, we put it in the pot. Now, granted, if anybody knows someone who has some pots, they could use a set. We had two pots, but it was actually still warm so it worked out all right, and we had some rice and some boudin.
> DONA: We come up with some food!
> TINA: So it was like the wedding, you know, when the loaves of bread were presented to Jesus and the bottle [of wine]. Honey, we fed seventeen buses with macaroni and cheese, everything we had left in the fridge from that

day; we started heating it . . . we served them their rice, their okra, and a
little piece of boudin on top. And it was great.

PAULA: . . . God bless you, God bless you.

TINA: As they were leaving, I asked one lady, "How did you enjoy that?"
She ended up with a hot dog, I think, because we ended up finding a pack of
wieners, . . . a pack of wieners and some buns . . . and she said, "Honey, I ate
that like it was a rib-eye and a stuffed baked potato!" And it's like . . . and I
don't know that any of us really ate the whole time we were here because it
was kind of hard.

This group narrative reveals a whole host of examples of why the Atchafalaya Welcome Center's Katrina response effort worked so well. In the
example, we can see the intimate banter and joking that demonstrate how
comfortable the people are working together. Throughout the effort, they
all kept a sense of humor characteristic of the fun-loving community.
Indeed, we were struck with how, despite the horrors of the experience,
elements of play and even of festival organizing were incorporated into
the relief effort with tents, tables, cooling fans, jambalaya pots. We are
surprised, really, that there wasn't a band on the porch. We are certain that
the collective understanding of play helped them to sustain their efforts.

This example also reveals their local foodways, their ability to throw
together a meal from what can be found in the "land of make-do." The
ability to make a plate of okra, boudin, and rice sound so appetizing isn't
found in just any town. And with the serving of this food there was a characteristic desire to please a guest. Ms. Betty's getting "so nervous that she
wouldn't have enough food" reminded us of the time Jocelyn's mother
cooked three 16-quart casseroles of cornbread dressing for our family at
Thanksgiving, just in case. And when the food was offered—sometimes
seeming as miraculous as with the wedding of Cana, as Tina said—it was
important to the hosts that the food please the guests, even a simple hot
dog. This, to us, is an authentic example of communitarian values of sharing with neighbors, not paternalistic condescension too often associated
with some volunteer efforts.

And, indeed, the food was appreciated; the evacuees knew to do their
part in being "good guests." Mr. Liney, the groundskeeper, said, "I've never
been blessed so many times in my life," and, as the woman in the previous illustration showed, they received hot dogs as though they had been
given steak and potatoes. Graciousness was a shared value between many
of the hosts and the guests, as was religious faith. Cyndi Wilkerson, at one
time, said that they marveled at how, in her words, they had "a direct line

to God's switchboard," that no matter what they needed, they were able to get it. (We would say that these workers showed that if God does have a switchboard, it's on the ground, with the people who dial the numbers on earth.)

We wouldn't be doing justice to this discussion if we didn't also say that one reason the effort worked so well was that the people in charge placed being flexible at a high premium. They were willing to "press the envelope" when it came to following rules. Someone's friend who had a daughter who was a nurse offered her help, and thus an unofficial triage area emerged to deal with minor cuts, scrapes, and "that rash" that started showing up. Had the state and federal bureaucracy been half so willing to operate according to their own good sense, perhaps we wouldn't have seen some of the horrors that we did.

And, to be realistic, the relief effort worked because each bus stop was short term. Had they been forced to shelter all the people they fed for weeks on end, we might have heard a different story. But, as Dona said:

> A good analogy . . . I told my mother . . . we're just a band-aid on the bobo. We don't do major surgery here. All we're doing is applying a little band-aid here. That's our job.

Yet and still, it was a very important band-aid, one which was applied with grace, compassion, and even tears. As Lieutenant Nick said, "I've never cried so many type tears in my life."

Can such an organic model grounded in values and traditions of family and community be replicated? At first, the questions seems about as unproductive as Baton Rougeons going to Austin to ask why it's cool and Baton Rouge is not—which some Baton Rouge civic leaders did do. However, at least their going to Austin posed the question. And, in the case of replicating the Atchafalaya Welcome Center's relief effort, while we can't march in and demand that communities possess the shared values and traditions of St. Martin Parish—values and traditions which drove this effort to, as Angele Davis put it, "give back to people who had lost so much"—we can look at some tangibles: gathering necessary supplies, developing lists of contacts, knowing your community assets and traits, communicating with civic leaders, getting the word out to volunteers, preparing food, providing restrooms and cleaning towels. These are all concrete steps that can be taken to prepare for disaster relief. And if other welcome centers can undertake their relief efforts with the competence and compassion that the people of the Atchafalaya Welcome Center did, they will have accomplished something valuable.

We noted at the beginning that this paper would unabashedly celebrate this particular relief effort, and we meant it. By the time we interviewed the people involved with the Atchafalaya Welcome Center, we had heard so many horrific stories that we wondered what kind of medication we were going to need to see our hurricane stories project through. But after we completed this interview, we felt fortified, and, dare we say it, proud. It has been hard to feel uplifted throughout much of this nightmare. As we all continue to collect hurricane stories, we hope we'll continue to make room for what worked *organically*, and to envision ways to turn our everyday cultural assets into future policy.

MARCIA GAUDET

"Don't Get Stuck on Stupid"

General Honoré as Culture Hero

When a kingdom or homeland is threatened, the people pray for a savior
or hero to appear to lead them.
—Lord Raglan

A major concern expressed by people in the first few days after Hurricane
Katrina's devastation of New Orleans and the Mississippi Gulf Coast was
the perceived lack of competent leadership, the absence of someone in
control. On the third day, Lieutenant General Russel Honoré arrived in
New Orleans and took command of the federal military operations. His
authoritative style in commanding his troops, his compassion toward the
evacuees, and his refreshingly sharp directness of speech with the media
soon raised him to the status of folk or culture hero. The context and the
characteristics of General Honoré made this elevation inevitable.

In "Some Varieties of Heroes in America," Roger Abrahams defined
a hero as "a man whose deeds epitomize the masculine attributes most
highly valued within a society" (341–42). Whether or not folklorists support the idea of a normative model of heroic action in our culture, the
"folk" recognize a hero when they see one functioning like what they
believe a hero should be. General Honoré clearly met the perhaps unar-
ticulated but not unknown cultural standards for heroic action. A hero
in this context was a person whose deeds epitomize the attributes of

leadership most highly valued within that culture as well as those attributes most desperately needed in the wake of the hurricanes—someone to take command, someone to lead, someone to give at least the appearance of being in control.

In *The Great Deluge*, Tulane University historian Douglas Brinkley describes the devastation and hopelessness in New Orleans in the first few days after Katrina. He says, "a glimmer of hope appeared on Thursday in the form of Lieutenant General Russel Honoré . . . He gave the impression of a man not overwhelmed by the magnitude of the job at hand" (524), and "He had the kind of cool strength for which New Orleans had been longing for days" (525).

General Honoré, commander of Joint Task Force-Katrina, was the perfect hero for post-Katrina New Orleans. He came to New Orleans as a three-star general in the United States Army in charge of all active-duty military personnel sent to the area, but he was part of the Louisiana cultural vernacular as well. Honoré's response illustrates the kind of practical, effective actions that emerged from the people—finding solutions to solve immediate problems of survival in spite of potential violations of boundaries or protocol. People in Louisiana and the Gulf Coast perceived him as the native son, returning to his threatened homeland to lead his people out of chaos and devastation.

The concepts of hero, folk hero, and culture hero differ not only among cultures, but within cultures as well. While the local people conceptualized as heroic what General Honoré was doing, they probably did not specify his actions as that of a "culture hero" or a "folk hero." But, they had no doubt that he was a *hero*. Neither did the members of the media. Patrik Jonsson of the *Christian Science Monitor* calls him "the Rudy Giuliani of the Gulf Coast," comparing his performance with that of the mayor of New York City after the 9/11 terrorists attacks. A Survey USA poll of 1,200 Americans voted General Honoré "the most effective leader of the relief operation." In *USA Today*, Donna Leinwand wrote: "Lt. Gen. Russel Honoré, a Louisiana native, has become the symbol of New Orleans' emergence from chaos to reconstruction." The *Washington Post* described him as "The Category 5 General." Jeff Duncan of the *New Orleans Times-Picayune* described Honoré as "Hurricane Katrina's reluctant superstar." Kyra Phillips of CNN hailed him as "large and in charge."

While General Honoré's deeds were certainly important, it seems clear that more is involved in the elevation of someone to hero status than a series of actions (see, for example, Roger Abrahams and John Roberts). The question is—what is it that people saw in this particular situation and this particular person that so quickly made General Honoré, without question, a *hero*?

Russel Honoré was born in Lakeland, Louisiana, in Pointe Coupee Parish, shortly after a hurricane in 1948. He is the eighth son and one of twelve children in a Creole Catholic family. Honoré graduated from Rosenwald High School in New Roads and earned a bachelor's degree in agriculture from Southern University in Baton Rouge. He also has a master's degree in human resources management from Troy State. Honoré is a three-star general, with an imposing demeanor—he stands six feet two inches. He also knows New Orleans well, having spent two weeks at Charity Hospital in New Orleans as a child, after he had been hit in the head with a baseball bat. At the time of Katrina, he was commanding general of the U.S. First Army at Fort Gillem, Georgia, near Atlanta. Though he was nicknamed the "Ragin' Cajun" by his troops, his heritage is Afro-French Creole, not Cajun (i.e., descendants of the French Acadians from Nova Scotia).

Three days after Katrina devastated New Orleans, Mayor Ray Nagin made an emotional national plea for help on local New Orleans newscaster Garland Robinette's WWL Radio broadcast. New Orleans was underwater. The only thing Nagin gave President Bush credit for was sending General Honoré to New Orleans. He described Honoré as "a John Wayne dude who can get some stuff done," and said, "He came off the doggone chopper, and he started cussing, and people started moving . . ." After this broadcast, media covered almost everything General Honoré did and said. As he walked around the city telling police and National Guardsmen, "Put those guns down, put those god-damned guns down," the response around the state was one of the arrival of the Savior, one who would not only lead the rescue and recovery efforts but would set the media straight in what Tulane University professor Gaurav Desai called the "rhetorical Third Worlding of New Orleans and Louisiana" by the national media during their Katrina coverage (Desai 2005, 6). General Honoré's appearance as a cigar-smoking general in fatigues and a beret, his trickster-like use of language with such phrases as "You are stuck on stupid," and his sometimes unorthodox actions drew admiration and confidence in a man who had the authority and structure of the U.S. Army. But people also saw on television another side of General Honoré—the compassionate father and grandfather who comforted a young mother carrying twins, taking the infants from her arms into the care of his assistants. In addition, he is a Louisiana native son who came "home" when a hero was desperately needed. Wherever blame may be placed most strongly—on city, state, or federal officials—one thing was clear. The situation lacked a strong leader.

It lacked even the appearance of leadership. In *The Great Deluge*, Douglas Brinkley describes Louisiana governor Kathleen Blanco as "shell-shocked, disoriented, and running on no sleep . . . She was near tears" (265–66). He also says, "The arrival of Lt. General Russel Honoré drew cheers from the Gulf South, which desperately needed straight talk from someone at the federal level. The three stars on his shoulders were the first tangible evidence that the Bush administration hadn't forgotten the region" (540).

Brinkley's comments mirror the responses of the local media. *Times-Picayune* reporter Jeff Duncan wrote: "Lt. Gen. Russel Honoré, the commanding general of Joint Task Force Katrina, is on the scene—and everybody knows it. Police officers, relief workers and medical personnel flock to him to shake his hand or pose for pictures. One by one, U.S. senators fight their way through the crowd to congratulate him for his efforts." Duncan says, "The Honoré legend began from the moment his boot hit Canal Street and national TV cameras captured him dressing down soldiers for carrying their firearms with the barrels pointed too high." He further says that "New Orleans Mayor Ray Nagin cemented Honoré's hero status during an emotional radio interview in the chaotic days after the storm." Duncan calls Honoré, "the white knight for those affected by Katrina, a salty-mouthed, cigar-chompin' guardian angel in camouflage."

In folk culture and literature, a culture hero is one who brings food, drink, and the arts to mankind. Barbara Babcock-Abrahams notes that the trickster is often regarded as a culture hero, and she points out the paradox of the trickster and the culture hero, where attributes of both are combined in one figure (Babcock-Abrahams 1975, 161–62). Trickster is also typically very smart, a taker of risks, a breaker of rules, and a transgressor of boundaries (Babcock-Abrahams 1975). General Honoré is more predominantly a culture hero, but with some clear attributes of the trickster (see Babcock-Abrahams 1975, 162).

When General Honoré arrived in New Orleans, thousands of people were stranded without food and water, and they were portrayed by the media as not only desperate but dangerous. He is widely credited with changing this perspective and bringing an understanding that they were engaged in a humanitarian mission. CNN Pentagon correspondent Barbara Starr reported to Wolf Blitzer on September 3: "What I can tell you is as we have traveled with the military today, General Honoré has ordered, at the top of his lungs, every troop that he comes across to point their weapons down. He has repeatedly gone up to vehicles, gone up to National Guard troops standing sentry, even gone up to New Orleans PD and said, 'Please put your weapons down. This is not Iraq.' Those are his words. He wants the profile here to very much be one of a humanitarian relief operation."

In his book *Survival*, Honoré addresses the incident where he shouted to National Guard soldiers to "Get those damn weapons down!" He says that his reaction to seeing soldiers' guns pointed at people in New Orleans made him realize that "the word had not gotten down to the soldiers' level about how they should carry their weapons" (132). Though he was criticized and reprimanded by National Guard leaders, he says that he feels justified in taking action by giving those commands because, "The message we were trying to send was one of humanitarian assistance, but the soldiers were sending a message of fear" (132–33).

Barbara Starr continued to report on General Honoré's leadership in delivering food and water to the people, appearing at times to attribute almost superhuman powers to him in her report to Daryn Kagan on CNN Live on September 9: "And what was so remarkable was to see an exercise of sheer will, sheer military leadership on the part of this man standing on street corners in New Orleans, barking orders into his cell phone, really by virtue of his sheer will making this convoy appear. Dozens and dozens of Humvees of a thousand National Guard troops, trucks full of food and water, going, getting to the convention center, finally, to help those people who've been in such desperate circumstances for so many days."

Broadcast and print media continued to report on General Honoré, portraying him as a hero. Brian Bennett said in *Time Magazine* (September 12, 2006), "Under his direction, the military has delivered 13.6 million meals, handed out 24.2 million liters of water, launched 24 ships and deployed more search-and-rescue helicopters than are now flying in Afghanistan and Iraq combined."

Brinkley describes a "showdown" between Lieutenant General Honoré and the Louisiana National Guard at the Ernest N. Morial Convention Center. When bottled water and MREs arrived, the leader of the Guard wanted an orderly distribution, with thirsty, starving people lining up in single line to get food and water. Brinkley says, "At that Honoré went ballistic, cursing up a storm. 'Get the fucking HEMTT's and dump all that shit,' he barked. 'What kinda fool are you?'" (567). Here is the culture hero who understood the people and what they needed *immediately*. And he did it in his own style (whether those are his exact words or not). Delia LaBarre is a local preservationist and Lafcadio Hearn scholar who lives in Lafayette Square near the French Quarter. She decided not to evacuate before the hurricane and refused to leave after the hurricane. She was cooking for her neighbors (since she had a gas stove). She told General Honoré that she was trying to feed her whole neighborhood, and she asked him for "Meals Ready to Eat." He sent her a whole truckload of MREs (personal communication from Frank deCaro and Rosan Jordan).

Lynne Duke of the *Washington Post* (September 12, 2005) comments on General Honoré's propensity to use colorful language, including saying "That's b.s." on primetime national television. Duke says that his speech is well known in the army, including a quote from Honoré in *Inside the Army*, a journal: "You are fielding pieces of crap. Is that clear enough to you?"

The culture hero/trickster hero not only comes to the rescue of his people, but he *entertains* them as well. And *entertain* General Honoré certainly did. In explaining the difficulties of getting food and water to so many people, he said, "If you've ever had 20,000 people over for supper, you know what I'm talking about." Babcock-Abrahams also points out that "literature's 'heroes' are always those who depart from the norm" (147). Honoré's quick responses and trickster-like use of language on national television departed from any institutional norms. In an interview with CNN's Miles O'Brien, about where blame should be placed for the disaster, he stated: "The storm had a vote . . . The storm had a god-damn vote, and [the] storm is still there. The water is there! You can't vote that water out of the city of New Orleans. That's reality, folks." At times, he showed his annoyance with the media, particularly their focus on him rather than the larger story, saying, "I can't swing a dead cat and not hit a reporter."

General Honoré's daily responses to the media became a part of conversations and part of his status as hero. As *Times Picayune* reporter Jed Horne points out, "As much as he was the darling of the media, Honoré was also their scourge. The TV crews were wild for a little face time with the man in the black beret and aviator sunglasses" (105). But, Horne says, Honoré "could also be a voice of moderation," and he did not hesitate to respond sharply to reporters who tried to unnecessarily sensationalize the information from the city.

Honoré understood the circumstances of the people, the majority of whom were African Americans. Many, though certainly not all, were also poor. Honoré understood that in any disaster, the burden is heaviest on the poor. Among the Honoré quotations that were often repeated was "We didn't pull anybody off those rooftops that said, 'Damn, I left my Lexus!'" He also addressed the media's obsessive reporting of looting, showing the same video clip over and over of black men breaking into stores. He said, "They call it looting; I call it survival." Honoré writes in *Survival*, "After Katrina we saw people breaking into stores and taking out food and water so they could feed themselves and their families. Some people call that burglary. I call it survival. Some of those people did what they had to in order to stay alive. That does not justify what happened in New Orleans. But if that food is there, and you're hungry, and your family's hungry, the human instinct is to eat" (45). Honoré also said in regard to commandeering other things, such as mattresses: "What's the big deal? . . . Are you going to let grandma lie on the ground when you've got mattresses right there you can use?" (45).

An iconic image of Honoré in action was recorded in the CNN television clip of him assisting the mother of twin baby boys. This was perhaps the image that completed Honoré's elevation to culture hero—the strong leader in military fatigues who cussed and smoked cigars was also a caring, compassionate man who understood human suffering.

Barbara Starr reported on this incident, which Daryn Kagan on CNN called the "baby lift":

> We were leaving the convention center area. It had been just terrible. The general was walking along and suddenly, he comes across this woman with two babies and another woman with a baby. These young mothers were just in desperate circumstances, hot, tired, hungry. And he stops . . . . He stops and he pulls his soldiers over and he makes every soldier take a baby, and then we walk down the street. He commandeered a Coast Guard vessel and he personally took them to safety across the river. You know, I don't know what to say, Daryn. When is the last time in the United States you see a three-star Army general in command stop on the street and even have to take the action of rescuing three hungry, thirsty babies. It was possibly really the most truly remarkable moment.

Honoré addresses this incident in his book as a time when he found it difficult not to become emotional. He says:

> My staff and I were walking north on Convention Center Boulevard with Barbara Starr of CNN when a young African American woman wearing a purple football jersey with number 16 on it and a purple and white hat came walking toward us. She could not have been much more than twenty years old, if she was that. She had twin baby boys, one in each arm. As she got closer one of the babies started to slip out of her grasp. Blood was coming out of the child's nose, a sign of severe dehydration. I took that baby and gave it to my executive officer, Lieutenant Colonel Ron Rose. Then I took the other baby and handed it to my aide, Captain Scott Trahan. We turned

the woman around and had her walk with us two hundred yards or so to the river, where a Coast Guard barge was tied up. (134)

Honoré had become a grandfather for the first time only two weeks earlier, and he says that encountering the babies in such peril reminded him of his own grandson whom he had not yet seen.

After a few weeks of rescue and recovery in New Orleans, General Honoré's focus shifted to another hurricane threatening the Louisiana coast. During a press conference at Camp Shelby before Hurricane Rita on September 20, 2005, Honoré responded to reporters who continued to focus on Katrina with the phrase "We're not stuck on stupid." After persistence from one reporter, Honoré's annoyance led him to say directly to the reporter, "You are stuck on stupid." This became the most quoted line from the hurricane aftermath, leading to postings on the Web, as well as bumper stickers. Honoré explains the source of this phrase in his book *Survival*, "I had heard the song '(I'd Have to Be) Stuck on Stupid,' by Blues singer Shirley Brown . . . and the words stuck with me" (181). The blues song "Stuck on Stupid" was written by George Jackson and is on Brown's 2004 album *Woman Enough* by Malaco. The lyrics include, "I'd have to be stuck on stupid, in a super market, shopping for a brain . . . to take you back again." The phrase has been cited since 1989, and is sometimes noted as "SOS." Honoré used the "stuck on stupid" phrase again at the press conference when a reporter continued to press him on the aftermath of Katrina when Honoré was focused on getting information to the public and preparation for Hurricane Rita.

After almost a month overseeing the recovery operations in New Orleans and the Mississippi Gulf Coast, General Honoré was called to southwest Louisiana to aid in recovery efforts following Hurricane Rita. He said, "Compared to Katrina, Rita was just a girl. Katrina was a big, mean woman." When Honoré arrived in Cajun country, he was already a hero. After Hurricane Rita, Cameron Parish had thousands of cattle stranded in flooded areas. The people—having learned a lesson from Katrina—had evacuated before the hurricane, thus avoiding any loss of human lives, but there was no time to move the cattle. General Honoré decided that he would oversee cattle recovery. At the Cow Island bridge, one of his soldiers was reported to have said: "General Honoré says that not one cow will die on his watch." This is part of the Honoré legend since General Honoré himself describes dead cattle along the roads in Cameron Parish (185).

As New Orleans and Louisiana continued to recover from the devastation of two hurricanes and a flood, it also prepared for Mardi Gras,
2006. A clear indication of Honoré's continuing hero status in Louisiana
was Mayor Nagin's Mardi Gras costume and performance. Nagin was on
horseback, costumed as General Honoré with a black beret, camouflage
uniform, and cigar.

General Honoré returned to Louisiana many times during the year,
and he received many honors. He was an honored guest at the traditional
New Orleans ceremonies commemorating Katrina with a jazz funeral and
a second line on August 29, 2006. He returned as well for the reopening
of the Louisiana Superdome on September 25, the heartbreaking scene of
so much suffering and chaos in the aftermath of Katrina. He returned as a
hero. In addition, he returned as a hero in southwestern Louisiana when
he led the traditional trail ride in Cameron Parish on horseback to mark
the one-year anniversary of Hurricane Rita.

General Honoré's status as a hero in Louisiana and beyond continues
today, seven years after Hurricane Katrina. He was described by Jim Engster of WRKF Radio in Baton Rouge on the Jim Engster Show on March
4, 2011, as "the man who led Louisiana" during the Katrina aftermath, "the
pride of Louisiana, who is heading the Louisiana Bicentennial Commission," and "one of the giants of Louisiana lore." This is reflected as well
in comments by national media on his book *Survival*. CNN's Anderson
Cooper calls him "a true hero of the storm"; Kyra Phillips describes him as
"a national hero"; and Jim Clifton (chairman and CEO of Gallup) refers to
him as "a true action hero."

General Honoré, of course, would never refer to himself as a hero,
and he is well aware of the criticism he has received from leaders of the
National Guard and others for overstepping his official role as commander
of Joint Task Force-Katrina, in command only of the active military personnel sent to aid in Katrina recovery. He points out in *Survival* that by
the Saturday after Katrina he realized that he "had become the face and
voice of the federal rescue and relief effort to much of the media and the
American public. I never sought the role and did not particularly want it."
He says the role was "unofficial and unintended" (136). He also says: "Some
people say I was successful. Some say I too often overstepped my boundaries and played outside the lines. If they want to beat me up about what
I did, that's an ass-whipping I can take, especially if I stand in the shoes of
the poor people who were trapped at the Superdome. I was trying to do
the best I could for them and if I broke a few rules and bruised a few feelings along the way, so be it" (228).

This is a hero personified! A culture hero is the one who knows what needs to be done when the situation calls for it, and he is not afraid to break rules and transgress boundaries to do it. He also uses language in creative and effective ways. Just as the trickster-hero is "paradox personified" (Babcock-Abrahams), contrast and paradox are the pivotal things in General Honoré's case—contrast with ineffective leaders and the paradox of a general in the U.S. Army who was both compassionate and tough, powerful and poetic. He uses different tactics, different language, and he galvanizes hope and trust—in contrast to the elected leaders and politicians who failed to provide even the appearance of leadership for the people.

Not only does he come to the rescue, but he does it with compassion and style. He understands that allowing guns to be pointed anywhere but down would force further submission from those who were already down. With words used with the precision of the bullets of a sharpshooter, he puts down those who have marginalized the people of New Orleans—the politicians who failed to provide help sooner, and the national media who, in general, saw Louisiana as a third world country. And, indeed, Honoré is one of us, the native Creole son who came to the rescue, not with the force of guns, but with the force of words and the style of a hero.

Author's note: As Hurricane Isaac approached the Gulf Coast on August 28, 2012, Honoré's status as a hero was evident in the media. New Orleans mayor Mitch Landrieu said in an interview on CNN, "Well, General Honoré is one of my heroes and he always will be."

SOURCES CITED

Abrahams, Roger D. 1966. Some Varieties of Heroes in America. *Journal of the Folklore Institute* 3: 341–62.

Babcock-Abrahams, Barbara. 1975. "A Tolerated Margin of Mess": The Trickster and His Tales Reconsidered. *Journal of the Folklore Institute* 11: 147–86.

Brinkley, Douglas. 2006. *The Great Deluge: Hurricane Katrina, New Orleans, and the Mississippi Gulf Coast.* New York: William Morrow.

Chappell, Kevin. 2005. The Aftermath of Hurricane Katrina: And the Man Who's Helping Put Things Back Together. *Ebony* 61 (1): 284.

Desai, Gaurav. 2005. Member to Member: In the Aftermath of Hurricane Katrina. *MLA Newsletter* Winter: 5–6.

Duke, Lynne. 2005. The Category 5 General. *Washington Post* online edition. Monday, September 12. http://www.washingtonpost.com/wp-dyn/content/article/2005/09/11/AR2005091101484_p.

Duncan, Jeff. 2006. Reluctant Hero of Katrina Recovery Aims to Keep Focus on Mission. *Times-Picayune*, September 20. (Newhouse News Service).

Honoré, Lt. Gen. Russel L. (U.S. Army Ret.) with Ron Martz. 2009. *Survival: How a Culture of Preparedness Can Save You and Your Family from Disasters*. New York: Atria Books.

Horne, Jed. 2006. *Breach of Faith: Hurricane Katrina and the Near Death of a Great American City*. New York: Random House.

Jonsson, Patrik. 2005. A Native Son Takes Charge in Gulf Coast. *Christian Science Monitor* online edition. September 9. http://www.csmonitor.com/2005/0909/p01s01-usmi.html.

Klapp, Orrin E. 1949. The Folk Hero. *Journal of American Folklore* 62: 17–25.

Leinwand, Donna. 2005. Honoré in Charge, Refusing Excuses That Slow Cleanup. *USA Today* online edition. September 12. http://www.usatoday.com/news/nation/2995-09-12-honore_x.htm.

Raglan, Lord [FitzRoy Somerset]. 1934. The Hero of Tradition. *Folklore* 45 (3): 212–31.

Roberts, John W. 1990. *From Trickster to Badman: The Black Folk Hero in Slavery and Freedom*. Philadelphia: University of Pennsylvania Press.

PHOTOS BY DAVE SPIZALE, BARRY JEAN ANCELET, MARY PERRIN, SHARON SUIRE, AND COURTESY OF REBECCA BROUSSARD

Images from Hurricanes Katrina and Rita

A Photo Essay

Volunteer rescuers coming into New Orleans on left; traffic on right has been turned around by authorities due to concerns about the safety of civilians in the water. Photo by Dave Spizale.

On Airline Highway near Sam's parking lot where Mr. Quibodeaux improvised control of available resources. Photo by Dave Spizale.

Volunteer rescuers preparing to launch on the ramp at the Interstate 10 / Interstate 610 split. Photo by Dave Spizale.

Rescuers idling under the Interstate, sorting through mixed messages from various authorities (New Orleans police, National Guard, Levee Board, Wildlife and Fisheries) most of whom were trying to discourage volunteers from heading into flooded New Orleans. This spot eventually was converted into a major triage drop-off point. Photo by Dave Spizale.

Boating down Canal Boulevard which has become an actual canal; the railroad tracks crossing was high ground that served as transfer point for evacuees. Photo by Dave Spizale.

Exposed railroad track serving as pickup spot for evacuees. Photo by Dave Spizale.

Evacuees on the back of Dave Spizale's boat; they had walked from the flooded convenience store where they worked in New Orleans East along the exposed ridges to reach a pickup point at West End near Lake Pontchartrain. They offered to pay the Spizales with some of the supplies they had taken with them from the store (energy drinks, cigarettes, candy bars . . .). Photo by Dave Spizale.

Another exposed railroad track serving as an evacuee pickup point. Photo by Dave Spizale.

Staging area for injured evacuees, with ambulances and helicopters standing by. Photo by Dave Spizale.

Heading down Canal Boulevard toward Lake Pontchartrain. Note the semiautomatic carried by one of the rescuers in the foreground. Photo by Dave Spizale.

Idling down flooded streets because of debris and to avoid producing a wake. Photo by Dave Spizale.

Staging area with volunteer rescuers picking up stranded evacuees. Photo by Dave Spizale.

A crashed rescue helicopter near Bayou St. John in Mid-City, New Orleans. Photo by Barry Jean Ancelet.

Storm damage on Harding Street in Mid-City, New Orleans. Photo by Barry Jean Ancelet.

On the road to Erath after Hurricane Rita. Photo by Barry Jean Ancelet.

The Erath/Delcambre Head Start Building after Hurricane Rita. Photo by Barry Jean Ancelet.

The school demolished by Hurricane Rita in Henry, Louisiana. Photo by Barry Jean Ancelet.

A meadow in Pacaniere (Pecan Island). The house in the background was washed off its foundation by Hurricane Rita's storm surge. The house was stopped by the tree line. Its foundation is in the foreground. Photo by Barry Jean Ancelet.

Blue boats wrecked by Hurricane Rita on the Intracoastal Waterway at Intracoastal City, Louisiana. Photo by Barry Jean Ancelet.

In the process of recovery, a crane moves a beached shrimp boat back into Intracoastal Canal. Photo by Barry Jean Ancelet.

Red boat on its side at Intracoastal City after Hurricane Rita. Photo by Barry Jean Ancelet.

Volunteer rescue operations in Abbeville. Photo courtesy of Rebecca Broussard, Vermilion Parish Office of Homeland Security Emergency Preparedness.

Volunteer rescue operations in Abbeville. Photo courtesy of Rebecca Broussard, Vermilion Parish Office of Homeland Security Emergency Preparedness.

Volunteer livestock rescue in rural Vermilion Parish. Photo courtesy of Rebecca Broussard, Vermilion Parish Office of Homeland Security Emergency Preparedness.

Rescued cattle at staging area in rural Vermilion Parish following Hurricane Rita. Photo courtesy of Rebecca Broussard, Vermilion Parish Office of Homeland Security Emergency Preparedness.

Staging area for volunteer rescuers along Highway 14, Vermilion Parish. Photo courtesy of Rebecca Broussard, Vermilion Parish Office of Homeland Security Emergency Preparedness.

Volunteer rescuers with a casket that they retrieved from the marsh near Erath where it had floated away in flooding during Hurricane Rita. Retrieved caskets were temporarily stored in this merchant's shop, one of the few places with electricity for days after the storm, to keep them cool until they could be returned to their burial places in the community's cemetery. Photo by Mary Perrin.

Suire's parents' residence at Jean-Marie Landing near Henry, Louisiana. Sharon Suire, her husband, and her parents survived by spending nine and a half hours in the live oak to the right. The floodwaters rose to just under the ceiling. They eventually were spotted when they made their way to the collapsed wall to the left. Note their life jackets still hanging on the beam above the wall. Photo by Sharon Suire.

Volunteer rescuer Glen Miguez and his sixteen-foot flat-bottom boat, Bayou Tigue, near Delcambre, Louisiana. Photo by Barry Jean Ancelet.

PART 2

Vernacular Self-Rescue
"Victims" Save One Another and Themselves

CARL LINDAHL

Transforming Endurance

In the wake of Katrina, through a series of rare chances, Houstonians experienced more dimensions of heroism than most of us had previously conceived of. As the storm surge and the collapsing levees drove hundreds of thousands of Gulf Coast residents far from their homes and into our city, we prepared a heroic response, only to be humbled by the selfless courage of the "victims"—who continued to save each other spiritually as we provided material aid. We witnessed our mayor orchestrating one of the greatest acts of sustained civic heroism in recent times, marshaling resources that the national government had failed to provide. Even as the mayor's office struggled to help, a host of congregations and individuals performed their own spontaneous rescue acts, thousands daily. And as the years passed and many of those who had been driven here continued to live as exiles in Houston, we were inspired daily by their courage of endurance, their power to accept their losses so graciously that they made us grateful to know them.

I witnessed the transforming endurance of the survivors from a privileged position, as cofounder and codirector of a project that employed them to record each other's experiences of disaster. The survivors them-selves acted both as interviewers and interviewees; it was my honor sim-ply to listen in, but also in the process to learn from their own lips how profoundly humble and heroic my new neighbors were.

New Orleans West

New Orleans and Houston: at first glance, an unlikely couple. Yet for a moment during the first decade of the twenty-first century, the two cities were twinned in American perceptions. In early September 2005, with New Orleans under water, as hundreds of buses emptied the Superdome into the Astrodome and the Ernest N. Morial Convention Center into the George R. Brown Convention Center, Houston's population grew by as many as 250,000 while New Orleans's dwindled to a few thousand. With stunning swiftness, Houston had become New Orleans West.

One year after the disaster, Houston's count of Katrina survivors was estimated at 150,000; arguably, more black New Orleanians then lived in Houston than in any other city, including New Orleans itself. The two cities stood together at the center of a national debate, a profound soul search over how generous Americans can afford to be. To put it simply, New Orleans is now known throughout the world as the site of Amer-ica's most gratuitous abandonment of its own people, and Houston, in the year following Katrina, represented a rare and courageous affirma-tion of humanity, responsibility, and hope. In the days of the deluge, with pathetically few exceptions (notably the heroism of the U.S. Coast Guard), the governmental response to the older city's need was at best inadequate and more often criminally negligent. Even years after Katrina, the norm remains inexplicable indifference, broken promises, aid presumably mar-shaled but as yet undelivered.

More than three hundred miles to the west, the response of Hous-ton was compassionate, bipartisan, generous, and smart—to my mind, a rare instance of institutional heroism and grassroots heroism working together. Bill White, the city's Democratic mayor, and Robert Eckels, the Republican judge of Harris County, worked selflessly in tandem to staff two enormous refuges, the Astrodome and the Brown Convention Center. At the Dome, Dr. David Persse and the staff of the Houston Fire Depart-ment Emergency Medical Service performed on-the-spot triage for tens of thousands of evacuees. The Second Baptist Church deployed more than 40,000 volunteers to the Dome and the Convention Center, and numberless other private citizens, from the Houston area and around the world, converged in the city to offer their time, their skills, and their hearts to the survivors.

Yet something was happening in these shelters that transcended the generosity of the volunteers. All of the volunteers who have shared with me their thoughts about those times told me that they left the shelters in the knowledge that they were bringing away much more than they had taken there: they had been transformed by their human contact with the survivors. My experience accords with theirs.

At the George R. Brown Convention Center I was assigned the job of sorting donated clothing and helping the male survivors find the shirts and pants and undergarments that they needed. Walking into that vast space, I was stunned by the superabundance of material aid: acres of tables piled high with clothes and surrounded by hundreds of still-unemptied cartons running over with more clothes. The National Holocaust Museum in Washington, D.C., displays a mountainous pile of shoes gathered from the Nazi death camps, each pair representing a life cruelly taken. The mountains that stretched around me in Houston conveyed the opposite message: the promise of life restored. Yet among these hills of hope, the survivors seemed so small, dwarfed by gifts that we had readied for them.

The material needs of the survivors were undeniably great, and they in turn expressed great gratitude for our gifts. Yet, in listening to these men and women, I discovered immediately that they needed something far less tangible and far more valuable than a second tube of toothpaste or yet another second-hand shirt. They needed to tell us their stories. And we needed to hear them. The tellers were transfigured in the act of speaking, certainly in our perceptions, but also in theirs, as they saw on our faces that we were finally beginning to understand something about their ordeals.

From my first minutes in the shelter, Katrina survivors were telling me their stories. As a folklorist, I've been asking for stories for more than thirty years, but this was one time that there was no need to ask. One man, in his fifties, six-foot-five, bone thin, was having a hard time finding trousers long enough in the leg to fit him. But he talked far more than he searched, softly and humbly as if unaware of the power of his words:

> There were eight of us, trapped upstairs for four days, old people. Water almost to the top of the steps of our floor, but we were dry. I was the only one young enough, strong enough to feed anybody. Every day I go out the second story window, swim through that junk, get into that empty drugstore—never broke into a store before—pull out some food, but mainly

water, cases of water. I twist up some coat hangers and rope, make myself a
harness, tie all that water and food to it and swim back dragging it behind.
Swim through all that *junk*. It took a lot longer to swim back than to swim
there. Did that for four days till good people got us out of there. We all got
out fine, thank God.

Looking at him, I couldn't guess how he had managed it. But hearing
him made me see it. I even thought for a second of a scene from *Treasure Island*—which I had not read in nearly fifty years—in which the boy
hero Jim Hawkins swims across a bay hauling a three-masted ship behind
him. A. N. Wilson reminds us that *Treasure Island* loses something when
we realize that no boy could have done that: "The hero in old literature
is attractive because he differs from us. Breca's swimming-match with
Beowulf is impressive because we could not have done it: Jim Hawkins'
swimming feat is impressive because (if we are caught at the right age) we
believe that he could" (Wilson 1980, 46). But there was no doubt that the
gaunt man who stood before me had done the things he said. It would be
as unforgivable as it is impossible to outgrow his story.

This man was both life-size and much larger. Looking at him, it was
easy for me to tell that he was as humbled by his own superhuman acts
as I was. Forced into the position of having to outperform chaos, he had
been inhabited by a death-denying immanence that had allowed him to
save seven lives besides his own. I had come to the Convention Center
prepared to find victims, but in their places I found instead the most
remarkable heroes I have ever been honored to meet. As the tall gentleman walked away cradling his new clothes in his arms, I realized that I had
not even learned his name.

Having received the gift of his story, I felt the need for others to hear
him, and to hear the other stranger-neighbors whose words so affected all
of us who worked at the shelters. The Surviving Katrina and Rita in Houston project is, among other things, an attempt to fill that need. The project
has no higher goal than to break the too-often disparaging and conde-
scending frames of the standard media accounts by engaging survivor-
interviewers to record the stories of their fellow survivors, and by getting
those stories out to the world at large, through live storytelling sessions,
radio programming, and publications like this one.

The need for survivors to tell their stories—and for the rest of us to
hear them—remains as great now as it was in the days immediately following the hurricanes. The national debate over how generous Americans
can afford to be is still raging—if often submerged below the surface of

diversionary scripts. Although reporters for the Pacifica radio network, director Spike Lee, Anderson Cooper of CNN, and a handful of other vigilant citizens with media presence have strived to keep us regularly posted on the continued failures of the governmental response to New Orleans, very few stories of the exiled survivors have emerged. The most "newsworthy" stories tend to conceal the realities at the heart of matter. For example, in early December 2005, wire services around the nation reported a "riot" at Houston's Westbury High School, which resulted in twenty-seven arrests (Guzmán 2005). No doubt some tensions were being aired on that day, but nearly all of the news reports failed to include one crucial datum: that in spite of the fact that Houston's Independent School District was at that time teaching some 5,500 hurricane survivors in addition to its huge native student body, reported incidents of school violence in the fall of 2005 were 15 percent *fewer* in number than they had been the preceding fall, when no Katrina survivors had been in town. Nevertheless, with no or scant or distorted evidence, the news stories have accentuated the negative effect of the survivors' presence in Houston—even while my project partners and myself have continually experienced the opposite: contacts affirming that the heroic individuals we have had the good fortune to know are exactly the sorts of neighbors that any of us would be lucky to have.

What is really happening with Houston's survivors? Katrina's second storm surge, more lethal than the first and, for some, not yet crested, engulfed even those who had left their homes before the hurricane hit and who once thought themselves safe on high ground. Of the million and more people driven from the coasts of Louisiana and Mississippi before, during, and after the storm, hundreds of thousands have not returned. Their sufferings in exile cannot be easily captured in dramatic photographs. Their catastrophes are invisible to most of us. Most of their stories have not been lost in the national memory, for they have never been recorded. Now relatively safe in their Houston homes, survivors continue daily to experience stresses and loss of a magnitude that most of the rest of us have trouble imagining. Yet they regularly respond to their situation with levels of nobility and decency that go unremarked in the public news outlets.

In January 2006, I attended one of the remarkable "hurricane breakfasts" hosted regularly by Houston mayor Bill White. At one side of a square of tables sat the mayor and his staff; at another side, representatives of the governmental agencies presumably present to help the survivors; the third side was occupied by representatives of various service agencies;

and the fourth by a large complement of the survivors themselves. Survivors came forward to present case after case of unmet needs. Dozens stated that they had lost their cars in Katrina, and had made available to FEMA (the Federal Emergency Management Agency), several times, all the requested paperwork that, they had been told, was necessary to obtain insurance and emergency aid; they further testified that they had not yet received the promised aid, nor any indication of when or if the aid would be forthcoming—and five months had passed since the storm. The survivors asked how, without cars, they could get to their jobs, or even find one, in this most pedestrian- and commuter-unfriendly city. People without cars were housed in complexes literally miles from the closest bus routes. The FEMA representatives answered unconvincingly. Mayor White stepped in to put the question more directly, using the power of his office to ventriloquize the survivors: "Let's say I am a survivor. I am phoning your office. I am presenting this information to you. Please tell me and the survivors gathered here what we can say and what we can do to break this log jam." Faced with a question that he clearly could not answer, the FEMA representative promised to have one soon, as survivors throughout the room turned to one another and groaned.

But Bill White did not give up. He would not relent before the various agencies delivered the services that they were supposed to provide. He hosted such 8 a.m. meetings daily for months after the storm, and then relaxed into a weekly schedule after the city had addressed most of the extreme emergencies. White's gesture—of bringing together FEMA, the Red Cross, the mayor's office, the survivors themselves on a regular basis, in a venue where everyone was invited to see them interact—forced the government into accountability. White's doggedness—in repeatedly asking the same simple questions of the same public officials, to the point that they eventually had to respond—earned the respect of those who filled the room. Survivor-activist Dorothy Stukes, of ACORN, called White, "A God-given man," and thousands echoed that thought with similar words.

Even with this brilliantly focused response, many of the most basic needs remained unavailable to thousands of survivors. At one of the January 2006 training sessions in which we were working to give the survivors the tools to record their fellows' stories, one woman asked if it would be okay for her to miss a few hours of the next day's session. Because we had emphasized the need for every survivor to be present every minute of every day during the training, we asked her for her reason. "I have a chance to have some furniture delivered tomorrow," she said. We had not realized that she had been sleeping on the floor of an empty apartment for months.

Yet the lack of material needs pales in proportion to the human losses endured by the survivors. In June 2006, one of the survivor trainees told us that her New Orleans church community had been her second family: she knew each of her three hundred fellow parishioners by name, and in so many more intimate ways. Ten months after the storm, she had reestablished contact with only ten of them. She missed the others every day. Even on those rare occasions when long-lost friends are finally reunited, they often share far more sorrow than joy. The words of survivor Larry Gabriel, recorded by the project in March 2006, flow slowly under the weight of his loss, "We steady drowning. We don't have nothing no-how. All we thankful for, we made it out with our lives. That's all we can say, 'Made it out with our lives.' As we sit around finding some of our friends, our neighborhood people, you finding out who's dying, that's all you finding out. Who done died here? Who done died there? After the storm, not during the storm. After the storm, they died of the pressures. A vessel bust in their head."

Among all these losses, the survivors are daily aware that still missing from the public record are countless accounts of heroism, determination, and endurance. For all the media documentation devoted to the disaster, the stories actually told by survivors emerged slowly. In 2006, in one of the first (and best) books to emerge from the disaster, Michael Eric Dyson warned his readers, to avoid forgetting the lessons of Katrina, "we must engage in memory warfare" (Dyson 2006, 211). But the survivor stories could not be deployed because they were not yet a memory for the great majority of Americans. Dyson himself printed pithy statements from some survivors, but most of the early books reshaped their stories into journalistic forms. The poorer survivors' tales were largely ignored (as in Brinkley 2006), or many survivors' tales were combined or intertwined to produce a sweeping narrative (Horne 2006; Baum 2009; Vollen and Ying 2008). Some of these accounts, like Dave Eggers's *Zeitoun* (2009) and Rebecca Solnit's *A Paradise Built in Hell* (2009), are masterpieces in and of themselves, yet they are not the verbatim accounts of the survivors. In 2010, Solnit could still say, in truth, "it's high time to start telling the real story of what happened during those terrible first days and weeks" following Katrina's landfall; survivors' narratives honoring the heroism of fellow survivors are "the key missing stories of the storm" (Solnit 2010). The tales that come from and speak to the heart of this event are only now emerging. For those hit hardest by the storm, these are the most important of stories because they bear witness to the strengths of friends, neighbors, and family in the face of an otherwise dehumanizing loss. It was for the express purpose of giving voice to the survivors that Pat Jasper and I conceived of the project, Surviving Katrina and Rita in Houston (Lindahl 2012). We saw a need for all of us to hear these stories as soon as they were told, at a crucial juncture in Houston's, and the nation's, history when too many of us did not yet know the survivors, and could too easily be led by the media into the illusion of seeing victims or criminals where heroes stand.

Survivor to Survivor: Training to Listen

Pat and I worked with the American Folklife Center at the Library of Congress (AFC)—to design week-long training sessions that would give survivors the tools that they needed to interview their fellow evacuees. Each trainee would share one crucial bond with her interviewee: both of their lives had been upended by Katrina.

As each session began, we asked the participants to consider and share their reasons for joining the project. Few mentioned money, even though, for all of them, even temporary employment and a modest paycheck represented a major difference in their lives. Unanimously, they spoke of the need for the survivors' voices to be heard; unanimously, they affirmed that the best person to interview a survivor is a fellow survivor. But beyond these points, emphasis varied. Some speak very generally of the historical importance of the stories they will collect: they wanted people who will visit the Library of Congress or the University of Houston a hundred years from now to see and feel the storm and its aftermath from the perspective of the otherwise nameless people whom it hit hardest. Some spoke abstractly of compiling a record of the social injustices that helped cause, intensify, and prolong the disaster. But the great majority spoke of immediate concerns in deeply personal terms. Some stressed the therapeutic aspects of sharing their experiences with fellow sufferers: one survivor told us, "I came here to heal." But most often, and most emphatically, they spoke to this effect: "We want people to know who we are. So many have been so generous, but even the most generous do not have a clue of what we've been going through. We are not criminals, fools, or deadbeats. We have honor, respect, and pride, in others and in ourselves. We don't want people either to scorn or pity us. We want them to see us."

The guiding principles of the field schools are simple, but their implementation involved levels of complexity, emotion, and work that all the participants found challenging. We began by telling the survivors that each of them was the world's leading expert in her or his personal experience, and that in Katrina, each had an experience that we, the teachers, could not fully share—most particularly, they had their own storm stories based on personal experience, they had told and heard hurricane stories as part of their daily lives, they knew how such stories unfolded in everyday situations, and they didn't have to be reminded how deeply important these stories were to those who told them.

We then presented them the goal of the ideal interview: a "kitchen table" story shared intimately by the survivor and told on the survivor's own terms. The trainees tended to recognize instinctively and value intrinsically what we were looking for. But then we problematized the situation, with words to this effect:

> Across the kitchen you are facing someone with whom you are sharing a profoundly life-changing experience. You probably feel an immediate bond with the person, and that person probably feels an immediate bond with you. But this particular kitchen table is cluttered with things that endanger that bond. There will be an audio-recorder and a microphone; you will be wearing headphones: both the storyteller and you yourself are likely to feel at least a little bit nervous in the face of this, especially as you position the mic, test the sound, monitor the room for ambient noises, and perhaps discuss with your host what measures you would like to be taken to ensure the best sound quality. Then, just before you begin the interview, you have to read your host a long "informed consent" form in legalese, and then get the storyteller to sign it. For survivors with numerous, painful recent experiences signing government forms that have as often as not brought them no benefit, the paperwork could well be more than merely inconvenient—it might be unsettling.
>
> And that is just the beginning, because at the same time that you are cluttering your host's table, you are trying to clear it: to turn a difficult and artificial situation into a relaxed and intimate one. While you are encouraging the storytellers to relax and find their natural voices, you have to be monitoring the sound quality of the recording. While you may feel the urge to jump in and correct the storyteller on a matter of fact or ask for clarification, your job is to let the storytellers go their own way and stay in spotlight. You do everything you can to let the storyteller be himself, while you are being three people: the friend across the table, the technician tracking the sound, and the listener who takes mental notes on the stories and thinks up questions to ask later, because you can't interrupt the story while it flows.

As the sessions progressed, we underlined our basic rules of interviewing, rules that often clash with those that govern other documentation projects:

First, stories are more important than information per se. It can be a lot easier for you to tell a story than to record one in the cluttered-table situation of the interview. The work of the interviewer is first and foremost to set the table for a storytelling session. After a story, you can always go back for more information, but if you start out emphasizing information, you may never get a story.

The ideal situation for getting stories is a "nondirected interview"; strive to reach a state where the "interviewee" directs the course and the flow of energy comes from the other side of the microphone. There is an art to asking, but at least as great an art in listening, in quietly coaxing the story out.

Therefore, ask as few questions as are necessary to trigger the story. The most vivid stories tend to be those that are most concrete. Therefore, instead of asking for emotions and interpretations (How do you feel about the hurricane? What is your opinion of FEMA?), try to set up descriptions of scenes and actions (What did you see happening in your neighborhood after the evacuation order came through? What did you do to prepare for the storm?).

Avoid words and gestures that might seem to pass judgment on the teller or the story.

Never push for a story. The storyteller has the right to withhold any words at any time. If the storyteller wants to stop the interview, the interview is over. If emotions overcome the storyteller, offer to pause the recording until he is ready to continue. These dicta are common courtesy, but they are also attached to our conviction that we want to record only those stories that it benefits the narrators to share. The healing potential of a story depends in large measure on the readiness or the reluctance of the speaker, and we believe that forcing a story can exert a negative effect on the teller. (In our project, we relied upon trauma specialists to advise us on the best methods to help stories heal.)

All of these precepts support our cardinal rule: the interviewee is always right. You may ask permission to record the story in a private, quiet room, but if your host wants to sit close to a noisy air conditioner with her children present, she is right. You may ask her to tell you about what happened to her in the Morial Convention Center, but if she doesn't want to talk about it, she is right. At the end of the session, you may be deeply disappointed by the content and the quality of the interview, but if your host is happy with it, the project is happy as well, and her words will go on record in the collection.

We ask the survivors to record, in the course of each interview, three separate but closely entwined stories. All three narratives center on the concept of community. Each storyteller is asked, first, to describe the community where he lived before the storm hit. Many of New Orleans's materially poorest neighborhoods were extremely rich in traditional culture. In the Sixth and Seventh and Lower Ninth Wards, shared memories and cultural creativity had crafted networks of religious, musical, and festive life. Church groups, social and pleasure clubs, and extended families had created some of the most resourceful and soul-affirming responses to poverty to be found anywhere on the planet. These communities, now shattered, often exist only in the survivors' memories, and they must be documented not only for the historical record, but also to aid the survivors in shaping their new lives from the rent fabric of the old.

Second, the interviewers ask for storm stories. We discovered early that storm stories are also community narratives, because they so often center on instant fellowships created by strangers in mutual need who worked together to save each other and forge common paths out of harm's way. We have found, unsurprisingly, that the storm stories are often the most coherent and well-crafted tales, because each interviewee has shared them repeatedly with others, fellow survivors and strangers alike.

Finally, interviewers ask the survivors to talk about their life in Houston since the storm: to record their ongoing struggles to rebuild damaged social networks or to create whole new communities in a foreign environment. These are stories still in the making; often, storytellers spoke of failed or incomplete efforts to build community. Often, their descriptions of their new neighborhoods quickly turned into catalogs of the things they most missed about their former homes. In New Orleans, they had known how to get from one neighborhood to another; in Houston, they got lost almost every time they took to the road. In New Orleans, they had felt security and goodwill living amid family and friends; here, they encountered mostly strangers and were often viewed with suspicion. Even in the largest supermarkets, they could not find the foods and spices that had been the staples on every table in the neighborhoods they had lost. But it was our hope that even in the act of mourning their old lives, storytellers were forming the germs of new communities. As survivor Shari Smothers has told me, "When you're sitting across the table from another survivor, there's something therapeutic about sharing even the losses. I feel closer to the people who are telling me their stories; and I believe they feel closer to me."

The one field school exercise most useful to the survivors is the peer interview. We divided the trainees into pairs. One trainee recorded his partner's storm story. Afterward, both survivors evaluate the interviewer. The next day, the person who told the story the day before now takes on the role of interviewer and records the story of her partner. Then another evaluation took place. Thus, before the end of the training sessions, each survivor had told her own story and recorded the story of her partner. By putting herself in the shoes of her future interviewees, she learned how hard it is to create an atmosphere of ease and comfort in front of a microphone and how important it is for the interviewer to set up a situation of intimate sharing.

The great strength of the project lies in the common bond established when one survivor listens respectfully to the story of another. This bond has proved stronger than any of the artificial impediments that we have placed in its way. Before leaving the field schools, many of the trainees shared their misgivings about the technicalities and technology involved in recording the stories. They worried most about the consent and release forms that the storytellers had to sign in order for the interviews to be recorded and deposited in archives. So many of the prospective storytellers had recently signed innumerable government documents attached to undelivered promises: What would they do when asked to sign yet another official-looking piece of paper? They also worried about the recorders, the headphones, and the microphones: Would a stranger really open up to them in the presence of all this official-looking gear?

Yet the survivors' experiences with their hosts were almost universally gratifying. Technicalities that might present overwhelming impediments if a trained folklorist were performing the interview, all but disappear when the host learned that the interviewer is also a survivor. To date, the interviewers have engaged in about 430 recording sessions; in only one instance did the storyteller decline to release the recording to the Surviving Katrina and Rita in Houston project.

Months before our first field school, while conceiving the survivor project, I leaned upon my prior experience of listening to September 11 narratives deposited at the American Folklife Center at the Library of Congress. While sifting through these accounts, I had noted that the stories that struck both the AFC staff and me as the most powerful were those that were told not to academic folklorists like myself, but rather to friends of the narrator (or in one case told by a woman to no one in particular, but simply to herself, as she pressed the "record" button on a tape recorder in her local library [see Lindahl 2004, 2, 653–62]). It was on the strength of this perception that I came to believe that fellow Katrina survivors would be able consistently to capture stories of a level of intimacy and intensity that my professional colleagues and myself could seldom match, in spite of our training. Seven years into the project, as I listen to the extraordinary narratives that the survivor-interviewers have recorded, I find that the stories they collect have exceeded my expectations.

The power of the narratives recorded by the survivor-interviewers relies, first and foremost, on the hurricane experience that they share with their hosts, but also upon another, closely related factor: the reverence with which they listen. They came to us saying that they were here because they "want people to know who we are." Because they were profoundly aware of the importance of their own stories, and equally aware of how seldom they had been able to tell them—all the way through—to strangers, they extended uncommon respect to the interviewees, allowing them to take control of the narrative and guide it by himself. At the outset, I had worried that a particular interviewer might saddle herself to a particular agenda and try to guide her host to tell her own story rather than his, but in fact I have seen little evidence that such a thing has happened. Many interviews conducted by seasoned professionals amount to no more than the record of the story that the interviewer has already fixed in his mind: the man with the mic imposes the plot upon the interviewee. The great majority of the survivor interviewers, however, offer the friend across the table an urgently needed space to speak. When survivor-interviewer Darlene Poole recorded Sidney Harris, she began with a few brief questions; after answering them, Sidney set out to tell a compelling story that stretched for more than forty-three minutes before Darlene needed to ask another question (Surviving Katrina and Rita in Houston interview number SKR-DP-SR04).

This is not to say that the project has been free of disappointments. Some participants have come to us eager to record the stories of their peers, but have subsequently found that financial or family needs were simply too great to allow them to continue. Others have hit emotional walls along the way and have had to drop their interviews temporarily or permanently because they found themselves "stuck" in the past and feeling the need to hold the hurricane experience at arm's length for a while. We began the project believing that most of the participants would finish their interviews within three weeks of the end of the training sessions, but learned from experience that six weeks is a more reasonable time frame.

But we have been continually gratified and honored by the efforts of our survivor-colleagues. One participant, a twenty-nine-year-old woman with three children, was also charged with caring for her seriously ill sister. Her partner, a truck driver, was often away from home many days in the course of any one week. She herself had no academic training beyond high school and possessed no computer: these realities stood in the way of her ability to compose logs of the interviews as well as to transcribe parts of them, as the project required. Given these impediments, it is not surprising that she needed three months rather than three weeks to complete her work. Yet, that said, there is no substitute for its quality: she recorded her fellow survivors' accounts in an intimate, compassionate, and open manner seldom matched by professionals.

As for the interviewees, a few of the people who were at first eager to record their stories found it necessary to demur on second thought. Survivor-interviewer Susie Cambre painstakingly arranged for a session with one woman, who, initially, was more than happy to host her. But when Susie showed up at the woman's apartment, she found her host dressed up for a night out. "I just can't tell that story now," she told Susie. "I need to go out and get some relief." Several other potential interviewees canceled their appointments, in need of respite from the burden of their stories. Some of those who canceled their interviews have later reconnected with the interviewers and put their stories on record, but others have not. Yet now that we have recorded well over four hundred interviews, we are buoyed by the knowledge that only one storyteller has sat for an interview that she, on second thought, declined to release to the project.

The overwhelming majority of storytellers have engaged eagerly with the interviewers and have reported that they were satisfied with the recording. Many have asked for copies of the interviews, and these have been provided. Some spoke of a need to get the stories off their chests; others, hopeful that their interviews will reach a wide public, have expressed the hope that we could help them put their experiences before the world at large. During his interview of May 12, 2006, Bernie Porché, one of thousands who endured the flood trapped on New Orleans bridges and overpasses, spoke passionately about the need for others to know how the bridge people suffered in the face of cruelty and neglect. Bernie recounted a catalog of horrors like the following:

> I'm telling you, you had dead bodies on the bridge. You had people with, I mean, people from different areas trying to survive the storm, well the storm was over, trying to survive this bridge action that's going on. And they had one Black cop, he was the only Black cop on the bridge. Everybody else was White, Hispanic, whatever. So, they had this one lady cop and she was a real

B, and I hate to say it, she came on the bridge, she had a pump [gun], she pumped it and she looked at everybody, like everybody on the bridge was suspect, you know, like did a crime or something. So, I mean, kids watching this, I mean kids saying, "Mommy, Daddy, she got a gun." I mean there was no need for her to act the way she did. (SKR-NE-SR11; recorded and transcribed by Nicole Eugene)

Bernie noted how, even during his days on the bridge, there were people who were trying to keep him and his fellow survivors from getting their story out.

And that time the news reporter . . . , white man, came [onto the bridge] and he was coming towards the people, you know, I guess to interview them or something like that. So, what they did, the police officers, they made a circle around the . . . newsman, and he could never get close to nobody on the bridge . . . and when he left they kind of like escorted him off the bridge. Like you couldn't, you ain't going to talk to this man here, so that's why I say [that people] don't know what happened on the bridge. (SKR-NE-SR11)

Seven months after leaving the bridge, Bernie was still looking in vain for evidence that the true story of the bridge was getting out.

I bought two Katrina books; they have never stated nothing about a bridge. You know, they never stated nothing about what went on on the bridge cause they don't know . . . .

All I'm saying is that if there's any way possible that you can get this tape and let them hear it because they need to know that what went on on this bridge was way beyond what happened at the Superdome.

Our pledge to Bernie Porché, and to all of his fellow survivors who have honored us with their words, is that we will do our best to get their stories out—not only to record the horrors that they have had to face, but also to show the dignity and courage with which they have faced those horrors.

The work of surviving Katrina in Houston is still in progress, and still charged with struggle, hardship, and pain. As Pat Jasper puts it, the survivors are living "big lives," lives so complex and difficult that we could easily wonder how in the world they have endured. The unfolding saga of their continued survival demands documentation. But if Pat and I sometimes wonder how the survivors managed to maintain, they daily put the answer in our hands: compassion, courage, faith, love, decency, and an abiding trust in their own humanity—square in the face of the media forces and the forces of ignorance that have sought to deny it. The survivors have become our friends, and we have been enriched immeasurably by that fact. The stories that follow explain.

Bibliographical references for this essay and all other chapters in Part 2 are found on pages 267–70.

CARL LINDAHL

Survivor to Survivor

Two Duets

[Revised and expanded from an article that first appeared in *Callaloo* Volume 29, Number 4, 2006]

Katrina stories were being told by those in its path before the storm hit and retold among survivors long before rescuers arrived. In New Orleans's Lower Ninth Ward on the eve of the hurricane, neighbors congregated in bars to verbalize a plot of betrayal: the rich and powerful would once more dynamite the levees and flood their homes as during past emergencies (Brinkley 2006, 45). And after the storm, as water filled the city's streets and topped its houses, those who fled to the high ground of the overpasses introduced themselves with stories: "We just got together, walking up and down the bridge, you meet this person, you hear a story, you meet that person, you hear a story," Henry Armstrong told Nicole Eugene in one of the interviews that follow.

No storm stories are more important, more compelling, or more true than those shared among survivors, and for this reason we have focused our training on strategies aimed at cutting through the red tape of release forms in order to convey the survivor interviewer back to a place where she has already been: listening to the story of someone who is important to her, in a situation of trust and intimacy, as if across her own kitchen table. Many complex difficulties stand in the way of this simple goal; for that reason the survivor interviewers train themselves to ask briefly and listen deeply. The thrust of these efforts is to give the storyteller sovereignty over the story, and to put that story before the public in a way that reflects the teller faithfully. If the interview succeeds, in the great majority of cases it is because the interviewer is a largely silent partner.

But the silence of the interviewer is anything but passive. The listener forms an active bond with the teller. To give an idea of the strength of that bond, to demonstrate that every interview is in fact two stories, and to let the untold story of the interviewer surface, the pages that follow feature two duets: in each a survivor-interviewer introduces herself, talks about her experiences with the Surviving Katrina and Rita in Houston project, and then introduces one of the interviews that she has conducted. In her introduction she speaks about the special qualities of the narrator and the aspects of the story that made this interview compelling to her. Through these two duets, we hope that readers will see something of the relationships that form between those who share stories.

Nicole Eugene, though born in New Orleans, has lived most of her life outside of Louisiana; she had just moved back to New Orleans to explore her roots when Katrina forced her to evacuate to Houston. Nicole was enrolled in Bowling Green (Ohio) State University when she began working with the survivor program, and she has since completed her M.A. thesis for Bowling Green's American Cultural Studies Program.

Nicole's "duet" is, properly speaking, a trio, because the main narrator, Henry Armstrong, insisted on having his mother present for the session. Although Dorothy Griffin speaks few words in the course of the interview, she exerts a telling presence throughout, for she was the focus of Henry's concern and the source of much of his strength during their days trapped together on a New Orleans bridge and their time in the Superdome. The obvious power of Henry's words (even when reduced to writing) was a major factor in influencing Nicole to undertake a collaboration to create a play based on the accounts of Henry and other Katrina survivors who weathered the deluge on the bridges of New Orleans.

Nicole and Henry were mutual strangers before their interview session. Shari Smothers had known Marie Barney all her life. Shari came to the survivor project with a degree in social work from Southern University of New Orleans as well as work experience in writing, sales coordination, and public school teaching, among other skills. She has spent most of her life in New Orleans, surrounded by family members and lifelong friends whose collective memories stretch far into the city's past. In 2006, when Shari conducted her interviews, many of these friends and family members lived in Houston, and Shari interviewed several of them for the survivor project.

Shari's duet with her godmother, Marie Barney, presents a remarkable family portrait of loss and endurance. On the day before evacuating New Orleans, Marie Barney buried her husband of forty-six years as Shari's extended family and many of the city's dignitaries, including Mayor C. Ray Nagin, joined in the ceremony. Within two days, already having lost her husband, Mrs. Barney would lose her home, her church community, her neighborhood, the entire city of her birth. Yet the strength of Mrs. Barney's dignity and character are echoed in this interview, which among many other things, testifies to the power of the bond between Mrs. Barney and her goddaughter.

On the surface, Henry Armstrong and Marie Barney represent two radically different kinds of heroism. Caught in the teeth of the storm, Henry acted in highly visible and dramatic ways to save the physical lives of many: most notably his mother and other relatives, but also, by liberating water and distributing it to hundreds of people trapped on an overpass, potentially hundreds of others. In Henry's acts, we see the "victim" transformed into the rescuer. In Marie Barney, we see at first a person who does not act, but rather is acted upon. As her narrative unfolds, however, her courage and endurance move to the foreground. After more than four decades, she lost her husband just days before the storm. In short order, she found herself in a place she had never lived before, living and fending for herself alone for the first time, making the best of it as she faces a new hurricane, and exhibiting an uncommonly heroic response to her new life in exile.

The initially opposed experiences of Henry and Marie—struggling for life in a flooded city versus watching the flood on a television in a neighbor's house—do not fully prepare us for how similarly their stories end. By the time they stop speaking, their unforgettable memories of Katrina's immediate effects have been followed by months in limbo, during which time they have reflected repeatedly on what they have lost and on what they still have. In Marie's and Henry's words of assessment, words of gratitude, and words of resolve, a shared quality of heroism emerges. This is the courage of transforming endurance: the courage with which they continue to face the unknown, honoring the past without surrendering to a hard and unsought present, finding grace and sometimes even humor in a place where they never planned to be and which they are only beginning to know. By sheer force of words and will, they reach a heroic balance of grief, hope, and resolve.

A New Orleans Life

Sharing Marie Barney's Story

I came to Houston with my family on August 29, 2005, fleeing New Orleans because of Hurricane Katrina. Houston was our destination because we have relatives here. We caravanned in three cars. The exodus spanned nineteen hours. To give you an idea of the snail's pace at which we crept, there were people walking their dogs, passing up the cars in which they were passengers in the bumper-to-bumper traffic all along the highways.

By the time we reached my aunt's home, it was nearly seven the next morning, but we were too wound up to sleep. Still there was little energy to do anything more than sit in front of the TV. We watched CNN all day and for days to follow, to see what was going on in New Orleans. This was not our first evacuation from New Orleans, but it felt different to me, so I waited expecting that things might be bad at home. Still, with only the flip-flops and jeans that I wore and a few pairs of shorts and a pair of sandals, I thought it might be a few days or a week before I returned. This was an excuse to go shopping and to be with my cousins.

What I thought would be days, quickly turned into a month. We were passing through survival mode like visitors in a museum. Surreal is the

Shari Smothers. Photo courtesy of Shari Smothers.

word by which I and many others named the experience. Every day was about taking another step to survive away from home a little longer. Houston extended much-needed assistance to those of us who had managed to get here. We were given food allowances, which was most critical. Health assistance and many other benefits were extended in the short term.

My family decided to stay here, especially after learning what had happened to our homes. It was a month before we really knew anything. The news media coverage we all found suspect, and at best it was inadequate to the task of addressing every individual's home.

October 2, 2005, was the first time any of us was able to get as far as my parents' home. I returned to New Orleans for the first time that day with a friend to see how bad or good things were. My friend's house fared the best. My home was devastated by rising water and roof damage, too. My parents' home was in bad condition from what I could see outside. I couldn't get inside because I'd forgotten my keys; I only saw the water lines etched around the house on the brick and the windows. I looked over their fence at the destruction of their yard and the oddly positioned things in the sunroom. Across the street I saw a tree that had fallen on a neighbor's house. I was taken aback by the sight of the city as we drove through; the desolation and destruction seemed to be mourning the devastation dealt out by Hurricane Katrina and, to a much lesser extent, by Hurricane Rita. I didn't see any animals or birds. The traffic signals that were still standing were dark. Instead, stop signs sat low on the corners propped up by makeshift stands. Some areas, like New Orleans East, where my parents' home was, still smelled awful even from the streets.

When I went to my home, I opened the door and the mold assaulted my nose even through my facemask. My friend was not able to go in with me because the smell so overwhelmed him. We returned to Houston the same day. I reported to my family what I had seen, with pictures and with the resolve that I was going to stay right here. In New Orleans I was a renter, so I didn't have the responsibility of managing the owner affairs that my parents and others had to deal with. There were a few things that I wanted to try to salvage from my home. The rest of my plan was to work and get a place to live because I wasn't going back any time soon.

October 8, 2005, I rented an apartment in a complex where my sister-in-law had rented ten years earlier. I had unemployment income from New Orleans and assistance from the federal government. That is how I survived while I was searching for a job. I went to a job search agency, The Work Source, and got information. It was suggested to me that I not put New Orleans on my résumé as prospective employers were reluctant to hire people "who might want to return home." I listed it anyway since there was really no escaping the fact, and I put it in my profile for their online jobs database. One day when I was searching the database I found a company that was searching for people displaced because of Hurricane Katrina. I received a call about this same job from a worker at The Work Source, and attended the presentation the next day to see what it was about.

After the presentation, things that had been weighing heavily on me seemed to lighten. I felt good about what I understood about the project's goal. After a group presentation, Carl Lindahl and Pat Jasper conducted individual interviews. My interview was with Carl and it lasted all of three minutes. He said that I would know something in a week. I walked away from the briefest interview of my life with a really good feeling. It wasn't just because I thought I got the job, but because of what the job entailed. A week later was March 13, 2006, and Carl called to let me know that I had the job if I was still interested.

From that time to this my enthusiasm for the project has not diminished. The scope of this catastrophe is larger than the individuals who survived it. Therefore, for it to be outside of the normal scope of others who may find it difficult to empathize, is not unbelievable. It's larger than each of us who lost the lifestyle that we knew. It's broader than the narrow focus of the ratings-driven news media can encompass. The story of this group of people—of us—is far-reaching and impacts a broad segment of the population beyond just us. People displaced by the storm represent the lifeblood of a world-renowned community. And who we are could be lost for all time, without a forum to be heard, to make a record of who we are and how we lived. The Surviving Katrina and Rita in Houston project seeks to preserve the record of our lives for all to see in the Library of Congress, the University of Houston Folklore Archive, and other useful repositories: a record for us to remember and recall, for others to read and hear and try to understand what happened to us and how we survived. And I get to be a part *that.*

As a member of this project, I was charged with the responsibility of finding and interviewing twelve people, family, friends and strangers. Through this project, I've met some good people who were separated from places and people familiar to them. They now suffer the task of starting over again, many from nothing; some in their thirties, some in their seventies and eighties. Some are not interested in returning to New Orleans in the near future or ever. Some wish to but can't for health reasons, or are uncertain of what will be the next phase of the city's reformation. I've talked with people who insist on returning to New Orleans, because it's home, and because they have hopes of regaining a past New Orleans that lives in their hearts. Without the information they need from city officials, insurance agencies and other agencies affecting them, it has been difficult to make life decisions, and so people remain here working to build a new future, knowing they are safe, but uncertain of whether or not they'll remain here ultimately.

I have heard enough stories to understand that only the broadest generalizations may be made. The stories of the individuals must be told because each is different and important and representative of a unique life. I hear the stories and I know that while my experiences are quite different from those of many with whom I've spoken, I am not alone. I listen to the stories to respect the presence of their individual souls. People don't readily see each other individually but in aggregate. Conventional wisdom is against recognizing the individual, I would guess, as a matter of self-preservation. It's not possible to let in everything and not feel much of it. And so, seeing people on a macro scale is acceptable, but only if you remember always that this distant view does not negate their importance or lessen the severity of their trials as individuals. Carl Jung put it quite succinctly: "Infinite nuances are needed if justice is to be done to individual human beings." Talking with people, sharing stories, seeing the devastation, all worked together in a healing manner, helping me to start to regain my perspective on my entirely new life. Listening to people, witnessing them tell their stories, being a part of giving them a forum has helped me, as my life gradually becomes more real than surreal.

When I was asked to share only one of the twelve interviews that I conducted, I didn't know which one to pick because I find significance in all the voices. I ultimately decided to share the interview done with my godmother. Hers is a story of great loss just prior to Katrina, a story of surviving and continuing, with no time for necessary grieving. My godmother told her story with only my initial question to get us started. She told the story of her life in New Orleans and her community life and the world that she and her husband, Clarence Lyle Barney, Jr., had created for themselves. In her words I heard the familiar ambivalence about returning to the home that she and her husband had shared for thirty years. Throughout her story of the losses suffered before the storm and after it, she found humor in her experiences: at times it seemed that she laughed almost in defiance of the difficulties those experiences presented.

It seemed the storm provided Aunt Marie some needed distraction from the loss of her husband just days before. And yet it robbed her of her time to grieve; it robbed her of many of the things that reminded her of him and the home that they'd made. It put immediate distance between her and Uncle Barney's final resting place, as well as the friends and family who would have seen to her in this time of mourning.

Marie Barney mentioned that people said her husband's funeral was the last major event in the city before Hurricane Katrina hit. In many respects it was. The services were attended by standing mayor C. Ray Nagin, National Urban League president and former New Orleans mayor Marc Morial, members of the Landrieu family, and other local political figures as well as dignitaries in the ranks of the National Urban League from as far away as Washington, DC. The remembrance dinner was the last engagement that would be hosted for months by Dooky Chase, a well-known, black-owned eatery specializing in New Orleans cuisine. Even the location of the funeral was of note, for this was the last major gathering to take place in Dillard University's Lawless Memorial Chapel. The next day, we were evacuating because of Hurricane Katrina. Both the restaurant and the chapel sustained major damages as a direct result of the hurricane. Dillard University was unable to reopen the campus in the fall semester due to the extensive damages suffered. When I interviewed my godmother, Mrs. Chase was working to get her restaurant repaired and operating for the 2006 New Orleans Jazz & Heritage Festival.

Marie Barney is setting out on an entirely new way of life. Her story is unique without a doubt, yet it possesses the familiar ring of finding one's place—and it embodies, as my brother Kemic put it, the natural desire to seek out homeostasis wherever we land.

For the interview, we sat at her dining table in her very nice apartment in the Houston Galleria area. Her high ceilings and white walls reminded me of the living area of her home in New Orleans. Her furniture is attractive. The apartment is comfortable and seems to suit her in this transition stage. She said that she was just coming out of survival mode and she felt that she really hadn't yet grieved. Shopping for necessities, being independent in new ways such as putting together some of her furniture, evacuating for Rita on her own, planning for tomorrow: these things are only about her. Aunt Marie talked about trying to find activities to give her life meaning and fulfillment. It is her way, I think, of reconnecting to the larger community.

Marie Barney Remembers

April 11, 2006
Interview recorded, transcribed, and edited by Shari L. Smothers

Well, I was born in New Orleans and spent just about all of my life in New Orleans, with the exception of maybe a year or so on educational leave or something along with my husband. And I've always had a real love and fondness for New Orleans. All of my family, extended family was in New Orleans; my friends were there, my church was there. And just various

Marie Barney. Photo courtesy of Marie Barney.

clubs and activities that I belonged to, they were all there. My career was there; I am a retired educator for the Orleans Parish School System. And I retired about ten years ago. I lived there with my husband of forty-six years. He and I both retired in 1996, so we spent much of our retirement years together in New Orleans. We went to a lot of restaurants; we went to a lot of activities. We went to church; we went to church activities. We went to our sons' school activities. We had two sons who grew up in New Orleans and who went to high school there, both of whom went to college for a while away. One ended up graduating from a school in New Orleans and the other one graduated from Howard University in Washington, D.C.

My husband was the president of the Urban League of Greater New Orleans for approximately thirty-five years. There were numerous activities, volunteer experiences and things that kept us busy during that time.

I was really active in my church. I was at one time a chairperson of the Board of Trustees. I was a member of the choir; I was a deacon. I belonged to a sorority, Delta Sigma Theta, and there were things, activities, volunteer kinds of things that also kept me busy. So there were a number of things that I did. All of those brought a number of activities that kept me busy and experiences that I enjoyed doing.

My extended family went back, the ones that I knew, I would say about three generations back. And in my early years when I was growing up, all holidays were spent with this huge extended family. We really had, you know, good, good times. And as the older people got older and passed on, then I guess eventually, when Katrina was here, my generation was the senior generation. And we still spent holidays together. We always had big family dinners. And when I was the person who became the senior of the group, I guess, they were held at my house. My children enjoyed it. My nieces and nephews enjoyed it; those persons who were still living; my husband enjoyed it. So, we sort of had just everybody around us. That was, you know, a lot of happiness; a lot of joy.

We enjoyed a lot of activities in New Orleans. New Orleans didn't have a tremendous amount of things. They had an occasional play or movie, I wasn't big on movies. Of course, we had our traditional Mardi Gras and our Jazz Fest; those kinds of things that we did and enjoyed. You knew that you would always have something to do; somebody to be with. I had two brothers, two sisters, one of my brothers died. I still have two sisters living and one of my brothers. And they were living in New Orleans. So, you know, even in our late years, we visited and spent time together, that kind of things. Always I knew where they were; could always call on them when I needed them. One of my sons lives in Florida. The other was in New Orleans so he was always around. So, New Orleans was just to me a really wonderful place.

My husband and I used to go out to dinner mostly or go to community activities. And after we retired, we were together much of the time except for an occasional meeting or something we decided, you know, that we wanted to do on our own. But for the most part, we spent every day in the house together, enjoyed it. My husband was quite a talker so you were never lonely around him because he talked all the time. And he was a person who kept up with community affairs—and I did too, so you stayed abreast of everything that was going on, so he always kind of had a hand in things that went on in New Orleans. And he was a senior citizen—I think he mentored several people. And that kept our house kind of lively because he always had young men, and even sometimes young women, who came in and met with him and talked to him. And that kept us both again busy. So, it was just a kind of fun; there was never a dull moment.

What happened, I guess right before Katrina, well my husband was sick for about three months. He was in the hospital before Katrina. And the week before Katrina, he passed on. So, that was kind of a really downer for me. But, yet I had no idea Katrina was coming.

We planned his funeral for August twenty-seventh, which was the day or so before Katrina actually hit. As a matter of fact, his funeral was the Saturday before we had to evacuate, before the Sunday that we evacuated. And again, during that week after he passed, before his funeral, the house was always filled with people, just lots and lots of people. And people, you know, would bring food and flowers and plants and all of that. And you never really sat down and looked at the TV during that time; at least I didn't, and my sons did not either. Our time was occupied; we were trying to plan the funeral. So we knew there was a storm but we had no idea of the severity. We had no idea that it was actually going to come in our direction. Matter of fact, we had heard it was going to go another way; that's how little we knew about it.

So, the day of the funeral—some people jokingly tell us now that that was the last activity probably in New Orleans, and I think maybe it was. We had the repast at a restaurant, local Dooky Chase, which was a local black [owned] restaurant. And that was probably their last activity. So it was a whole thing again while we were going through this and we were just really surrounded by family and friends and community people and just about everybody who cared about us, cared about him and loved him, loved us; they were all—everybody was there.

So we did not realize—even that night after the funeral, our house was filled with people. We didn't realize that this storm was as near as it was and that it was actually going to hit our area. We had planned to go down to a hotel in New Orleans if we had to, that next day. But we were going to make that determination that Sunday.

Well, when Sunday morning came, my son who lives in New Orleans called me and he had taken one of his friends to the airport. And he was supposed to go back and get the minister from his hotel and take him to the airport because he was from Chicago. And he called and he asked me, he said, "Mom, you think the minister"—he called his name—"could get a cab out or something?" He said, "Because it's really bad out here." He said, "The traffic is so heavy." He said, "I don't know, even if I got back, I don't know if I could make it back in time for his flight."

So I said, "Well, why don't you just call him and explain and see what he says." I said, "Well, what's going on?" He said, "And by the way, we're going to have to leave; we can't stay in New Orleans." So, I said, "Well what is happening?" He said, "Well the roads are just filled and everything is just," he said, "The highways are just cluttered," he said, "and really—I think we're going to have to leave." So, I said okay. I put the television on and tried to listen to it. Meantime, I got online trying to find reservations someplace. And my oldest son, who lives in Orlando, Florida, well he and his wife were there for the funeral. So he started boarding up, and his wife started gathering up a few things for us to take with us. And well, my online quest was just futile because the closest that I could find any reservations was Oklahoma City, which just seemed too far out of reach for me. So, I felt really defeated.

Well, when my younger son got home, he called a friend of his here in Houston and asked if she could help. And she did. She managed to get us a real nice hotel suite. So that was really helpful. And we left New Orleans about eleven thirty or twelve o'clock, somewhere in that neighborhood, and got on the highway. Well, the highway is something else when there is a hurricane evacuation because you get nowhere fast. We started at around eleven thirty or twelve o'clock, and we must've reached Houston probably about four thirty the next morning. So, it was really a snail's pace, you know, just maybe stopping for a bathroom break or something and that's about it. And, when we reached Houston, we had reserved our hotel suite so we did have a place, you know, to rest and to stay.

Well, we didn't really know what was going on in New Orleans at that time, so the first thing we did, four o'clock in the morning, no matter how tired we were, we put the television on, to see what was going on. And much to our dismay, we got very little locally. Well, we didn't expect to get New Orleans stations, but we expected to see, I guess, scenes from New Orleans. But I don't think we did. I think we saw, you know, like what national commentators were saying, for the most part. And I don't think any of them at that point were broadcasting from New Orleans, maybe other places, but not from New Orleans. So, we still had very little idea.

But, the following day, when the water started to come, that's when we started really seeing what was going on. And it was very discouraging because we had each left with [so little]. I had on a pair of tennis shoes which I rarely wear. And I had a pair of summer sandals, like little flip-flop sandals, and two pair of pants, one on me and one in the bag and about two shirts. Because we thought we'd be gone for a day and then we would go back. And my sons had the same thing, my son's wife, she had the same thing. As a matter of fact, my son and his wife who were from Orlando, had not even brought any of their dress clothes, because they had brought them to our house for the funeral and enough to last like a week. So they were all still at our house. Well after about that Wednesday, my son and his wife had to get back to work because again they lived in Orlando. So, they got a flight from Houston, still with nothing, and went back home.

Well, I had my car, my husband's car, because my car was totaled. We had driven his car which was convenient because it was an SUV and I could move things back and forth. I was a person who never nailed a nail or anything before, but I learned to assemble the furniture I had [she laughs at her expanding abilities]. And then my son helped. And then after I saw him do it as I bought more things, I kind of learned how to do it myself. So, I put together quite a bit of furniture. I did a lot of things I probably normally would not have done.

I was not cooking a whole lot because, well, for one thing, once [my son] went back I really had no urge to cook for just me. So, I think I was probably eating sandwiches, occasional restaurants and like that.

I did find a church, which was a very wonderful church with a pastor that was just outstanding. But, it was a mega church, it was this huge church. I was not accustomed to that; I was accustomed to my own little small church where I knew everybody and everything. So I would go to this mega church, because it was convenient, close to my [apartment], the minister delivered a good message, so I kind of liked it. And it was easy to get to.

That's the other thing, I did find a church in my denomination where I occasionally went; it was a little further out. So, between the two—those were sort of, I guess you could say, my church homes. Although, I did not change my membership or anything, I just attended occasionally.

Between that and finding my way around Houston, that was the next thing because if you know New Orleans: New Orleans has one interstate that you get on and you pass straight through. [She laughs.] You don't have to worry about going down this way, that way, that way, because if you were on the interstate, you were just going in one direction, coming back in one direction. You had exits, I guess, but you didn't have any cross-belts and all of that kind of stuff. When I got here to Houston, the interstate looked like spaghetti to me.

And that was the other frustrating thing because I knew New Orleans. I guess my car knew New Orleans and we could both drive it with our eyes closed, or whatever, and get to where we were going. And, New Orleans was not that big. You could go completely across New Orleans I guess in about ten minutes, or fifteen minutes if the traffic was pretty good. And I knew it like the back of my hand; and Houston, I didn't. So, whenever there was a need for me to go somewhere, I would have to get on the Internet, find the directions and then try my best to find it.

Well, Houston has—its interstate tends to change its names periodically. So you get on and you're on one highway, and when you look again the signs will say something else. And you wonder, "Well, when did I get off the other one?" Actually you didn't; if you keep driving you'll find that it's still the other one. Or they would have these little, I guess you would call them sub-highways, or some other highways, where the bigger ones had the two numbers, the interstates. And then it must be local highways that had three numbers or whatever. And directions will tell you, "Well you start on this interstate but then you change to this, to 257 or 277," or something like that. And, the problem was that you rarely saw those little signs until you were right up where you're supposed to exit. And if you're in a four-lane highway, and you're a couple of lanes over, then it's extremely difficult when you get to that road, you know, to get across and get off. So, I spent a lot of time being lost and finding my way. [She laughs.]

I would go places and it's interesting because I don't mind driving. And as long as things go smoothly, it's pretty good. Like, a lot of friends I know would not drive. But it was a necessity because here I was alone. You know my son had gone back to New Orleans and if I wanted to get anywhere I couldn't wait until the weekends when he came. So, I'd get on the highway and go.

Well, to make a long story short, Rita appeared. And when Rita appeared, I was here, and by myself. My son was not here and he called and said that maybe he should drive in. I said, "No, because if you drive, you're driving along the coastline and no telling where Rita will hit. So you'd best stay put and I'll find a way." So I decided to drive to a niece's in Dallas.

Well, when I went to Triple A, they charted me a map and then the man told me, "Well, Miss, you're going to find that 45 North is going to be extremely crowded, so I'm going to give you a substitute route going this way." Well, he gave me one of those little three-letter highways, and I'm like, "I don't want to do that because I don't know that and I'm going to get lost. So I'm going to stick to the tried and true." Well, big mistake. [She laughs.]

When I got on, I was told to somewhere to 45, I don't remember even what it was at this point. Oh, I also got my Internet directions. And when I got to 45, there was this police car that crossed the highway and [a sign that] said "45 CLOSED DUE TO THE STORM." Well, that did it. I sat there and there was no policeman, I couldn't get out. I didn't know what to do. I saw the car, but I didn't see a person. So, I'm like, "Well, what do I do now? I have no idea where I'm supposed to go." I literally had no idea what to do at that point.

Why they would close a major highway, I don't know. But, for somebody like me who didn't even know the area, and they were told that 45 North takes you to Dallas, you want to go 45 North. The sign didn't say, "TAKE THIS ROAD" only [that it was] closed because of the storm. So here I am in tears at this point because I really had no idea what to do, where to go. I tried to find people. Well, there was nobody to find.

So, finally, I ended on what must have been, what appeared to be [U.S. highway] 59, but I didn't know it at the time. And traffic was so slow that you could literally talk to people next to you. You know, you didn't have to stop, you could just talk to them. So I'm rolling down the windows: "Am I on the way to Dallas?" And they looked at me, "No. No way." [Her highway predicament makes her laugh again.] So I'm like, "Oh, what do I do now?"

I didn't know what to do. So I thought, "This is a crisis, this is an emergency, you call 9-1-1." And I called 9-1-1. They were very courteous. They were going to try to help me and they put someone on the phone. "Where are you?" Of course, I couldn't tell them because I had no idea where I was. So they did their best to help me. It didn't help.

Aunt Marie didn't get the help that she needed, so trying anything that came to mind, she called information. They tried to help but it was also to no avail. Finally, she came across three police cars in a cluster and one of the officers drew for her a map that she could use.

I had left like seven something that morning. I drove and drove and drove nonstop. There were people—it was like Mardi Gras on the highway because there were wall-to-wall cars going nowhere. They kept telling us to use the contraflow or whatever. But nobody told us how to get on the contraflow.

Throughout the trip, there were constant traffic issues and dramatic scenarios over the scarcity of gas. She hesitated to get gas because there was only regular available. Everyone, friends and family, who knew what she was trying to do, kept calling her cell phone to make certain that she was alert. At a filling station at six in the morning, she waited in a line to get gas not due to arrive until three in the afternoon. She got to a good gas line and waited for four hours. She got her gas and continued on. She heard information over the radio about shelters where she might rest, but she wasn't familiar enough with the area to find them. Eventually the highways loosened up as she neared her destination just outside of Dallas. It was four o'clock the next evening when she got really sleepy.

I thought to myself, it's going to be one of two things that will happen. "One of these eighteen-wheelers is going to push me off the road. Or, somebody's going to call the police to come and get this drunken lady, she's weaving over the highway."

Aunt Marie spent a few days with her niece and returned to Houston. That episode put her in mind of needing a game plan for hurricanes and what she would do. She settled into making her new life and finding what she would do with it. She spent Christmas traveling and then returned to Houston, her new base, to continue plotting her future.

I had left New Orleans when I had real bad problems with my back and my legs, you know, just painful. I couldn't stand or walk for long periods of time. Well, not even a short period for that matter. So I needed medicine to be refilled. So, I called my healthcare group and they referred me to a doctor. And I found a doctor who's pretty good. I had tried calling some of my doctors in New Orleans but that proved futile.

Anyway, I went to see him and he kind of hooked me up with a surgeon and with some other doctors that I needed to look at my back and all of that. So, I ended up—I guess one of the plusses about being here was that I found that my medical care was pretty readily available. So, I knew had I gone any place else, I probably wouldn't have gotten some things done as quickly as I did. With coming here, that was a blessing because I had surgery on my back. And I had some other little challenges and they were corrected or worked on, that kind of thing. So, that was a plus; I can now move around, walk around without a whole bunch of problems.

So, I'm going to still, I guess, pursue some type of volunteer activity; I don't know what. I have all of these nice, new clothes that I spent all this time shopping for, with nowhere to go. [She laughs at the pleasant predicament.] So, I said, "Well, maybe I can get into some of these new clothes and do some of that." So, I probably will.

I've made about three trips now to my house [back in New Orleans]. The first trip was just, I guess, an informational trip to see what had happened to it. And I, of course, needless to say, when I got inside, I didn't recognize it. Everything on the first floor was topsy-turvy, full of mud and muck and dirt and everything turned upside down, nothing in its place. My husband in his illness had kept most of his things downstairs, in the closet downstairs. So, all of his clothing were wiped out. My oldest son was about his size, and I had already told him to look in there and take what he wanted. Well, he had planned to when he got back, but, of course—too late. Everything was washed away, and just full of dirt.

It was interesting because things you would have thought would have been broken, were not. And things you would not have thought would've been broken, were. It was like, I had a sofa, well, in my living room and then another one in a den—those sofas sat there. We'd been in that house for about thirty years, and those sofas had been there all of those thirty years, just like new because we rarely used those two areas.

When we left, we had received lots and lots of plants because of my husband's death, so we had plants just all over everywhere we could put a plant. And then food; people had brought food like you could not imagine. The refrigerator was full, the freezer was full. We had caboodles of soft drinks and everything in the back and inside and everywhere.

And we had cakes. I shall never forget, we had so many cakes you could not imagine [she laughs at this reflection]. Every surface we could put a cake, we had a cake. And when I went back, it was like one of these—if you ever went to the haunted house at Disney World or someplace and you looked around, how it looked, that's what it reminded you of because we had these shutters. Now our living room was full of light but the other rooms—We had one room called the play room, it was dark, very dark because the shutters were down and it didn't let in a lot of light. The living room had skylights and all of that and a big open window, so it let in a lot of light. But that other room looked like a haunted house kind of room or something, where you had nothing but gray and everything. And if you looked around the floor, a lot of these cakes were still in these plastic containers. They had not opened, had not washed away. You look down and you see this, look like, cement cake that was just sitting there. And cakes were all over. And we had a bar my mother had given us, oh, years ago that my daddy had brought from overseas. And it had bottles of alcohol in it—some were open, some not. And then we had another bar that we had bought some years ago. Now this was a very heavy thing, but the water had just toppled it over. So, besides the cakes, the other interesting thing that we saw a lot of was these bottles of alcohol that had floated out or when our furniture turned over, they just came out, and they were everywhere too. None broke but some were still unopened; some were opened [already] but they had stoppers, and all of that was still intact around the floor, you know.

And then, the refrigerator had turned over on its side, on its face. And it was—well, we didn't open it because we were afraid it would be full of flies and everything. So, my minister came along, he and another church member and helped my sons to take it out and put it on the curb. They had a problem getting it out, I don't know why, because it got in there. But, for some reason, they had all kinds of problems getting it out. [She laughed at this recollection, too.] And they didn't want to take the doors off. So, they took the handles off. But they had the worst time trying to get it out. So that's about all we did that day. I looked upstairs and upstairs was pretty much intact. It didn't have any water up there or anything else. And, I spied a picture of my husband. So my son got over and got that for me. And everything else I think, we more or less left. We just locked it up and then we left.

Well, we went back another day. My son from Orlando had come that [first] day. Well the next time we went was a few months later, my other son and I. My son and I went, and a nephew. We gathered up some things that we could take or salvage and things that we were going to try to have redone. My husband had lots and lots of awards and plaques, so we got as much of that as we could because the water hadn't gone all the way to the ceiling downstairs. So, some things that were high up were dry.

And my church—you know, after a funeral, you look forward to having all your family and your friends and your church members and everybody surrounding you with a lot of love. But after my husband's funeral, everybody scattered. We had nobody. [Laughing in spite of the stark reality of it.] You know, I came here—with the exception of my two sons and my daughter-in-law, I was almost alone. But my church ended up with somewhere in the neighborhood of twelve members that are back in New Orleans. So the church—well, we were in the process of renovating, so they couldn't use it anyway, but it didn't have water; a lot of its properties got water.

And, all of my friends went various places. So for a long time you didn't know where anybody was, you know. That was the other challenge where you had some numbers and if you managed to have a person's cell phone number, eventually you could contact them. So it's amazing how fast people hook up. But, I'd say within a month, we had a list of all of our church members, just about, where they were, and they've all gone. Well, we had an elderly church, so most of them are gone for good, because they've gone to sons and daughters out of town, and they aren't coming back.

Some friends I have that I've hooked up with—as a matter of fact, here in Houston your mom and dad and I have one of my high school classmates here. And I have friends who live here in the complex, a church member I know who's here. Well, we get together and talk, you know, sometimes on the phone and stuff. And then I have friends elsewhere who I talk on the phone a lot with.

So, I guess you count your blessings and everything. And I think Katrina: trying to just survive those first few days kind of took my mind away from my husband a whole lot. And, I don't know if I ever really had any grief time, to tell you the truth, because things moved so fast. You just had no time. I lamented the fact that I had never gone back to the mausoleum where he was buried; when I buried him there, I thought, this was this nice serene place and a place I'd be comfortable coming just to sit awhile and stuff. And I thought I would be there all of the time, and here it was like almost six months and I had not gone back at all. And I'm like, "Oh, this is terrible," you know. I mean I keep thinking, what if dead people know. [She laughs at the idea of such a thing as this crossing her mind.] You know, *what if he knows I'm not there*, that kind of thing.

It was interesting having a place I'd so carefully selected, where they had little waterfalls and some other things. And, you know, it was so serene and so nice. And then all of a sudden you don't get back there at all. And that's another reason why I don't think I want to be this far away.

The other blessing was that my husband—I had no idea that he was going to actually pass on; I really thought he was going to make it. And he had been—he went in just for, like, a little minor surgery which had some complications. And he stayed in; he went from ICU to the, what do they call it, therapy places, which were really where you can't stay any longer in ICU, they could be closely monitored in therapy places, I forgot what kind of facility they called them, but it was like another little kind of specialty hospital. And, he stayed there from June thirtieth until he passed on August eighteenth. And, you don't want to see anybody pass away. And I didn't think he would. I really thought he would make it because by the time he finally died, maybe a day or so before, he started having problems with his white cell count and I remember that was like a little crisis. But actually he died from having a blood clot move to his lungs.

And I look at it, and I said it to my sons, that I guess it is a blessing that if he had to die—and we didn't want to see him die—that he did when he did because I don't think he would've made it through Katrina from what I saw of the sick people. And he was in one of the hospitals that was inundated with water. What I saw there, I don't see how he would have made it because he was on a respirator much of the time, and he needed much of that kind of thing.

Another blessing was that I waited a week to have the funeral and I think—don't know why. I guess I just thought that was a good time to have the funeral. And I was glad we did because one more day, and it would have been impossible, you know. So, I guess we were blessed to have gone on with that. And for him, if he had to go, to have gone before Katrina because that would have been just a terrible thing that he would have suffered.

I miss my church. You know, I used to sing in the choir, I miss all of that. I guess I just, I miss everything. I miss my husband [She laughs in spite of the pain.] I miss a lot of things. And really, I had my husband taken away from me, my home of thirty-one years, everything, friends, family; everything just disappeared in a matter of twenty-four hours. And, I'm like, how could this happen? You know if somebody told me this a year ago, that you would be alone with nothing—none of what you had or nothing or nobody you know: my sister—one is going to Atlanta; my brother's already moved to Mississippi. My friends are everywhere; church members are everywhere. Then, what do you do?

After her 2006 interview, Marie Barney lived in Houston for another year before returning to Louisiana, where she now lives just a few miles from her husband's grave. Shari Smothers continued to live in Houston until 2011; she has now returned to New Orleans.

NICOLE EUGENE

Bridges of Katrina
Three Survivors, One Interview

[Revision of an article that first appeared in *Callaloo* Volume 29, Number 4, 2006]

My Katrina Story

I moved there the week before Mayor Ray Nagin called for everyone in the Crescent City to evacuate. I left reluctantly. I had only been there for a week. I wanted desperately to stop moving around, to stop living out of a bag and to finally stand still long enough to get an honest accent. I had yet to unpack any of my bags from all of the traveling I did that summer, so I put that bag back in the trunk of my car and joined the pre-Katrina exodus down I-10 West. I drove to Houston alone because my dad had decided to go to Atlanta, and although the freeway was packed with cars and SUVs, this extended yet all too familiar drive foreshadowed what the next few months would feel like.

Once in Houston I returned to the house I grew up in, and although the house and myself have changed I have always resisted the way that the house changed because it looked less and less like the home of my adolescence. Sixteen years after moving into this house my parents are divorced, my mom is retired and two of my sisters live there, one was expecting a

Nicole Eugene, Houston, 2006. Photo by Dallas McNamara.

baby girl in December and already had a two-year-old son staying with her. There was very little room for me in that house, but regardless of the uncomfortable quarters I was happy to see them and be with them. Since this was supposed to be a brief visit, I didn't mind sleeping on a futon in an unkempt room.

Like so many evacuees and non-evacuees I was overwhelmed with disbelief and shock when the footage of the flood started appearing on the TV. I remember looking at the first footage of the Superdome that they kept showing because for the first few hours there was no other footage. Those first few days were saturated with captivating images that were accompanied by the sound of talking heads. Now I realize that, for the most part, these images had no voices. So many of the people stranded in New Orleans were not given voice.

At the time, I didn't know enough about the geography of New Orleans to know if all my belongings sat underwater or on dry land. Weeks later, even after finding out that East New Orleans was hit really badly, my mom and I still could not know anything for sure. There were no New Orleans neighbors that I could call. I didn't have a real relationship with anyone in New Orleans, besides, of course, the aunts and uncles I rarely saw or heard from. All we could do was wait, and so that's what we did.

My uncle's family evacuated Metairie after the storm hit and then stayed with us for a few weeks in the Houston house. While there my uncle and his wife would spend all day dealing with FEMA, Red Cross, or the Department of Human Resources after which they had many stories about how long the lines were and how difficult the whole process was. My mother and I were merely spectators of their tragedy; we didn't know how this affected us and we didn't know what to do. It was my mom's first house that I had just moved into in New Orleans, but since it wasn't her primary place of residence she didn't know the extent of the damage, or even that there was damage. I took my mother's lead and was apathetic about the matter until it finally hit me: I had nowhere to go and all my belongings were gone. Luckily we had flood insurance so we were given the full worth of the policy. Even after the insurance adjuster went to the house without us, we still held on to the possibility that something could be salvaged. Maybe it was not a total loss.

I didn't have to deal with Katrina, it was something I was able to just put aside, as if I was on vacation and Katrina was something that I would have to deal with once I returned to the real world. In the meantime, catching up with my high school friends was a convenient distraction. I didn't have a social network of people who were grappling with Katrina and struggling to keep moving, I was the only one in my immediate family that lived in East New Orleans. I was the only person that lost so much of my belongings. Since most of the people around me were unaffected, it was a bit too easy for me to not deal with Katrina. I can now see that, for me and perhaps many others, Katrina was more of a non-experience than a real experience. This is because when Katrina hit New Orleans I was not there, rather it has presented itself as so many absences and losses scattered throughout the landscape of life. Other than being a lacuna, Katrina existed via the constant flow of images and stories that the television spewed. It was not a real experience until I was finally able to return to New Orleans in January 2006. Seeing the damage, smelling the mold through a facemask, climbing over my mountain of belongings, taking pictures, and finally opening some of my unopened boxes to find out that nothing was salvageable: all of this made Katrina real.

In the days before Katrina, after completing a master's program in the Midwest, during which time I had longed for the South and the family that lived there, I decided that before continuing my studies I should take pause and learn and live in New Orleans. Although I was born and raised for the first few years of my life in a New Orleans suburb, moving to Houston at a prepubescent age left me not knowing much about my parents' home city. My childhood memories of New Orleans paled as I grew up in Houston. Our Houston suburb was too sterile, too new and too perfect to feel like a community. By August 2005 I had been to several countries and was a part of several communities but still longed to experience a sedentary community. I wanted to tie my identity to a unique culture and a unique people. I longed to be a part of the New Orleans community and to strengthen familial ties but ever since Katrina approached the Gulf

Coast, I've been here in Houston. And up until I began working with the Surviving Katrina and Rita in Houston project, I was dealing with Katrina in isolation from the many other Katrina survivors in this city.

I was still a stranger to New Orleans when I left it, but I since have come to know it through the eyes of those who lost their communities, their livelihoods, their homes, and the closeness of their family. Through working with Carl Lindahl and Pat Jasper in the Surviving Katrina and Rita in Houston project, I was able to train as field interviewer and talk to other evacuees about how they experienced and dealt with hurricane Katrina and the events that followed the storm.

Before being sent into the field as an interviewer I was able to bond with the other evacuees in the field school. This is where the healing began. In the context of the project the survivors had a commonality that allowed us to forge friendship and provide support to one another. Our differences were quite vast but the same tragedy wounded us all and no one would dare to allow these differences become a source of tension. Although the dynamics of the field school were amazing this didn't stop me from worrying about how I was going to find interviewees. After all, I hardly knew any other evacuees, especially ones in Houston. Most of the school participants were already a part of tight social networks. For them, finding a good interviewee would be as easy as asking a mother-in-law, a sibling, or a friend.

As it turned out, I found that Katrina survivors were everywhere. I merely needed to tap into the social networks that I was already part of because, although they may not be in Houston or survivors, they inevitably led to a person that came to Houston as a result of the events that followed Katrina: I found evacuees in my church, one of my best friends was dating a displaced Tulane MBA student, and a nonprofit art gallery that I was a member of gave me the contact info of a displaced artist/art professional. Yet, by far the most fruitful inquiry came when I found out that the father of a former classmate of mine was a presiding pastor of Houston's Franklin Avenue Baptist Church, a New Orleans congregation that now holds services in Houston. One Sunday Pastor Mack was so gracious to make a brief announcement so that people who were interested in sharing their Katrina stories with the project should come and see me after service. After this I had more than enough prospective interviewees and several new friends.

The project gave me a reason to connect with a network of fellow survivors. It has allowed me to experience Katrina vicariously through these stories and these relationships. After hearing one survivor confess that she dealt with depression during the months that followed Katrina I knew that I was not alone; I also laughed with her as she declared how she was "sick of shopping" because I too had felt that same frustration with the magnitude of trying to replace everything; I remember the loneliness of those who, like myself, live alone in Houston without family and without a social network and still carry empathy for them; and yet still I feel the hesitant joy of those who are better off in Houston, people who have been dealt a good hand and have a brighter future than they faced before the storm. With these stories and many more I've been unable to be despondent and aloof about Katrina. They helped me deal. Finally, I've been able to cry, fret, laugh, and mourn with my fellow evacuees. I can only hope that the act of sharing has been a source of relief and healing for them as much as it has been for me.

Henry and Dorothy

I met Henry Armstrong at the First Baptist Church in Houston because this was where Franklin Avenue Baptist Church held Sunday's service. A tall, solid, almond-colored man in his fifties was the first to come up to me after service. I introduced him to the project, letting him know that I would tell him more about it over the phone. He didn't say much in his raspy deep voice. I struggled to make sense of his resolute stature and resolved that I would get to know more about him soon enough.

My interview with Henry and his mother, Dorothy Griffin, was my fourth interview and it's one that holds a lot of significance, for me personally and for the project. Henry, fifty-nine, and Dorothy, eighty-two, are both native to New Orleans. When I arrived to meet with them, April 5, 2006, they were staying in a spacious three-bedroom apartment in the Big Bend Retirement Community. During the interview I sat on an imitation leather love seat and Henry sat across on the matching couch while the microphone and recorder sat on the glass coffee table that also held salvaged pictures of Henry's children, Dorothy and Henry. Although protocol recommends one-on-one interviews, Henry insisted that his mother be a part of the interview because she was such a big part of what he went through. So, while Henry is the main storyteller, Dorothy shares her experiences in the beginning and end of the interview. The sound quality of the interview is somewhat compromised by the presence of two interviewees that are unable to quietly sit still, but the story has so much character and content that outweigh these shortcomings. There were several times when

I had to press the pause button throughout this long interview, many of which because Dorothy was unable to stay seated for an extended amount of time; this is one of the many ways she continued to suffer from the aftermath of Katrina. The exchanges between Henry and Dorothy that were captured during the recording testify to the devotion and spirit that inhabit the content of their story.

As mentioned earlier, this was an early interview in my development as an interviewer and so it possesses some novice awkwardness. After this interview I learned the value of ensuring that the interviewee knows that I'll want a lot of background information before getting into the storm story. From the start of the interview Henry was ready to get to the meat of the story—the experience of surviving the aftermath of Katrina while waiting on a bridge—and so I had to really focus on getting the details of his life before Katrina. But as you will see, these interviews are not just about Katrina and the flood that followed it. The scope of these interviews is much wider than the great deluge. To get listeners and readers to connect with the story of Henry and Dorothy the narrators must first be introduced to the audience. For this reason I include many of the details of Henry's career, family, and life in New Orleans. This is what makes the experience of interviewing so intense; it's not just about Katrina, it's not even limited to the whole individual; rather, it is about all of the relationships and lives that were affected by Katrina and remain augmented as a result of it.

This is also very important in the context of hero and rescuer stories because an antihero is more believable than a pristine hero. When Henry responded to a question about his family and sons by explaining that he has beautiful loving children and, "the only problem I have with that is that my children are not by one woman. I have four sets of children," something in me froze. Was he really saying this? I didn't ask for all of that information, but he volunteered it and in doing so he presented me his humanity. Henry is human and has the flaws to prove it. But what Henry really values, and is proud of, is his ability to say that, although "they all seem to be as if they collectively came from the same spot. I guess—they all, they all love and respect each other, they're very close" and that "and so far, they all seem to think I did a good job."

Hannah Arendt's *Eichmann in Jerusalem* comes to mind because it chronicled the details involved in her revelation that the atrocities of the Third Reich was not a testament to the existence of radical evil, rather it was precipitated by the existence of mundane evil. Within Henry's story and within several others' stories, told and untold, about Katrina there is a lesson that flies in the face of America's superhero mythology, which is that many of us survived Katrina because of acts of mundane kindness and mundane goodness. Perhaps the radical charity of Houston and large organizations was precipitated by the mundane goodness of everyday people. This analogy is unarguably a gross simplification of Katrina, but it is nevertheless appropriate because it is the lens through which I, the interviewer, view Henry and his story. Another way to describe this mundane goodness is in the words of Henry, "Katrina brought the best out of even the worst of us."

The Bridge: Connecting through Our Stories

As an evacuee, I know from experience that Katrina is not merely an event that, for a time, captivated the media and through them captivated the whole world. For evacuees it is not merely a mediated event but it is quite real—yet it is just as fleeting as time and memory. I would love to explore the ways Katrina intersects with Baudrillard's postmodern concept of simulacra, but I'll save that for another day and another anniversary. This recollection is dedicated to the bridges of Katrina: the bridge I found through the Surviving Katrina and Rita project and the stories of waiting and traveling through Katrina's aftermath on a bridge. This is my bridge to New Orleans. This is my community. Each interview and each narrative brings me to a particular way in which relationships, place, and memory work to keep people connected, whether it is the displaced New Orleanians, the dislocated transplant like myself, or the distant reader. We are all profoundly connected to this moment in which Henry, Dorothy, and thousands of others were abandoned on a New Orleans bridge.

Henry's narrative offers a glimpse of what life on the New Orleans bridge was like, and as he says "it wasn't nothing nice." As Henry recalls, the day after Katrina passed, when the water started to rise, he took measures to get several people, including his mother and other family members, out of the projects on mattresses. Once on a New Orleans bridge they were in need of food and water because, to their surprise, no one was going to help the thousands of people on the bridge. Henry and his friend, Wilfred, would leave the bridge to go out and find food and water to bring back. After several days on the bridge Wilfred, Henry, and his mother got to the Superdome where they were then evacuated to Houston's Reliant Center. Eventually his elderly mother was hospitalized for the injuries sustained while waiting on the bridge. Within this interview there is a touching and inspiring narrative that begins and ends with a need to protect and provide for Henry's elderly mother. Throughout the Katrina ordeal Henry helped many people, but what is most memorable is his humbleness and ability to fully commit himself to his mother.

There were others on the bridge, and I have met and interviewed several other Katrina survivors that were brought to the bridge: one woman spent one night on the bridge, another woman spent a few hours on the bridge, one gentleman spent a few hours on the bridge before asking to return to his flooded house where he stayed until the rescuers returned him to the bridge. Each survivor offers a different glimpse into that catastrophe and a different way of experiencing and dealing with the trauma of being partially rescued. I am adapting Henry's interview and other interviews that deal with the bridges into a play that will bring these stories, and the lessons within them, to a larger audience. Yet, even more moving than these stories and their lessons is the experience of sharing the narratives. This is what my play aspires to present with help of illumination that only a stage can provide.

Henry Armstrong and Dorothy Griffin Remember Katrina

Interview, April 5, 2006
Recorded and transcribed by Nicole Eugene

Nicole Eugene: Let me first start by asking both of y'all, where were you born?

Dorothy Griffin: I was born in New Orleans, Louisiana March the twenty-sixth, 1924.

Henry Armstrong Jr: And I was also born in New Orleans, some time later, in 1946 in May.

Nicole: So, can you tell me a little bit about what it was like growing up in New Orleans?

Dorothy: Well, it was nice. People were friendly and they shared and they cared about one another. And everybody was—just to get together and be nice to one another, and stuff like that, went to school, went to church and all. And I graduated from McDonogh 35, and I continued going to a Lutheran church. I used to help serve food to the hungry once a month at Mount Zion Lutheran Church, and help them with other things around there if need be. And I used to belong to a little Christmas savings

Henry Armstrong Jr., Houston, 2006. Photo by Dallas McNamara.

club, and I would go out socially, visit with friends. I could get around then. I wasn't using a walker or nothing like that. I had *no* problems, I had never been sick.

Nicole: Can you tell me a little bit about your family?

Dorothy: My mother and my father, both of them died. My father died in 1960, my mother died in '82 and, you know, they were working parents, and they cared for us, my brother and I. And we had a small family, just the four of us, and we got along well together, no problems. Had nice friends and everything.

I married in '45 to Henry Armstrong Sr. And he was nice. We had nice life together, we stayed together for about seven years. Then we divorced and he went away and each time that he came here, to New Orleans, he would always come and see us, come see Henry [Jr.]. And all we shared, I let him know what things he was in, things he was doing. I stayed with my parents and he moved to L.A.

Nicole: Henry, can you talk a little bit about growing up in New Orleans?

Henry: Oh, yeah, I had a beautiful childhood. I grew up in the area called Sixth Ward, which is downtown, about eight blocks off Canal Street, and we lived on Dumaine Street. It was a close-knitted neighborhood, everybody knew everybody; everybody looked out for everybody else's kids. When we were running around it was like we were always under the eye of some parent, so that if we did anything wrong, that if anything bad happened, it didn't take long for news to get home.

I moved to L.A. to live with my dad, I went to school out there for a couple of years and I came back here to graduate. My mom wanted to see me graduate from high school. I was an above-average basketball player. I finally graduated and moved off back to L.A., and then I came back here to be with my mother and grandmother—my grandfather died in the early ages—and I lived with them, my mother and grandmother. And, everything was smooth, especially as long as my grandmother was living. I could do no wrong. But as things would be, God took her away from us, and left me and my mother to fend for ourselves.

And so, I was a merchant seaman from about 1970 to 1989. So, I was always in and out and I have to accredit a lot of the experiences I had with Katrina, I guess I'd have to credit a lot of that, to the merchant seaman industry: being out, traveling different oceans and whatnot. A lot of people say, "Ooh, all that water!" Which is one of the things that she [Dorothy] said that morning when she looked out the window: "Ooh, all that water." So I guess that helped to keep me from panicking. But I was concerned and, first and foremost, I talked to God and I tried to make a deal with him, and it seemed that the deal worked. I told him if he let me get my mother out of this I'd be forever committed to her, which I was already. You know, and coming up in school, I mean, and going to Lutheran school: if you didn't go to church you couldn't go to school.

But at any rate, up until Katrina life was beautiful; I had stopped shipping and became a professional waiter and was doing, I guess, okay at it. And then: well if I could get into this pre-Katrina thing?

Nicole: Can you tell me a little bit about your family and your sons?
Henry: Oh, my sons? Well, I have a beautiful set of children, you know. I have a lot of them. And they all love and respect me and I love and respect them, and their grandmothers. Most of them are grown and gone: Thank you, Jesus. And coming up with them we've had a lot of things to share in New Orleans. The only problem that I have with that is that my children are not by one woman. I have four sets of children. But even at that, they all seem to be as if they collectively came from the same spot. They all love and respect each other, they're very close, even though some are in California, some in Texas, some in Louisiana, some in Georgia. And since Katrina, I mean, most of them were living away, but since Katrina we

done picked up Georgia. I got my grandkids spread all up and down Texas. We were about to have a family reunion before this. I'm thankful that it happened like it did because I don't know what would have happened if all my daddy and brothers and sisters would have been down here. Thank God that it didn't turn out to be like that. But, as for my kids, we share in activities, we hang out when we're together, when I get a chance to go home especially. My oldest son, he's in New Orleans working and now my third son, Kevin, he's down there also. And so when I get to go down there it's like déjà vu; I get to be daddy. I get to find out what it was like coming up under me and so far, they all seem to think I did a pretty decent job. Coming up to Katrina, anyway.

Nicole: Can you tell me about the area and places you'd stayed, before Katrina? And your everyday life before Katrina?

Henry: I'm a professional waiter: hotels such as the Hyatt Regency, the Marriott, the Convention Center, the Monteleone, the Fairmont—all these people, when they need waiters, I'm usually included in the fold because of my talents and abilities. As a matter a fact, up until the day Katrina arrived I was supposed to be working at the Fairmont hotel. They were going to pay us because they were going to have workers and people who were in the hotel at the time, and they had to be taken care of. They were going to pay us to stay there during the storm, they were going to provide housing and provide a room for us. And I just thought about my mother. And the more I listen at the news and the more I thought about it, I just decided that with those winds and with where she was living at—which was like, the house she was in was a rear apartment and it was wood. And I often use this term: I'm reminded of the three little pigs and the big bad wolf—the wolf being Katrina. And with her living in a wooden establishment I merely thought about this, I left work: *I don't think I'm going to go. I'm going to stay here with her.*

And thank God that I did, and I got her from her apartment where she was and moved down about five blocks to where my oldest son, Henry (the third), where him and his wife was staying. And it was up on the second floor, and it was brick. So I thought that's where I'd take my mother under those circumstances. And I brought her over there and we went to gather the grandchildren, and whatnot, and everybody—which is where his mother was living, oh, about three blocks away but in the same projects—and so we gathered by them. We went to all the grandchildren that we could get together, everybody we could get together and family, and we had them there and we were here.

And then came Katrina. Well, we sat up during the night and we watched. You know, we listened at the wind hollering because that afternoon it started raining. The sky got gray but nothing happened until the darkness of night. And I remember coming out the apartment and stepping in, what you call a breezeway, I guess, looking out. And I could see the wind was just taking air conditioners, everything. Just pulling them out, Lord, and I'm not talking about small, I'm talking about large air conditioners: *zoom zoom* [Henry moves his hands around in a roller-coaster-like loop]. And I think after about my third air conditioner I got pretty, for lack of a better word, afraid. Just imagining the wind bringing one of those into that window area where I was. And I went back inside. I had seen enough and I went to sleep.

We woke up that morning. No water, beautiful sunshiny day. We knew that it was all over. And so everybody was out and they were talking, mingling and suddenly your feet start getting wet. Well, you didn't pay no attention to it; still got a little rain going, you know, off and on. But for the most part, that morning broke with sunlight and then it got dark again, gray; then it started raining. By the end of the day it's kind of hard. I don't know if my mind blanks out a lot of stuff or whatnot, but I noticed one thing—I had a friend who was working the pumping station. And they couldn't go anywhere. You know, these are the guys that were working in the pumping stations that pumped the water off the street. I used to bring food back to him daily, because they had no way of eating. This is when the water started rising, and every once and a while he would call the house—when the phone was working—because, by now, you know, we've lost lights, we're losing phones eventually, and the gas. These were things we had lost, after a while. So, what you do is you try to cook up all the stuff that you have before it spoils. I would bring him [food] and he would keep me posted on the conditions. And he said, "Man, there's going to be a little lightweight flood." Well, lightweight floods, we been through lightweight floods; that's when the water gets up to your ankles. So you know then not to wear shoes. But Katrina didn't turn out to be that. Because it got to the ankles, then it got to the calves, and then it got up to the knees, and then nightfall came.

This is when I made my first efforts to take my mother out of the projects. So at that time there was looting going on around the city. So we had the opportunity to confiscate a mattress from somebody who had been looting. They were using a mattress to carry the stuff off. And the family up on the third floor—my mother's friend's children and grandchildren—they were getting scared because, the water was, about then, up to our knees. They wanted to go.

"Well, okay, and if y'all want to go, I'm going to take my mama out too." But when I got ready to put my mom on their mattress she had so much fear in her face. And she was so afraid because—and I could understand why—because it was pitch dark. You couldn't see anything but water. You knew there were buildings out there. I imagine, I don't think she's ever been in that kind of predicament before, so we took her off the mattress and said, "Don't worry, we'll get you out in the morning, Mom." We went on and brought the other family out and we came back, my son and I. So we called it a night as far as that was concerned. This was when I made a pact with God that if he would help me get my mother out in the morning—because I had talked to my friend and he told me that the water was going to be rising.

That morning, when I got up, I never dreamed I'd see what I saw. But during the night you hear people talking, I mean, it's just, just you could hear blocks away; that's how quiet it was, if someone hollered loud enough, because nobody was walking around in the water. All you could do is holler across the court or holler down the court to try to see if everybody was all right, which is the way we communicated. However, I fell asleep. But I was awakened that morning with the sound of, *"Oh, my God. Look at this water.* Where all this water come from?" That's what my mom was saying. And so, I got up and I looked out and, sure enough, the water was at least waist high *on me*, and I'm six [foot]-four.

What did we do then? My son, he went back to where his children were, and I decided that I was going to go and try and to get another mattress. And at the same time this water is steady rising because I remember leaving in waist-deep water and coming back and the water being chest deep. So when I got back with that I went upstairs to get my mom and my son's mother. And I called for my son and then I told him, "Well, here we go, this is what we're going to have to do. We'll put them on the mattress and we're going to have to swim and push and guide these mattresses so that they don't get away from us." And try to keep them from going into the middle of the parkway where the water was much deeper. My son, at first, was a little shook up; I imagine he had never been through nothing like that. But we got them on the mattresses and we went up and as we was going up something I recall is my mama just sitting there and the people asking us to, "Come back, now, come back and get us." And my mama said, "Oh, they're good boys, they going to come back and get y'all." At the time—I don't know what I was acting on. Whether it was fear or adrenaline or what. I just knew that everybody was looking up to me to get them out. My mother, my son's mother, my grandchildren, and I just knew that I just had to, I had to, I had to come through. Excuse me. [The recording was paused until Henry was ready to continue.]

Well, I knew that they all would be depending on me and I couldn't let them down because I was Daddy, I was Papa. And everybody knew that Papa would get them through. So anyway my son and I, we pushed and swam, I guess about seven blocks until we got my mother and his mother to dry land, which was on the Claiborne overpass, this is the part that sits across from the Dome. And, at the time we didn't know it, but we weren't going to have any help on that overpass. Anyway, we went back and got my grandkids and we went through the same things: put the girls on the mattresses, two of the boys [who were about ten or eleven years old], had them in the water beside me. And I had them, "Just keep one hand on the mattress and kick your feet; if you get tired, let me know, but don't take your hand off the mattress and don't stop kicking your feet." I remember giving them those instructions. And so we managed to make it out on the mattress and got them up to the same area. And went back one at a time and after that I was just physically spent.

We went and got maybe three or four, maybe four more people, elderly people, and we brought them over and then I couldn't—I told my son he could take the mattresses and if he wanted to go and help somebody else, it was okay. But I couldn't, I was, I was spent. But by this time my son—it had become obvious to him what he had to do now so he went back and he helped some of his friends and some more people, whoever, I don't know, while I sat up on the bridge there with my mom. Now mind you, we sitting on the bridge, no food, no water, no port-a-potties, you know—and you can see her age, and at the time it was taking its toll on her. Katrina's beginning to take its *toll* on her then. If you had told me two days prior to Katrina that I would be sleeping in a gutter I probably [would have] cursed you out and told you you're crazy as I don't know what. But turns out that even on the bridge, that helped. And what it did for New Orleans, I feel, is that first of all a lot of it had to be God's work because it taught us to be humble, it taught us to be kind to one another, it taught us to help one another *any* way we could, because we were all in the same boat, so to speak. And while we were up there they had other ladies, my mother's age and whatnot, who had no one but themselves.

And then there came a need for food. There was a need for water. And over in the Superdome there were helicopters coming in and they were depositing water and food, but all this was going in the Dome. The people on that bridge, which was thousands, who were coming from downtown and uptown: they sent us nothing, no food, no water. We're standing up there, when the helicopters are coming in, waving our hands, we asking, "Bring some over here, give *us* something." And the folks in charge over on the heliport, they just looked down on us and turned their backs.

So we decided—a guy that I knew, a good friend of mine before Katrina, it seemed like we just bonded right then and there. Between my mother and these other senior citizens that we had, we decided, man, we got to do something, so we left. And we started going across over to the Dome to get food and water and these MRE [Meals Ready to Eat] packages were what we were able to come back with. And as we were making trips backwards and forwards we was, you know, dispersing it amongst the people on the bridge: it wasn't just for my mother or just for him and I. We were just taking care of everybody that we could. We run into another family who happened to have food that they were cooking and they in turn got along with us.

(As a matter of fact, I saw him at the FEMA place [in Houston], and they wound up in—oh, it just goes to show you because they was a family—he had his family together like I had mine together: some wound up in Arkansas, if I'm not mistaken—Katrina just really tore up a bunch of [families]. Even those that survived the storm paid a price. The price was when it come time to evacuate, [being] taken in parts: the elderly, handicapped, women, pregnant women, women with kids, and the men came last, I guess, which is understandable. But a lot of people for a lot of months didn't know where one another was. I'm glad that I was able to stay with my mother because the toll that it took on her was unbelievable. After we got here she had to be hospitalized and she came out and she had to be hospitalized again for [congestive] heart failure, fluid—and then she was put in a nursing home. Well at first, after we did get here, in Texas, I was able to start working again as a waiter downtown.)

Dorothy: Excuse me. [The recording is paused while Dorothy sits down].

Henry: So, what we would do is we would go and get food and water, and we would bring it back and divide it amongst the ladies. And if there was enough for us, then we would eat. At the time we didn't know that those MRE packets could be heated because we were eating it as is, and with water. And let's face it, a box of MREs and a couple of bottles of water, because that's the way they were dispersing it, in little miniature bottles of water. But anyway we'd take that back and forward, and for some reason the people got tired of seeing us coming off the bridge telling us that we couldn't come that way any more: water contaminated, or whatever. But, I think if you tell somebody to cut off their meal supply, you think they're going to accommodate your wishes? No way. So what we would do is, we just kept on coming down, and we didn't go near the Dome, we just stayed over to the other side on the fences. And this went on, like I said, for three days and two nights. This is what we had to do to survive, to eat.

I think this was around the beginning of the third day [on the bridge]: I noticed a Kentwood water station, which is housed under the I-10 area. And I just went to thinking, say, "Well, I ought to go down there to see if they got water in those trucks." And, lo and behold, trucks had been stocked and left. And so, as a child I recall being able to hotwire cars and whatnot, and as fate would have it, some of the trucks had keys in them. So I helped myself to a truck, and I drove the truck up on the bridge and I emptied a truck full of water and drove it back down. Got another truck, went up and did the same thing. I was going up the ramp that you come down on but they had no car traveling on it so I had no problem with that. And after the second truckload, after unloading that which, like I said, this was like going into the third day. And we were always trying to wait and see, or find word on about whether we were going to be evacuated. Looking at all the buses, and whatnot, up on the overpass, and they just sitting there.

So, this particular day we found out through walking around—you know, when you got nothing to do and you're just looking to see who else has made it, if you knew anyone that has made it. We just got together, walking up and down the bridge, you meet this person, you hear a story, you meet that person, you hear a story. You sit there and you're watching the people trickle into the Superdome. So, they were trickling into the Superdome, and I mean, I've seen Katrina brought the best out of even the worst of us. I mean that I've seen some flotation devices that you would not believe. I mean we got some geniuses in our race who don't even know it. I mean, you'd be surprised: empty barrels, telephone posts that's fallen down—they'd ride them, you know. There's things that before then you would never have even thought they had use for. But, anyway, when I got back to this water situation, after the second truck, unloaded it, it seemed like by then the people on the bridge had enough water. Evidently they had too much, because I saw one guy taking a bath with it, you know.

But anyway, we went back down and around and we got my mom, me and my friend, Wilfred. (He stayed with me through the whole ordeal, even when we got ready to evacuate: we came to Texas together. Him and

I took care of my mother and those other ladies while we were in that fix under that bridge, or on that bridge. Him and I slept side by side in that gutter, and now that this is over I see him whenever I go back to New Orleans, and he's there now, he lives in Missouri. And when he and me are there he comes down in the morning early and picks me up and we spend the day together. Wherever I got to go or he got to go, we'll do it. It just created a bond with him, and I don't think we'll ever be separated again, because we even talk on the phone now, and you'd think we were two women the way we're doing that, because I'm not a telephone person. I'll call him or he'll call me. As a matter of fact, even my kids, everybody: it's the one good thing that Katrina has left us with, is my kids and my friends. We have a bond now that, you know, we talk. It may be long distance, or it may be some of them are here, but we call one another and we talk, "Now, you all right, man?"—"Yeah, I'm cool," you know, and this is the one thing I like about it.

But the thing that I hate the most is what Katrina has done to my mother. Because my mother would always like to get up and get on the bus and take care of her own business, independent. And now she's been through a couple of heart problems and fluid, and it's left her now where she can't walk a half a block. But thank God she's still breathing, and she's still here. But we here, and since we've been here, well, FEMA has made it comfortable for us, I guess—or convenient. But, we're still longing to go back home to where we was born and raised. You know, Texas has been good to me, I must say, but I would much rather be able to go back home now.

And the area where I lived at, first of all let me say this: where my mother was living I had the opportunity to go back and to go into the house, and the waterline was three quarters up the wall. And the house sits, like maybe two feet off the ground. So if my mother had have been in that house she wouldn't have made it, at all. It would have been over her head, even when she stood up, even if she stood up. So she's got absolutely nothing to go back to. We have a family dwelling, the house that I live in, was passed down from my grandmother to her and now me. That house sustained roof damages and siding, got wooden floors—and they didn't have a lot of water out in Metairie, which is where the house is located, near the airport. But the water was up high enough to where it could touch the bottom of the floors. The water filled up so much in there, let me tell you this, it went through the floor. The weight from the water—water is heavy—and by it coming down through the roof and whatnot, the house was declared a major disaster. And at this time I'm waiting to see if FEMA's going to give me enough money to repair that house.

FEMA did a lot for us here, monetarily speaking, but how do you start all over again at my age? I'm fifty-nine years old. And I know, if it's hard for me, I can imagine what she's going through. But as of now this is our greatest wish, that we could somehow—I'm waiting to hear from them, I haven't given up hope—if I could somehow come up with the monies needed to repair that house. And she don't have anything to go back to, and as I say, this was a family dwelling, through succession, and this is all we got now. We have furniture and stuff that we can go back with, but that's not the problem. The problem is the roof over your head. You know, if we can get that there then you could pretty well call us a Katrina survivor. Up until then, we're just evacuees.

Nicole: Can you go back to the bridge and tell me how you got off the bridge and got to Houston?

Henry: Well, we were on the bridge for two nights [and] three days. And that was miserable, for me, to see my mother having to go through this, because she's a proud woman. She didn't want to go to the bathroom and she didn't want this, that, and the other. But the best thing we could find was for her to sit on was the sides of the concrete where you would walk, if you were walking on the bridge. This is where they had to congregate, they had to use the rails and all this for their back support. Life on that bridge was—it wasn't nothing nice. But to get her from the bridge to be evacuated we [used] the trucks that I told you about, after emptying the second truck.

These trucks have these partition-like spaces where they keep the water. And going to the Dome from where we were, there was a lot of water there; I bet the water that was there was at least waist high or better. So, if you're a person who was able to stand up straight and walk it's no problem, you'd just walk along the fence, but at this time my mother was hardly able to walk and, like I said, Katrina's taking its toll on her. Well what I did, Wilfred and I, we put my mother in the truck and he got alongside her and I was driving and we drove that truck in the water, because it was a big truck; we drove it in the water until we got up to that end of the Superdome, and that's the New Orleans arena, which is where the Hornets play basketball, and it's about three flights up from the ground. And so I back the truck up as close as I could to the steps so that when we took my mother off of there, it was probably the first time she was in the water, thank God. It probably was up mid-way to her calf. And then we got her on the steps and between him and I, and my mother, we went up three flights of steps, she never once complained. During this whole Katrina ordeal she never complained, I got to give her that. Which I'm glad that she didn't: that means that I was doing okay taking care of her. We would go up and let her catch her breath, and we'd go up a little more and let her catch her breath, and so on and so on until we got to the top, or where we needed to be. And after then, we went across the walkway, which is like crossing the street, but up in the air, and then we got into the Dome and she still never complained. She had to go in there, she wanted to go in there, I guess she wanted to go to the bathroom *so* bad. And she had to really want to go bad because the scent from walking inside that Dome from the toilets being inoperative, and whatever else was out of whack out over there. That's the only time I had to leave my mama. I could not take it, it was just making me sick. And so some lady was going in. I asked her to bring my mother and she went with her and I waited right there till she came out. And we came back out and we found my oldest son and he showed me where the grandkids were.

We got all them together and then we heard that they were about to evacuate. And we had everybody in one group and we're steady moving up with her. And the heat and I guess the pressure from being within the crowd, people were falling out, you know. I'm glad that, if it did happen, it didn't happen while we were there, that panic and chaos and how people were just trampling one another; or maybe some people, you know, just so out of it, just start fighting or something like that—it had never come to that. But we got everybody up close, and soon we got them all together, I was faced with a situation that I hope never happens again: where I got to decide am I going to go with my mama and am I going to leave my children and grandchildren behind. Am I going to stay with them or go with her? Well, evidently, my mother won hands down.

That life on that bridge, them two days and them three nights were, oh man, ridiculous. I'm telling you, but like I said, it brought everyone together, it had us feenin for one another. Whereas, you know, I recall a situation between a white gentleman and myself. He was there, oh, he was just, "Oh, I done lost everything. I don't know. What am I going to do?" *Man*: blah, blah, blah, blah, blah. I had to just tell him, "Look around, man. Just look around. You up here, and the way you talking." And, you know, I wasn't heated or anything, but I was just, "Look around, man. All of us done lost stuff. You're talking about your house and your boat and all this here, man, *but you're breathing.* You know, that's the thing to be thankful about." And I think, by telling him that, it kind of woke him up or something. Man, all that's material that you're talking about. I remember floating in the water and bodies passing by. You know. What you think that person got to complain about?

However, I hope we never have another Katrina or tsunami. I hope another human being never has to go through what the people of New Orleans had to go through. And I understand that was a tri-state affair because it's hard to realize that anything of that nature was happening anywhere else other than where you were. Because you thought that this right here, in this project area, is where everything is until you got up on that bridge and you talked to people from downtown. You talked to people from other areas of town and how they got there, and you hear about the lady whose baby fell off that boat when they were trying to get them out. I wonder, too, if they ever found that baby. This was life after about the second day on the bridge, when the guys on the boats started so-called plucking us from out the projects. They dropped one baby. I have the mind of another.

It's kind of hard to just sit down and in an hour or so and put down everything that you went through. I remember sitting around, and one lady was hollering, "Oh, my baby!" She had her children on a mattress and one fell off, and I think this was in the beginning where I injured myself—this was when the water was coming up—but I dove out in the water and the first thing I hit was a grocery basket. Which is why, when I get ready to stand up, I can't stand up straight because my knees [Henry rubs his knees] are almost decimated. And so it never got well. I've been so banged up I don't know what it is. But every once in a while, if I go to stand up I got to take my time and get my legs underneath me. But we got there. I got to the little baby, the lady was so, I mean, you know: trauma, panic, whatever, I don't know what to put it on. But I know from some of the experiences, some of the things I've seen, and things I've heard about, you know—this lady got her two kids, she done forgot about the baby that I went under the water and got. She just walking away with the babies. I'm calling, "Miss, I got her, I got her." She just gone. And when she got to the porch I gave her her baby. Oh, man, mind boggling, you know.

And I'm reminded about hurricane Betsy, you know, that happened years back. I'm glad I wasn't here for that one, because a lot of people then had a lot of stories, but this was more or less downtown in a predominantly black area. And that was done to save the white areas at that time; I don't know what happened to the levees this time. I don't want to think like a racist, I don't want to sound racist, but I know, in the past, that's what's happened. I don't know what happened this time, but I do know that—as big as that storm was, like they say Louisiana, Mississippi, probably Alabama, I don't know—I know that I hope it never comes through [again] in the next two, three, four, five hundred years. And that's about it for me unless you want to hear about something else.

Nicole: What do you think about the rebuilding efforts, what are some of the problems?

Henry: Well, so far from what I see when I go down to New Orleans, I have to go back on business trying to pay house taxes because you know that eventually politics and government is going to be back in it. So, I go down for different reasons.

Recently, when I was down there, the projects that we went to for my mother and them: that's fenced off. The St. Bernard project, it's fenced off. Where are these people going to come? When they come back, where will they live? Because now all we worrying about is the business district, the parks. You want the people to come back. See, a lot of people, even this guy, my friend—he stayed there the whole while pumping that water out of the city, he got nowhere to stay right now.

You know, trailers and all this; I have a trailer but I'm not used to a trailer, I mean look, it takes me at least four or five bumps on the head to realize that I could never make it in a trailer. But it's what I got. It's what they give me, and I make do with it. It's sitting on our property and it's somewhere where if it rains you got a roof over your heads because we can't go inside the house, which is right across from the trailer. FEMA's been good far as that's concerned, but I wish they'd allow me—if they don't give me no money, let me sell that trailer and get to use the money to fix the house up. I could bring my mother back to New Orleans, and she can live out the rest of her days in her home where she wants to be.

My mother still talks like you can go across the street to the store. Baby, in Texas, y'all got a lot of room here. They say "right up the street," but they talking about *a mile* away, because when we say "right up the street" we in the same block or the next block. So, it took me a while to get used to that vernacular, and when they tell me "right up," now I point "Where? How much? Let me know," you know, and then I'll tackle it.

But, you know, I know we're going to overcome. We're going to live this out, we done been through too much—huh, Mom?—for it to take us down now, no way. And I do hope that these experiences that I'm sharing with you—that if it helps somebody in any way, I'm glad that I was able to. And to let somebody know, one thing I can say. No matter how bad off you are, there's always a worse situation somewhere. I'm reminded of what my grandma used to tell me as a little boy. I'd come in hollering. "Boy, what you hollering about?" she'd always tell me this, "Boy, I want you to remember this throughout life" (and I mean it has helped me out a bunch of times): "I cried because I didn't have any shoes, until I saw a man that had no feet"; you don't want to thrive off the misery of another; but no matter how bad things get there's always something worse going on somewhere in the world. And with that thought there, I guess that's about all I have to say.

Nicole: Did you go to the Astrodome when you got here? Where did you first go when you got to Houston?

Henry: Yeah, yeah, we went to the Reliant Center. Not to the Dome but the Reliant Center.

Nicole: How was that experience?

Henry: Oh, that was an adventure at first, but what the deal was that this is where we had to be, because this was where we got our benefits from. Now, my mother, at this stage, she couldn't stand there, because she had these problems with her legs and the cots, the legs on them were too low, which is a point here I forgot to make. My daughter, the one in Wichita Falls, she went to college and she had a friend of hers to come and get her grandma and they brought her to their house where she was, you know, able to sleep in a bed, and stuff like that. So, until we were able to get to the George [R.] Brown [Convention] Center, that's where accommodations were made. Those people, I must say, those volunteers, they really, really gave a lot of assistance in helping me with my mother. All I'd do is bring her upstairs and that's where they got her a wheelchair—by this time she was able to be assisted, and then that's what I mean by those people were good to us. I'd bring her up there and, "Oh, okay, you can go," 'cause I'd have things to do within the building as far as trying to get our benefits or whatever you want to call it. And I could go stand in line and not have to worry about where she was. Everything I had to do I had to do it twofold, because if it was a benefit I would have to sign for me and then sign for her. And that was the thing that helped us [get] this far. And then again, I'm grateful to the state of Texas for accepting us like it did. The people, the volunteers, they were wonderful, they were friendly, they had smiles on their faces. They kind of helped you get out of the position or the predicament that you're in. Because, you know, you're wondering, how the heck do y'all come to work everyday smiling? Friendly, but it takes its toll on you. And this was remarkable how the city opened up to us. I guess I'll forever be indebted to the city of [Houston], or Bill White or who's ever responsible for what all transpired once we got here.

Nicole: So how is your life in Houston? Have you been able to adjust, and can you also tell me how you found Franklin Avenue [Baptist Church]?

Henry: Okay, now life in Houston for me—and you got to remember you're speaking about a native New Orleanian, and I just got finished telling you about how I owe them a debt of gratitude—*it's boring.* It's boring because, for number one, here I have no transportation; it's boring because everything is too far. Okay, I mean, even when I was working, the Metro system is beautiful but to get from here to the Metro system is about eleven blocks, so by the time I get to work I've already done a day's work, you know, which I guess has nothing to do with the things that have transpired and the people who have helped us out along the way. But you know New Orleans is a eight-day-a-week, twenty-five-hour-a-day town; things shut down here at two o'clock. We never close, so this is where the boring part comes in, and I would imagine that probably if I had transportation—because I mean there's a lot of things you used to do that you can't do no more—like the old song say, "It's hard for me to be me and be here."

Now how I came to First Baptist Church is that, I think maybe some six to eight months prior to Katrina I had been baptized Baptist. I was Lutheran and I have this friend who's a preacher, that's about maybe three, four blocks from where my mother was living at. Where I was going to church. And so, since I've been here I've been trying to find me a church, especially a church with some good singing and good preaching and I've been to a couple of churches and I'm still trying to find, not still—I mean, and that's how I got to First Baptist. First of all, that's a New Orleans congregation, which means that eventually you go there with the anticipation that maybe I'll see a friend. My mother has a—

Dorothy: A cousin.

Henry: A cousin that goes there. And you know, in New Orleans, but I haven't been able to see her yet. We haven't gotten in contact with them yet. And, I enjoy the services, I enjoy the preaching and besides I don't have to worry about transportation, there's a couple that goes there that I can ride with. So, that's basically how I got to the church, and you know I went there the first time, but if I go anytime after that it's because I enjoyed it. The Sunday we met I think that was like my fourth trip and each time I go I meet somebody new, I meet somebody special, you know—I'm speaking of you. And then I'm amazed at the building. I don't know about you but I'd never been in a building of that size, you know—and that's about it.

Nicole: Are there any other things that you miss about New Orleans, or in the community that you're from?

Henry: I miss being able to go in and out my house. I miss my grand-children, I miss not being able to be around them. I miss how my work ethics have been, more or less, demolished because I had to stop working again on account of my mother. When she went to the hospital, and I had to be there, I had so much on my mind I probably stopped working the way that I should have. I miss that and I miss, I miss working. I miss get-ting a check every week. There's a list of things I can tell you I miss; boy, my lifestyle. I'm existing.

Dorothy: I'm sorry.

Nicole: So, Dorothy, is there anything that you'd like to add to Henry's story?

Dorothy: Yeah, and like they said, I lost all my clothes, all my belong-ings in the flood back there. When I left home—you know, the house filled with water—and couldn't get back in there. It stayed there for some days with the water around. But, the people were nice to me at the Center, the George Brown Center. They were nice, you know, with me. And they had people that was dead; they had them laying on chairs over there, at the foot of the overpass behind the posters in the back.

Nicole: In New Orleans?

Dorothy: Uh huh. They had about, I saw at least five of them dead, you know, they had them laying on the chairs. People just brought them back there. But it was a rough ordeal, you know, getting from there, the Super-dome, being over there because it was really filthy. When the helicopters started flying next morning trying to rescue people we was in the window, but they didn't see us flagging out. They were just flying over, going ahead. They went up to LaSalle and Jackson and picked up people, but they were going. But we just thought they were coming to get us back there, you know.

But I never would have made it hadn't been for my son, and my grand-son. I guess I'd have been on a chair somewhere.

[In the background Henry replies, "Don't talk like that."]

Yeah, but I appreciate the assistance that I did get, you know.

The words of Henry and Dorothy played an important part in inspiring Nicole to envision a play based on the words and experiences of survivors who had been trapped on the overpasses and bridges of New Orleans in the aftermath of Hurricane Katrina. In 2007, the Cynthia Woods Mitchell Center for the Arts sponsored a collaboration engaging playwright Nathaniel Freeman and actors from the University of Houston Drama Department in dialogue with the survivors recorded by the Surviving Katrina and Rita in Houston project. Freeman listened to the recordings of more than a dozen survivors and joined Nicole in recording some follow-up interviews.

Nicole writes,

Nate Freeman traveled to New Orleans with me and met several of the people behind the voices in the interviews, including Henry Armstrong. The play opened in the fall of 2008, at a time when the wounds in Houstonians and Katrina evacuees were still scabbed over. The performance and the discussions following the showings captivated the imagination of many of the viewers and participants. The play ran from October 3 to October 12, 2008.

In the years that followed the play, I hesitantly welcomed the coming recession because it turned my personal misfortune of unemployment into a collective one. There was nothing cathartic about turning unemployment into a shared experience. The situation did, however, echo the need for community I felt before becoming an interviewer and meeting fellow evacuees. It is worth noting that Henry also, without being prompted, described his misfortune as a part of a larger condition that several people are suffering through. My search for stable employment led me to becoming self-employed. Being an online bookseller allows me to set meaningful goals for personal and business growth while also supplying me with the tools needed to work towards them: books. My mom's duplex, which was flooded, was finally put back into working order just in 2011 and will be fully occupied soon.

Since the interview Henry and Dorothy continued to hope that FEMA would help them fix the roof damage on the family's only house. When Nicole interviewed Henry again on December 8, 2007, he spoke about the pain that his memories continue to evoke, and he expressed his gratitude to Nicole for the opportunity to share his story with her:

Well, it helps to relieve. I don't believe in whining and crying and all of that. And I got so many looking up to me, I don't really have time. But it is a relief to relieve yourself of some things sometimes. And, actually, I find that when I do this in the times that we've been together, this has done a lot for me. Like I said, I'm not familiar with psychiatry and all that, you know. Actually, I don't want to fool with them unless I'm crazy, and I don't think I am crazy. So, you know, I do this; this really is relief for me. It helps me out a great deal. And then once I've been with this, I don't have to worry about going [to] these stress classes that come around here. I just feel like, that's just a waste of time or just some people here being exploited—my mother included—where they sit around and talk. I never been to them. I can sit down and talk about things, but I don't want to talk about things openly in front of a large crowd. Especially things that sometimes might get next to me, might—how my children say it?—might punk me out: "Daddy sitting up there crying again." But they haven't been through it, and they don't know what it's like, and I don't think they would hold it against me now that they know what I've been through. I've enjoyed both your company and knowing the feeling that I have when you do leave. You know, wow, that did me some good. It's like a burden been lifted. So, I don't know the medical term for it. It's been sort of like going to—what do they call it?—my therapist. Yes.

In 2008, before Henry was able to take his mother back to New Orleans, Hurricane Ike bore down on Houston, and Dorothy—who had endured so much in an earlier storm—passed away during the evacuation. Henry has returned to New Orleans. Nicole continues to live in Houston.

JOSEF BROWN

"We're a real tight family, and can't nothing break us apart"

The following survivor interviews are arranged roughly by order of the narrator's age. The Surviving Katrina and Rita in Houston project was restricted from interviewing children under the age of fifteen. Thus, Josef Brown, fifteen years old when survivor interviewer Phylicia Bradley recorded his story on April 1, 2007, was one of the project's youngest story-tellers. At the time of the hurricane, he had been fourteen.

    Josef was thrown immediately into a role of adult responsibility for the lives and well-being of others. He embraced this role, for it was already part of his upbringing, as his accounts of family life attest at every turn. Barely a teenager at the time he was recorded, Josef views his family as an entirely interdependent organism in which every individual is responsible for the acts of all others. He helps his brother break into an unoccupied house to save his family from drowning. He expresses concern that his aunt, in her seventies, had to lie on the cold concrete of an overpass for even a short time. In Houston, after the storm, as his mother becomes depressed over being unemployed, he acts as her caretaker.

Josef Brown (center), age fifteen, in Houston, with his older brother Cedric and his mother, Debra. Photo by Dallas McNamara.

Well, I grew up in New Orleans, and as a child I always had fun, because I could hang with my friends. They were close around, and I always had something to do when I was in New Orleans. I grew up downtown, Mid City. Went to McDonogh 35. So.

I have two brothers and one sister, and it's a real close family. We like to keep in touch with each other. We talk to each other almost every day. We're a real tight family, and can't nothing break us apart, especially a storm.

I miss the surroundings and the homey feeling that I always had, like I always wanted to go to school. I never had a day where I didn't want to go to school. I always woke up, got ready to go to school, went to school, did my thing, caught the bus home, might have went down the street, talked with my friends, and played basketball, just laugh, just have fun. Things wasn't so tight; it was more free, and I could just be free, so that's how I felt. That's pretty much a basic day. I come home after playing basketball, talk to my mama, call my big brother, see what he did that day, and watch television.

I feel that New Orleans just, it's a wonderful place if you, if you ever been there, ever visited, went to Jazz Fest, Mardi Gras, anything. It's a wonderful place and even with the stuff that went on there it's a very wonderful place. It's so homey. Everybody's like family there. You can hang out with people you don't know, for hours, and they ain't going to even tell you nothing. It's really close-knit in New Orleans. Everybody: you ain't got to be nervous around them, and you ain't got to put on airs. You could just be yourself and that's what I like about New Orleans, you know. You always want to do something, you could always be with your friends, you go to Canal Street, they always have something to do. It wasn't too big. It wasn't too small. It just, it was perfect for a person like myself. Always had somebody to be with, always. Always knew where to go, and I knew my surroundings, and that's what I like about it. And I feel that everybody should know that.

The schools were good. You learned what you had to know. It was real friendly schools. The schools were good. The teachers didn't really pound unnecessary stuff into your head. They taught you what you needed to know, and they taught you anything you needed help with, like family. They could be your counselor: if you ever needed to talk, teachers wasn't just going to run away from you. If you had a problem, they were there for you. Like they were your own mother. If you couldn't talk to your own mother, they would be your mother for you. And just things like that: that's what makes a life. If you had that, you wouldn't want nothing else. You wouldn't want it to change. It just changed on me. After that, I didn't know what to do. It was lost.

During the time of the hurricane, I was in New Orleans East with my brother and my cousin, and I didn't really know too much about the hurricane. I didn't even know there was a hurricane coming. My mother called and said she was watching the news and there was a storm coming, and she wanted to know what we was going to do, because the place that I was at, we was right by a levee, and she didn't want us to be that close. So she came, got me and my brother, my cousin, and my aunt, and we went to the house. We went to her house, and we didn't have enough gas to leave, and all the gas stations were closed, so we decided that we was going to sit out the storm, and see if we could hold it out. And so we called my aunt in St. Louis, and she just went crazy. She found out we wasn't leaving, and called newscasters trying get us helicopters to get out. It was crazy. But we stayed.

When the storm hit, we was just looking at it. It was a good four and a half feet of water, or five feet at the time when I woke up. And we felt that we survived another one. But a hour later, we seen that the water was getting higher and higher. So we figure if the water was getting higher, we would have to leave our house, because we couldn't stay in our house. Because we had a one-story house.

A house across the street had two stories, and the man wasn't there, so we decided to get in this house so we could have safety and dry land.

So me and my brother, we finally went into his house. And my mother, she was shaking. She didn't want to go into nobody else's house. She wanted to just sit there. But we told her we can't wait till the water get up to our knees and up to our chest in here, in our house, because then outside it's going to be over our heads. So we would have to leave then.

So we finally convinced her to leave, so we got our stuff. We carried food and a couple of changes of clothes to the house across the street, and we just sat there and watched the water rise till it got dark. We tried to flag planes down 'cause planes did fly above us, but no one seen us, and we heard the neighbors down the street. They were going to get a boat. They were going to get a boat and find a way to the bridge where we could be on dry land, and hopefully get a bus to the Superdome or Convention Center. But when they got their boat, they left and told us they was coming back, and another boat came. And we got in the boat with the other people. That was with people that came from Canada or something. And we got in the boat with them.

They took us to the I-10 [overpass], the St. Bernard Bridge, and we stayed on the I-10 for about five hours. We went to sleep on the I-10. My auntie, she's seventy-four. She slept on the I-10, and that was really shocking to me, to see her, at her age, walking on a cane, just sleeping on a rock, a cement bridge. But then the buses came and took us to the Superdome.

The Superdome wasn't what I expected it to be. I thought it was going to be real food, not the Army Reserve food. A whole lot of [it] wasn't what I expected. [When] I got to the Superdome, wasn't no lights in the bathroom, you couldn't see where you was going. It was real crowded. They wasn't giving out soap or nothing, where you could wash yourself, and it was just waking up, getting in line, knowing what time they was giving out the packets of food. It wasn't really nothing you could do in the Superdome to make it better. You just had to [live]. And we stayed in the Superdome for about six days. We stayed until, I think, it was September the fifth. And they were getting the yellow buses to take us straight to Houston or take us to the airport and fly us in a plane to San Antonio. My mother, she got on the bus with my aunt the day before. We stood in line for about twenty-four hours, me and my two brothers. And while we were waiting in line fights broke out. It was hot. They didn't give you too much water. They just had you stand up in the line. And it was hard for you to catch a breath if you wasn't standing in the right spot. You know.

And eventually we got on the bus. We got on the bus that took us to the plane. We flew to San Antonio. We didn't know where my mother was because she left the day before us. And we were trying to find her. We were trying to get a number to contact her. And luckily one of us had her cell phone in our bag. And we looked through her phone for the number for my auntie in Houston. And we called the number, and luckily she was over there. And we got in touch. We said that we were going to come down there shortly after we get clothes and stuff from the shelter.

We stayed in the shelter for about three days. They gave us what they could and they fed us. They really helped us out, and I really appreciate that. But we left to be with our mother. We seen our mother, and it was just a wonderful experience seeing our mother after the storm, 'cause we didn't know what happened to her. And we finally seen her. I was real [grateful]. And we started our life in Houston.

We stayed with our cousin for about two months. And it wasn't the same. You couldn't go to the park and play basketball. You didn't really know everybody around. You uncomfortable. It was really big. We had to catch the bus everywhere we go because our car was in New Orleans somewhere. And it wasn't like the RTA [New Orleans bus system], what we used to. It took much longer to get us where we had to go. We was going to the Reliant Stadium and all that where they were sheltering New Orleans people because my mother, she was an activist and helping the people, so she went down to there to do things and get in touch with people, important people to help. And my mama didn't want me to start school, because she was looking at the news and New Orleans kids was getting in all kinds of fights with Houston kids and they were raving, and she didn't want me to have to go through that just yet.

And one day we was in church and a pastor told [her] about a school called Barbara Jordan, and she felt he was trustworthy, so she enrolled me in Barbara Jordan. And I started going there. It was all right, but it wasn't what I'm used to. It didn't make me want to get up in the morning and it didn't start my day like I wanted to. I always just wanted to get up out of bed saying, "Oh, I got to go to school, I got to go to school. I can't miss a day of school." And when I got enrolled, I didn't want to go to school. I ain't never not wanted to go to school until I got here. And it just rattled me because I didn't have any friends. It was the first time I went to a school where I didn't know anybody. And I always knew at least two or three people that introduced me to everybody else, but I didn't know anybody. So I was nervous; I was scared to make friends. I wanted to just stay to myself, be a loner.

But I met these two females, and they refused to let me be alone. They introduced me to everybody. They were real exuberant in their quest to get me friends and quest to get me known with everybody. And me being six-seven, it's hard to go unnoticed in the school. Everybody going to come up to me and say, "Oh, you're tall. How tall? What's your name?" And all that stuff. So I really couldn't do what I thought I was going to do. I made friends and it wasn't so bad once I got into the groove, but it still wasn't what I was used to.

And eventually we got a house—apartment—three bedrooms. And me, my brother, and my mother stayed there. We had both my brothers here. It was more comfortable. I know I could talk to my brothers. I could go see my brothers still, because they were still with me. But then my brother left. He went to Dallas, and my other brother went to New Orleans to rebuild his house. And it hit me again. I didn't know what to do, because I was just here with my mother. And I was just stuck. It felt like I was stuck in a place. Stuck in a box. Stuck somewhere, and it was hard just being here by myself for so long, just here with my mother. But I know I couldn't leave her because where her mind was; she needed somebody there to hold her and keep her straight. And she didn't have a job for a long time. She was just an activist. She went to the mayor's meetings and stuff like that.

But once she got a job her head got on straight. She worked at the Ripley House, and what they did: they made sure New Orleans people got clothes and [that] they knew when they was giving out clothes and food and furniture and things like that. They told them about it and got them jobs and things like that, that's what they did.

That's where she worked. So once she got a job she was really more comfortable to be around, you know, she wasn't always rattly or shaky or didn't want to be bothered, or down. So that really helped for a while. And when my brother came back, it really helped too. He came back from New Orleans, and ever since then we've been good. My cousin also lives here. We found out my cousin lived here. Me and my brother used to drive up by my cousin every night. We used to stay till two o'clock in the morning because it was the closest we were going to get to home, going by my cousin every day, so that's what we did every day.

And when I was going to Barbara Jordan, a person, she played basketball for Phyllis Wheatley High School, and she asked me, could I come play basketball for Wheatley. And at the time I didn't want to play, as I was just out of it, and I ain't played in a long time either, and I ain't really want to go through that. And she gave my number to this guy Arthur, and she said to call him, and he would make sure I got home every night and make sure I got my hair cut, and things like that. He would take care of me. So I called Art and Art gave me the number to the coach and I called coach, and me and coach got to talking. So I decided to play.

When I joined the team, I seen somebody I knew from New Orleans that I had played basketball with, named Henry. And that really comforted me also, just knowing that I found somebody else that I knew and enjoyed being with. So I played basketball with them, and we had a good season and things like that but it still didn't give me that bounce, that swagger I'm used to having. But other than that Houston has been a really great place. But it's just not my home. I could live here, but I want to be home.

That's just where I have to be in order for me, the entire me, to be at one. I just need to be home in my abode, waking up, going to McDonogh 35, Warren Easton, one of them schools—and just enjoying life again. But I'm going to make the best of it while I'm here. I'm going to stay with my mother. Me and my brother, we're going to go play basketball, do things.

I found my little cousin in Katy [a suburb of Houston], so I go out there and visit him and make sure he isn't going crazy, doing bad in school. I keep him straight. And he's been a real joy to me, just knowing that I feel like I'm the big brother when I go see my cousin. My cousin and my aunt: she recently passed away. On February the twenty-eight, she passed away. And we went to the funeral in New Orleans. I love my aunt. She always took care of me. She wanted to be my godmother. She always called herself my godmother if nobody else did. I love my aunt. I miss my aunt. All the memories of her I have were in New Orleans. I didn't really get to know her in Houston, but all the memories I have of her is in New Orleans. I'm going to miss my aunt. But I see a piece of my aunt in my cousins, my mama, and my brothers, I see a piece of her everywhere, so she's going to be in our lives. Whether she here or not, she going to be in our lives. I'm going to keep continuing going by my cousin and taking care, making sure he's all right, making sure he's not missing my aunt too much and well—not missing her, but doing crazy things because she's not here. So I'm always taking care of him, being his big brother—and make sure he's good. While I'm here in Houston.

When [my mother] got here and she started interacting with people, she always came home talking about [how] people just ain't friendly and they not what she's used to. Well I just didn't like that. She could have got her job back in New Orleans, but she don't feel that it's the right place for her to be at the moment. And every time that she come home talking about [how] they're not treating her right at her job, and all kind of stuff. And it just hit me hard, because I know she never had to go through that in her job in New Orleans. She never came home complaining about the people. She came home complaining about the work, but she never came home complaining about the people.

And that was real hard for me to see her, especially when she didn't have a job. She would just lay on the couch and just sit there. Sit there all day not doing nothing. That's not my mom. That's not what she does. She always gets out, do stuff. But when I see her just laying there and not doing nothing, watching TV, I knew that wasn't my mom. I knew something was wrong in her—where she could just sit there all day and watch TV. My mom never was able to sit there all day and watch TV.

And I wound up talking to her about it. And we got to talking. She told me that she was going to eventually get a job so she could get off the couch and do things. She eventually did. I seen a major change in her, in her spirit. It just uplifted her spirit knowing that she had something to do. And when she had something to do, that brightened up my day just knowing that my mom's happy. If she's not happy, I don't know what I would do. I don't know what I would do without her.

Phylicia: And how were your teachers at school? Were they eager to help you like your teachers back home?

Some of them, knowing my situation, they branched off and tried to help me, but some of them just pushed away, thinking I was a certain way without getting to know me. But a lot of teachers tried to help me. Like when I first got here, my first class was biology, and I went to biology and they were taking a test in biology that day, the quarterly exam. And the teacher said, "You could just read or do whatever—I'm going to let them take the test." I said, "No. I want to take the test. I want to see where I'm at." And we took the test. And she went to go grade them, and when she came back, I had the highest score. Everybody failed, but I had the highest score, and ever since then, me and her been real cool with each other, and she always decide to help me, Ms. [Galvan]. And she always did help me.

A lot of teachers helped me, but some of them were a little shaky, and they didn't quite hear me out or know where I was. But a lot of teachers tried to help me, knowing my situation. I really do appreciate that from them.

Phylicia: Okay. I hear you're missing what you're used to. So tell me, what are you used to?

I'm used to being able to walk down the street, have a lot of people that I know in my neighborhood, and just going by their house, sit in their house, and just talk to their friends, and their mothers and sisters and brothers like I'm part of the family. But I'm here. I don't have no friends in my neighborhood. I know a few people in my neighborhood, but I don't really know a lot of people what I'm used to. I'm used to just knowing everybody in the neighborhood, being able to just go next door and sit in their house when my mama's not home. If I get bored, just sit in [their] house and just do something until she get home. So I could talk to her about my day. I always ask her about her day, how her day went. And things like that. So I'm just used to liking school. Even though school is good out here, it just doesn't give me the same satisfaction that school used to give me. I always did like school, and I still do, but it still don't give me that same satisfaction of going to school. I always used to wake up and say, "Something going to happen. They going to have a free dance or something and I'm going to miss it if I don't go." And usually nothing happened, but just the suspense and knowing that it could happen [made me go]. And out here, it's just slow-paced. It's not what I'm used to. I'm used to being able to go to dances all the time. I don't really like going to dances out here. They don't play the type of music I listen to. They don't have certain things at dances—or DJ's like I'm used to. And I'm used to going to a dance and hear bounce music the whole dance. Bounce music—out here, they be like, "Bounce music? What is that?" You know. They getting hip to it now because we started to come to school and play it for them. And they get their little bounce and see if they can keep up.

I'm used to being in a family-oriented neighborhood. And I ain't in no family-oriented neighborhood now. If I [were], I might have to try and get to know the other people. But I just didn't make an effort because that's not in my head. I'm just trying to make an effort. I'm trying to stay to myself until I be able to go back home. All the family's home. I have one brother out here now with me. But my other brother, my other aunts, my nieces [aren't here]. My nephew—he's in New Orleans. I haven't seen my nephew in a year and a half, since his birthday. And it's just been hard. I want to see my nephew. I want to see those people, but I can't see those people because they're six hours away. I'm used to being able to see everybody within the week, see my whole family. But all I see is my mother and my brother.

Phylicia: Your aunt that just passed away recently, was she the same aunt that was with you all during the hurricane?

No. My aunt that was with me during the hurricane, she's my mother's auntie, but my aunt that passed away, she was like my mother's best friend. And it hit my mama harder than it did me, because they was friends for thirty years, and she lost a friend for thirty years. The first week after she heard it, she couldn't stop crying. And I always hurried home so I could console her, talk to her, be like, "It's going to be okay, she's in a better place." But it really hit her hard until the funeral. She went to the funeral and finally seen it was over; she couldn't do nothing about it.

And my aunt always took care of me if I didn't have any food in the house. She lived across the river, and I lived downtown. She would come all the way from across the river just to bring me a hamburger. That's just how my auntie was. And she always tried to help people. She had a whole bunch of friends. She could call friends in Chicago and things. Like my mother said at the funeral: everybody, when they was around my auntie, they just felt so special because of the way my auntie treated them, but she treats everybody that way. That just how my auntie was. I loved my aunt.

Phylicia: How do you stay strong these days, with everything that you've been through? How do you just maintain?

Well, I know that I'm here. I faced the fact that I really can't do nothing about it. It's my mother's decision where we're going to be. The housing situation is not good enough for my mother to say, "Hey, we're just going to go back." We would have been back, but my mother didn't want me to be in a trailer, being that I'm six-seven and the trailer is really small. And, you know, I just maintain, just knowing that I have a mother that cares for me. She's going to be here no matter what. I have a brother that care for me. He's going to be here no matter what. And my brother in New Orleans, if he hear that I twisted my ankle, I bruised my knee he would try his best to come out here just to see me to make sure I'm all right. That's just how my brother is. And I stay strong because I feel that if I'm not strong, why should they have to be strong? You see.

So I feel that if I'm going to be strong, my brother going to be strong, my mother's going to be strong, my other brother going to be strong: then ain't nobody going to pull us apart. We going to stay together. We go to put on this mindset where can't nothing bother us. We going to be here. We got to face the fact that we're going to be here. We got to make the best of it. And we're going to do what we can to live life and make it the best, best we can. Ain't nothing we can do about it right now. It's just where we at. It's nothing we can do. We here. We going to be here until something better—or something—happens.

Phylicia: That's a nice outlook. Now, I know you hear a lot of negative things in the news or through the media, but what would be one thing that you would just have people to know about where you come from, where

you're headed, and just about you? You told me a great deal already, but if
you had to pinpoint just one thing, what would it be?

Well, when I was watching the news, they tried to make New Orleans people seem bad or ignorant—and all of us aren't ignorant. We're really good people and they made us seem this kind of rowdy, uncontrollable type people. And when I went to school, they thought of me as a rowdy, uncontrollable person. Until I proved to them—I talked to one substitute in our class one day, and she said, "You're not like I thought you would be. I thought you were going to be crazy, but you're really friendly." And that's how a lot of people in New Orleans are. We're real friendly. And speaking of myself, I plan to go to college and if I don't go to the NBA, I'm going to be in accounting, be a banker or something that's just going to help me. And I feel as a person out of New Orleans: we're not bad people. I'm not a bad person. And if you get to know us before you think about us (and put this card on us, or this tag on us), you'll notice that we're real good people and all that you have to do is talk to us for a while and understand where we at and you'll really see that we're a great people. That's what I have to say about that.

In Josef's story, the family continually emerges as the ideal. The love, dedication, and indebtedness that he feels toward his relatives underpin everything that he says about them. And when Josef speaks about the things he most admires and misses in New Orleans—the people and the schools— he describes them, too, as "family." Living away from New Orleans was clearly a challenge for him.

Although his brother Cedric moved back to New Orleans by 2007, Josef and his mother continued to live together in Houston for the educational opportunities that the city afforded. On the strength of his athletic prowess, Josef went on to become a star basketball player at Houston's Phyllis Wheatley High School. Upon his graduation in 2009, and on the basis of his academic strengths as well as his playing, he was awarded a scholarship to Dartmouth College. At a ceremony held in his honor at Wheatley at the end of the school year, his minister and his basketball coach both acknowledged the power of the mother-son bond that had brought him such success.

CHANTELL JONES

"What happened to my mom and my grandmother and my uncle? That was . . . the thought that took over everything"

Chantell Jones recorded her story for her friend and fellow survivor, Phylicia Bradley, on February 27, 2007, nearly eighteen months after Katrina's landfall. Chantell and Phylicia were both from New Orleans East, and they had gone to middle school and high school together. The last time that they saw each other before Katrina was at their high school graduation in 2004. They found their ways to Houston at different times and along different paths, but reconnected via Myspace a few months after the storm.

Chantell's narrative is a profile in selflessness. She was just nineteen years old when the hurricane hit. She was trapped in the flooded city and endured the extreme conditions of Baptist Hospital and the Morial Convention Center. She spent four days at the Convention Center in the company of as many as 20,000 fellow survivors, making it through each day with little or no food. Yet she gave away the food she had brought with her to strangers (mostly children) and a pregnant friend. She was most troubled not by the heat, hunger, or squalor, nor by the rumors of rapes and murders flying around her, but rather by not knowing where her mother was.

Chantell Jones at the piano, Global Impact Ministries, 2011.
Photo courtesy of Chantell Jones.

In this last detail, Chantell is typical. Separation from loved ones is the most often-reported disturbing experience expressed by the survivors interviewed in the Surviving Katrina and Rita in Houston project.

Chantell narrated her own selfless acts matter-of-factly, in a quiet monotone, as if there were nothing remarkable about them. Her understated account, however, cannot conceal the fact that throughout her ordeal, Chantell, like other survivor heroes, was continually thinking about, and doing for, others.

In her narrative, Chantell refers to many of the legends and rumors that overran the city in the wake of the storm: murders, rapes, and a room full of bodies in the Convention Center. Such accounts were continually reported and generally believed, by New Orleans city administrators and ordinary citizens as well as the national media. On September 6, New Orleans Times-Picayune *reporter Brian Thevenot published an account echoing the horrors that Chantell had heard about: a freezer stacked with "thirty or forty" bodies in the Convention Center and the corpse of a seven-year-old child with her throat slit. Later, Thevenot wrote that he had fallen for unsubstantiated rumors. The final documented toll from the Convention Center was four bodies, one of which was a homicide. Toward the end of her interview, Chantell mentions that she had stayed in the hospital where, "The nurses killed a lot of the people; I heard on the news. You know, gave medicine to put them to sleep, whatever. But I didn't witness any of that." Here she repeats a rumor that was rife in early 2007, when this interview was recorded. A doctor and two nurses had been arrested in 2006 and charged with euthanizing patients at the hospital. But charges were dropped in the summer of 2007 and the state of Louisiana, acknowledging the false charges, paid the legal fees of the accused.*

As is typical of other narrators, Chantell speaks of crimes that she heard reported, but that she did not in fact witness. She is clear in separating what she merely heard from what she actually saw. At the same time, she reports acts of goodness and heroism that never made the news. Her experience, then, runs exactly counter to the common media accounts. Although she was exposed to horrors and did indeed witness criminal behavior, she personally witnessed far more acts of goodness than of violence or nihilism.

Chantell and Phylicia end their interview by sharing memories of Mardi Gras as celebrated in New Orleans before and after Katrina.

I stayed in New Orleans East. That was like middle class. Most of the things I miss in the East is going to corner stores that was right around the corner, and I miss my middle school, high school years; I miss my friends; you know, I miss the teachers, the things I did in high school, homecoming, volleyball, stuff like that. I have a small family. I only got along with my mom's side of the family. My dad's side of the family, I never really knew them. But everybody in my family, all my first cousins, we all went to school together. We went to Fanny C. Williams Middle School and then we all graduated from there and went to Sara T. Reed Middle School.

I [lived] off of Bullard and Hayne, in New Orleans East. And there was really a lot of one-story houses around that area. But before the hurricane it was real peaceful. When it rained it didn't flood; after the hurricane we still didn't get much water. There was a lot of wind damage. And it was just like when I went back after the hurricane for the first time, the tree, we had like a real big tree that was in our backyard, it basically fell through the house so the house was basically split in half after that. And that was like most of all the damage we had besides the mildew. So after that I went back, like maybe a couple of weeks ago, and the neighborhood still looked the same. Nobody is really rebuilding on that block.

A typical day [before Katrina] was all the boys playing football, and my little nephew was writing on the house walls with chalk. And I really miss it. On a typical day after I left school, I used to go home and run on the levee. I stayed close to the levee, so I used to run from Bullard two miles, three miles up the road. It wasn't that hard to run. Yeah, I miss days like that because now I try to exercise and it only take like five minutes to do it. I don't run [now] as often as I did then, because it was convenient. You know, it's a stress reliever.

When I first heard about the hurricane, I didn't pay attention until two days before it was about to actually [make] landfall. I was sitting up in the bed about five o'clock in the morning and it was just on my mind. My mom and my auntie was who I stayed with. They didn't pay attention to the hurricane, and I had to just like, "A hurricane's coming. Are y'all going to stay here or y'all going somewhere else?"

Where else was we going to go? You know, we didn't have enough transportation to actually get out of town so what we did was nothing. So about five o'clock two days before the hurricane I was sitting on the bed, and it just kept dawning on me that we really needed to go somewhere, so I called my dad. He worked Uptown at Baptist Hospital. And me and my auntie, we went up there, but my mom she wanted to go by my brother who stayed two miles from where we was at. And he stayed at some apartments off of Read [Boulevard]. Anyhow, after I went to the hospital (me and my auntie and a couple of my cousins), my mom went to go stay with my grandma by my brother's house.

When the hurricane actually came—Uptown at the hospital where I was at—there was not much water. It was just a lot of like loud wind. And after the hurricane, like the whole day after the hurricane we was just sitting around waiting to go back to our house. And then eventually we seen water just like coming from nowhere because we went to go see if we could find something to eat, and we seen a lot of people looting and setting stuff on fire, people just doing all kinds of crazy things. Looked like we was in the *War of the Worlds* movie. So we get back to the hospital, and the water just rise about ten feet. Like right before our eyes.

So then I start to really think, because it didn't really hit me until after I seen the water rising and I couldn't get back home and I couldn't call my mom and make sure they was all right. So you know, I was like real sad, disappointed at that point because that's when it actually sinked in that we just had a real hurricane. At first it wasn't really a hurricane to me; it was just about the rain, that's all.

But eventually, after spending two to three days in the hospital where my dad worked, somebody came with a boat and he was taking out all the sick patients, bringing them to another hospital. Then finally they finished doing that, so they took us to the Convention Center on the boat. And, well, before they took us all the way to the Convention Center, they only could take us so far. It was on St. Charles where the water wasn't high anymore, so we had to wait on a tool truck to come and we rode in the back of a tool truck with like hammers hanging from the top, and it was like a hundred people in back of a tool truck and hammers falling on your head as you're riding in a tool truck and they driving really fast. We were like, "What the heck, what is wrong with y'all?"

So they drop us off at the Convention Center and told us they was going to have a bus [come] for us in a couple hours. The Convention Center had about ten thousand people, and I'm like, "Is buses going to come for us, and not everybody else?"

Eventually we find out they lied to us because we was stuck in the Convention Center for five days. We didn't have food, we didn't have clothes, we didn't have anything that we went to the hospital with because they told us on the boat we can only take one bag. And the one bag that I took was like a box of Chinese noodles that I had already had from before the hurricane. And when I got to the Convention Center, I basically gave out a lot of the noodles to the kids that looked like they was real hungry. When I opened them up, everybody started coming around like little mice for noodles so I gave them to a lot of the kids.

So after being in the Convention Center the first day, I had about as much as I could have. I walked around the Convention Center from the first hall to the end hall looking to see if my mom and my grandmother had made it to the Convention Center, because I never heard from them since they went and stayed by my brother. And as I'm walking around the Convention Center I see like a lot of people that I went to school with. And I see a lot of people that I just knew from my community, and I'm asking them did they see my mom. And everybody was telling me no. And so I'm walking around the Convention Center for almost a day. Back and forth, and as I'm walking around I see like a lot of old people sitting in the corners. I seen a few dead bodies. So, after the second day in the Convention Center—I used to work there, like two years prior to the storm—so I knew where the employee lounge was and where they kept a lot of the food. So me and my boyfriend, he was also with me at the Convention Center, we went to go see if we could break into the employee lounge. But by the time we got back there, they already had like a hundred-plus people back there. And where they kept the snack machines was where they kept all the dead bodies at. Somebody was storing the dead bodies back there where the snack machines was located at. So, we didn't get no food because we wasn't about to go over the bodies to get to the snack machines. On the third day in the Convention Center I ran into a friend that I went to school with. And she was pregnant. And I was just about out of my Chinese noodles that I had on me. I had two bags left. And she was telling me that she was having like a lot of contractions. So I gave her my last bag of noodles and told her eat that because she told me she hadn't ate in two days.

So I went to go look in that River Walk, because they had the River Walk right next to the Convention Center. I went to go walk in the River Walk to see if I could go find some food for her and for me because she—it was just her and her mama. So I went looking through there. I didn't find any food; only thing I found was like clothes and toys still laying around the floor. So I was out of luck with that, but eventually the army crew came through, and they gave us the army packets of food that you heat up. And that was like the best food I ever tasted. I don't drink cranberry juice, right, but that day they gave us cranberry juice, and it was the best thing I ever taste in my life.

But after that—it was the fourth day at the Convention Center—they came. Somebody was throwing strawberry milk [from their] car. They had gallons of strawberry milk. So I'm thinking, why is they giving these people strawberry milk? They haven't ate in a long time, you drinking strawberry milk, strawberry milk's going to make you have to poop. So, eventually after everybody drunk all their strawberry milk, you could not go to the bathrooms, for nothing. You couldn't get close to the bathroom door without walking in somebody's vomit or somebody's bowel move- ment. So eventually, after everybody drunk down the strawberry milk, they had a lot of people running to the back of the Convention Center with like little boxes of anything they could use to use the bathroom in. It was like the worst sight I have ever seen. I didn't drink the strawberry milk because I already knew what the strawberry milk was going to do to me.

This is not a funny matter, but I guess it helps to laugh. At the same time—my dad, he drunk the strawberry milk because he was hungry. So my dad drunk the strawberry milk. We had a little brown box that we had something in so we could sit on it to keep from sitting on the floor. And after he drunk the milk, he had to take that box and go handle his business.

So later on that day the army people came back out there and they told us they was going to have a helicopter [come] for everybody. That was another lie. I already knew it was going to be another lie because there was too many people just for a helicopter, nobody would get in line and stand in line until the people came like they told us. But on our first day in the Convention Center they'd had a group of white people, it was like five white girls and one white man. And they was like standing in the corner literally shaking like they was just terrified of all the black people. So some kind of way the police came up in there and they took the white people, and we don't know how they got in contact with the police or whatever, but the police skipped over all the black people and took the whole group of white people. They put them in the car and it was gone; we didn't see the police until like two days after that. And that was like really weird to us, like why did that happen?

But from what I heard, I didn't see this with my own eyes, but they was like abusing the white people on the other end of the Convention Center. I know there was a lot of boys walking around with brass knuckles and bats, and they was just beating up anybody that they wanted to beat up on, you know. And one night when we was trying to sleep—we was sleeping outside the Convention Center doors, because inside the smell was just like real polluted. They had this man and this woman [come] running around screaming for their daughter, and they was screaming out her name, "Daja." They kept saying, "Daja! Daja!" And then eventually, another man came out and said they found Daja's body in the back of the Convention Center. And she was raped and she was beaten.

But they had a little boy who was missing too, and they said the little boy, he was raped; it was Daja's brother. And like after that, the man and the woman, they went crazy in the Convention Center, so we moved from that location because we didn't know what was about to happen, and we went to another part of the Convention Center. And that was all I heard about that.

And later on that day in the Convention Center we was just sitting outside hoping somebody come around looking for us. Somebody took a U-Haul truck and a school bus around. And they was [picking up] people but you had to have money; they wanted some money from you because they had stolen a school bus and a U-Haul. And if you had money they was going to let you get on it. But we didn't have money.

We didn't have nothing but ourselves, we didn't have enough money for all of us to go, so we didn't want to separate. So we stayed there and they took off with about twenty or thirty people on the school bus and on the U-Haul. It was real packed and they said they was going to Houston, so I don't know if they ever made it or not. But, that was my experience in the Convention Center.

But the day they did [come] and get us, it was on the fifth day we was in there, and I had basically gave up luck. I had a little broom and I was sweeping my section where I slept at the last four nights. Because I had done basically gave up on actually getting out of there. I wasn't really hungry too much because I was so mad at the same time. So I couldn't really be too hungry. So as I'm sitting there waiting, the army people come back out and they came down. One man came down on a helicopter, and he was like we going to start moving people out.

(On the first day we got there, they had some buses came but they had so many people that bus drivers were scared to open up the door. Like they didn't open up the door, they just pulled off. Because once the people got up to the bus they was pushing and they was literally pushing a bus. Imagine people pushing a bus. It was literally rocking side to side so the bus drivers, they pulled off, they were scared to open up the door but they didn't never come down to our section. I just seen them from where I was at.)

But on the day we got out the helicopters came. And my auntie was with me; she had cancer. And she couldn't really walk because her feet would swell up. So I had found [a shopping] basket. I had put her in a basket and I had put her in line where the helicopters was coming to pick us up from. And we stood in line for like maybe twelve hours until the helicopters came back because they was taking small amounts of people, probably like twenty people at a time. And mind you they had like ten thousand people out there so we thought that was going to take days before they actually got us out there on helicopters, but because my auntie was sick they was able to take us in the beginning batch.

But they told us they wouldn't be able to take all of us; they was only going to take some of us. And we didn't want to be separated so my auntie didn't want to go on with the very first helicopter, because she didn't want nobody to be separated. So we missed out on that ride. But the next man came along and he let us all go as a family on one helicopter and they flew us down to Austin, Texas.

When we got to Austin, Texas, we got to the Convention Center, took a bath, washed our hair, and we ate. They had Chicken Filet, a lot of food there for us, so you know, we was actually happy. But my auntie, she was still sick because she had gotten sicker because she didn't have her treatment, she didn't have her chemotherapy, she didn't have none of her medicine on her, so she was real sick. So they had admitted her in the hospital out there in Austin soon as she got there. So she never made it to the shelter with us.

Then after the shelter, we called my boyfriend's parents and they took us back to Houston. We went to Houston after that and my auntie, she eventually came down there with us after she was released from the hospital. And then she was admitted right back into another hospital in Houston. But when we got to Houston, I finally got a phone call from my mom.

They was on the bridge by the Superdome. That's where they was at all the days they was missing. So when the helicopter finally came for them, it took them to Shreveport, Louisiana, but our phone services was actually working once we got to Texas. And she called and let me know where she was at, and our whole family met back up in Houston. And this is where we stayed at.

But before we actually got an apartment and things, we was staying in AmeriSuites hotel for like four months. And we was staying there for free. It was comfortable but, you know, it was like real sad because you never imagine living your life out of a hotel. But it was better than living life out of the shelter like a lot of people was doing, so at the same time we was still blessed. Because we didn't have to actually go through being in the shelter, we was only in the shelter the one day. One day after they came and got us from the Convention Center. And that's how things went for me after the storm.

Phylicia Bradley: What were your thoughts like when you were at the Convention Center? You just felt like you [weren't] going to [ever] leave? And were you worried?

See, when I was at the Convention Center, I was just angry. I was worried about my mom, because my brother, he didn't stay at the house with my mom. He worked at a hospital downtown, so my mom and my grandma and my uncle was the only people at the house, so I'm just assuming that they all are old and they all probably drowned, died. So instead of me really being hungry at the Convention Center, I just think that I'm never going to get out of there. I was basically just thinking about, what happened to my mom and my grandmother and my uncle? That was like the thought that took over everything. I was angry most of the time. As far as me getting out of there, like I said, when I was cleaning up my little area I got kind of comfortable in my area because I was so angry. I was so down that I didn't really look forward to nothing because I had already heard so many broken promises that the bus is coming, that the helicopter's coming. And nothing ever happened, but something did happen one day, on the fifth day that we was there.

So you know, that's my five days, there in the Convention Center, and I spent three days in the hospital. And even though it was a hospital, we didn't have no electricity, we didn't have no food, we didn't have no medical service, anything. The only thing we had was a roof over our heads, but we didn't have no air. We had to open up a window. It was stinky, smelly, and hot, you know. We couldn't see where we was going because the generators [had given out by] this time, because [they] wasn't designed, I guess, to last as long as they did. So life was more miserable in the hospital than it actually was in the Convention Center, believe it or not. And that was [the] hospital where they had a lot of people that actually died, you know. The nurses killed a lot of the people; I heard on the news. You know, gave medicine to put them to sleep, whatever. But I didn't witness any of that. I just heard about it after the hurricane.

Phylicia: Your friend, the one that was pregnant, how did she make out?
Yeah, well I actually found her after I gave her the food. I tried to get her help. Like they had a police officer, not an army man up in the Convention Center. And I was trying to tell him that she was going into labor, you know, she needed help or whatever. And he said he couldn't do nothing for her because that wasn't his job, he was just there to do what he had to do, and he couldn't call nobody to come in and get her or nothing. So, you know, I was real upset about that and I couldn't believe it. But they had a lady out there who was a nurse. At the same time that [my friend] was actually having contractions they had another lady, another girl that delivered her baby in the Convention Center, on the floor. And this lady after she delivered, after she delivered this [other] lady's baby, she helped out my friend. And like maybe a few hours after that a police car came for her and they took her. They took her on a helicopter so she was the first person to get on a helicopter.

But I found her months later on Myspace, and she's doing good, she's doing great. She has a beautiful little boy. Yeah. So everything worked out good for her, her mama, and her baby. She didn't go into labor. She was just having contractions from being in distress like that. But she didn't deliver her baby until maybe a month later; that was good, everything worked out for her.

Phylicia: Well, how has it been for you out here in Houston?
Out here in Houston, it's good. I can't lie. I miss home a lot, but every time I go home I'm ready to come back to Houston. I think this is like kind of my second home. I'm comfortable here like I used to be in New Orleans. And I go to school. I was working but now I just go to school and come home. And I'm comfortable with it, because every time I go home I'm looking at the destruction. You know, how it still looks out there, and it's depressing to me. And although all my family moved back, it just me, my mom, and my boyfriend down here in Houston, I'm still comfortable. You know, I miss them, but I still don't want to be back because every time I'm back I'm just not happy. You know, I'm not as happy. And I just rather stay out here until everything gets back to normal.

And, other than that, it's like the crime is escalated out there. So I like life out here in Houston. I don't plan on staying here forever, but even before the hurricane, before Katrina came, I couldn't wait to get out of

New Orleans. I used to always say that I want to go into the navy, move to Virginia, San Diego, somewhere because I want to get out of New Orleans.

[But] after the hurricane came, I changed my mind. I just wanted to be in New Orleans all the time because I never imagined having to leave like that, you know, being put out of the city like that. But once I got to Houston, and got used to being out here, I still want to be back home. But I'm ready to stay out here in Houston and finish school, and then after that I plan on going back to school out there sometime, maybe another two years, three years from now.

My mom, she's a homebody. She just stays at home and she just waits on me. I think she lives her life through me because I go to school and she's at home all day. She only goes places when I ask her does she want to go somewhere. She likes to just be at home. Just her and her TV. It's like she's still in New Orleans because she's still in the house. She don't go outside of the house unless she got to go to the store or a doctor's appointment, you know; she's not really missing nothing because she do the same thing she always ever did. You know, she's happy, she's fine, and that way I'm fine. But she wanted to go back to New Orleans, though, because she has grandkids out there, and she was real close with them because they always lived with her. So once I go back is when she's going to go back, that's what she say. So I guess I got to hurry up and go back. I'll go back and then leave her again, whatever. As far as my boyfriend: he don't want to go back right now. He like Houston. You see, out there the crime's too high. And he have his own place out here. If he go back to New Orleans, he don't want to have to live back with his parents, and he likes the job he has right now. So he's comfortable down here in Houston also.

Phylicia: That's really good. Well, I know you hear a lot of things in the news or through the media. What do you think will be most important, or what would you like other people to know about where you come from, where you're headed, and just you, period?

A lot of people stereotype everybody that's from New Orleans. And you know, they always out here in Houston, they think that all the violence is because of the people from New Orleans. You know that's not true because there is a lot of ignorant people in New Orleans, but there's a lot of ignorant people in the world. And everybody from New Orleans is not like that. You know, everybody [is] not drug dealers, killers, or everything else that you know they have out there in New Orleans. And, far as me, I just want everybody to stop really stereotyping people from New Orleans, because everybody is not the same.

Yeah, and what I want people to know about where I come from is: New Orleans, it's a really good city. We got Mardi Gras, you got soul food, people really know how to cook. It's just like the heart of the South to me. That's what I believe where I come from is.

Phylicia: Now, you saying Mardi Gras: you went to Mardi Gras this year. What was it like?

Well, I didn't go to no parades when I was down there. I went strictly to Bourbon Street. Anybody listening should know about Bourbon Street. It was all right, it was cool. One thing I have to say: the down side about it was how many murders they had for Mardi Gras. I don't really remember how many it was, but I did hear about three of them, when I was actually on Bourbon. But on the news I heard it was like twenty the whole weekend or something. Twenty plus. That was like the only down side about it.

But me, on Bourbon Street, I had fun. I was in my old world, I felt like I was at home, and I *was* at home. And I enjoyed it. But, Mardi Gras. I could tell you about last year's Mardi Gras. Last year I went to Mardi Gras, and I did go to a few parades, and it was the Mardi Gras right after the hurricane. And everybody was really trying to see how Mardi Gras was going to be after the hurricane since a lot of people wasn't living there, and see if people was actually going to pay for their beads, you know, throw the stuff off the floats.

But last Mardi Gras, I was like really impressed because a lot of people showed up, a lot of people came home for it. You know, that was real, that was real good because I didn't think many people was going to actually come back for Mardi Gras, and a lot of tourists probably was going to be scared to come. But a lot of tourists was excited to come just for the fact they wanted to see what happened with their own eyes, see how it really look. So Mardi Gras last year was good, Mardi Gras this year was real good. And they had a lot of people, lot of fun. You know, one thing about New Orleans is Mardi Gras never change. After the hurricane, before the hurricane. It always been the same. You know.

Phylicia: What do you remember most about Mardi Gras, like some of the traditions?

Zulu parade. Like when I was younger, my mom and my uncle used to get up every day about six o'clock in the morning, and we used to go sit outside with our little chairs and our schoolbook sacks, our Winn Dixie bags, or whatever, just to go sit there and try to catch coconuts and teddy bears at the Zulu parade. It's supposed to start at like eight o'clock in the morning, but it never really got to where we was at until about twelve in the evening. So we used to be out there all them hours waiting on the Zulu parade to pass on. Now, the Zulu parade is all black people. You know, and that's the only parade that actually gives out coconuts. And they have the Indians in the Zulu parade, you know; New Orleans is known for the Indians who march and they dance, they do their little thing.

And you know that's what Mardi Gras was when I was young. It was just waking up too early, but I used to get excited about it when I was younger. Well, see, when I became a teenager, about fourteen, fifteen years old, I didn't want to do that anymore. I didn't want to go to the Zulu parade to actually catch beads. I just wanted to go out there because it was a fashion show to me then. So I stopped going with my mama and them. I let them go with the younger kids. Six o'clock in the morning I would stay asleep until the afternoon, and get up and put on my clothes that I spent my whole check on, and just go walk up and down, whatever, Orleans and Claiborne. That's where all the black people was at and that was the fashion show area. And, you know, that was Mardi Gras week.

To the people from New Orleans, Mardi Gras is a fashion show. Now to the tourists, they wear all that silly stuff. Them costumes and, you know, wearing beads around their necks. But you won't catch the Black people that's actually from New Orleans with a costume on, not unless they special. So it was cool. I do miss those days.

Four months after being interviewed, Chantell went on to train with the Surviving Katrina and Rita in Houston project. Like her friend Phylicia, she became an interviewer. Chantell ultimately recorded thirty-eight interviews, more than any other project interviewer.

Chantell's mother returned to New Orleans in 2007, but—except a five-month stay in New Orleans in 2008—Chantell has spent her post-Katrina years in Houston. She has worked in many jobs, including as a seasonal driver for UPS and as a security guard. For more than a year, she owned and managed a local cafeteria. She currently serves on the leadership board of Global Impact Ministries.

ANGELA TRAHAN

"We really did not think that we would make it"

On January 23, 2006, less than five months after Katrina's landfall, Surviving Katrina and Rita in Houston held its first training session. On the first morning of that five-day session, the sixteen trainees paired off and began sharing storm stories. Each person told her or his story to a fellow survivor, then the two changed places as the listener to the first story became the teller of the second. Afterward, the whole group reconvened and each survivor summarized his or her partner's story for all the others; the group then chose one person to be the project's first interviewee. Angela Trahan was the person chosen for that role.

Fourteen of the first sixteen trainees were New Orleanians. Angela, by contrast, faced Katrina from Bay St. Louis, Mississippi, in a presumably indestructible building that stood less than fifty feet from the beach where, on the morning of August 29, 2005, Katrina hit with the full force of its 135-mile-per-hour winds, pushing a twenty-two-foot storm surge. The storm found Angela, her mother, her three children, and her fiancé, Sam, in "lockdown" in the seaside dormitory of a Catholic boys' school. As Angela explains, the building had withstood the power of Hurricane Camille, the

Angela Trahan, her husband, Sam, and their three children,
Bay St. Louis, Mississippi, 2007. Photo by Dallas McNamara.

benchmark for destructiveness on the Mississippi Gulf Coast. (Camille was
stronger even than Katrina when it hit nearby Gulfport, Mississippi, on
August 18, 1969, bearing 180-mile-per-hour winds and twenty-four feet of
storm surge.)

The drama of Angela's narrow escape from Katrina's head-on fury and
Sam's role in saving the lives of his fellow survivors were the obvious reasons
that the trainees chose her story as the first to record. Yet, over time, listen-
ers have been equally moved by accounts of Angela's family's resourceful-
ness and resilience in the days following the storm, and by the concluding
episodes, in which Angela recounts the kindness of the strangers who aided
her family on the course of their long escape to Houston.

Angela was interviewed by David Taylor, folklife specialist for the
American Folklife Center at the Library of Congress, as her fellow trainees
looked on.

I was born on May 20, 1977, in St. Louis, Missouri. We lived there
until I was about a year and a half, and we moved from St. Louis here to
Houston, with my mom, my grandparents, and my aunts and uncles. My
grandfather was in the air force, and he got re-stationed here in Houston
because he's from Houston, so he came back home.

Well, my grandfather passed away and my grandmother wanted to
be back home in Mississippi. She was born there in Bay St. Louis. And
her father was not doing very well healthwise, so she moved back home
to take care of her father. I don't think she wanted to be here in this big
city, without my grandfather, anymore. She felt more comfortable being
back home, and in her hometown, with her family. [She] and my oldest
uncle went first. And then my aunt and her family went, and my mom

and myself and another uncle were the only ones here. So after everybody else was gone—our immediate family—we started to miss them. My mom decided to move back, my mom and my uncle. I think she was missing her mommy. So she moved back to Mississippi to be closer to Mom.

I actually used to go [to Bay St. Louis during] spring break and summer to spend time with my grandmother and her parents before they both passed. So, I was familiar with Mississippi also. [Bay St. Louis] was a really nice town. Very big on sports, an athletic town really. They supported the kids in football, basketball, baseball. They had a lot of city leagues as well as the school leagues. And just a friendly town. You know, everybody knew everybody. If you didn't know them, you were related to them, or you went to school with them, or your kids played together, you went to the same church and store. I mean you cannot get, literally, five minutes down the road without waving at somebody like fifty times. So it was that close-knit for everybody: just knowing everybody, and knowing that you don't have to watch your back everywhere you go, just feeling safe where you are and not having to lock your doors if you don't want to. Knowing that nothing is going to happen to you in your hometown. Because either you're related to them or they know you, you know, so it really was a good quiet neighborhood. The whole town. Really was not very much crime. You know, the kids could play outside at night and still be fine. I like that aspect of living in a small city, for the kids.

[At first we weren't worried about Katrina.] At first we all thought it was like every other [storm] that had hit, the three other times before. We didn't think it was going to be nearly as bad as what it was because for the [previous hurricane,] Ivan, I stayed there in Bay St. Louis when the rest of the family came [to Houston], and I was on the lockdown crew at work, at the hospital, and [we] just [got] a little bit of wind, and a little bit of rain; we were on lockdown for three days, basically for nothing.

We were all on lockdown, just making sure that the rounds were still getting made, patients were getting taken care of, things like that. We had to do that for three days, and it really was not bad at all, outside. So, we just didn't think that Katrina was going to do half of what it did because the three storms previous to that didn't do anything, not to us. I think we were all in denial that it was going to happen on the Gulf Coast.

My mother and my aunt worked at a college prep school, a Catholic school for boys. They had international students that they could not get out before the storm hit. So they had to be there on staff to make sure that those boys were taken care of and fed properly and things like that. And my mother was a nighttime supervisor in the kitchen, so we decided to stay there, which was not a smart thing because it was right on the beach, you know. And so we stayed there with her in the kitchen, so she wouldn't be there by herself. Her and another co-worker, they were the two who had to stay there to make sure that the boys were fed. So her co-worker brought her two daughters and grandsons, and there was our family. We were the only ones that were in the kitchen, and we just assumed it would be safe because everybody has always said, "St. Stanislaus [the school] is one of the safest places to be when a storm hits; it withstood [Hurricane] Camille. It's 150 years old. There's nothing that could tear it down." And they were wrong.

The night before, it was like a calm, you know. A little bit of rain and the waves were kind of heavy, but when you have a high tide, when you're used to living right there on the beach, there's nothing abnormal about it. We thought that we would be okay.

Well, we were all asleep except for my fiancé and my sister Shelby, she's fourteen. And they were outside when the storm started coming in, the heavy rain and the winds. And they were standing on the back porch. And they saw the house across the street—that was a beautiful, three-story house. They saw it just get ripped apart from the top all the way down. And once the water started rising, they still didn't think it was going to get that bad until it got on the steps where they were.

And [my fiancé] Sam told Shelby, "Maybe we should go back inside now. The winds are picking up and everything." And before they could get all the way back up the steps, the water was just coming really fast. And so they ran back in and they closed the double doors—steel doors—but by the time they got from the door to the sink, the back doors were ripped off and the water started coming from that point. Everybody else was sleeping. You know, they had two dining rooms, one for the students and one for the teachers and the faculty; and half of us had made pallets in the faculty room, and half were in the boys' cafeteria. All I remember hearing is Shelby and Sam running through screaming, "Get up, get up, we have to get out of here now." And by the time I opened my eyes, I was drenched, I was soaking wet. I didn't even realize it. You know, I was like, "What is this?" And he was like, "It's the water, it's the water, we have to get out of here now."

And when my eyes focus and I look around, I see tables floating and chairs, and it was just crazy. It was like everything was crashing in, all at once. I mean the windows started breaking, it was glass flying everywhere. And I was panicking because we were all sleeping. I mean, nobody had on any shoes. Nobody. We were disoriented, at the moment, because we just couldn't believe that it was coming in that fast.

And I remember, the only thing I could do was grab my purse. And we started heading out that way. I have two sons who are fourteen and twelve. So we're making sure that we have the kids—and at the same time, we have supplies. We had brought a little basket with changes of clothes and everything, and it was sitting on top of the table. And, before it floated away, [Sam] grabbed the basket.

And the boys were going, "Daddy, I can't find my shoes," and he's like, "Just get out. Don't worry about shoes. We have to go. We have to go."

Well, as we start to try to get out the door that was already broken, [the water] was just coming in from everywhere. And I mean glass. Nobody had on any shoes. I remember I had flip-flops there, and they floated past me, so I was able to grab them, but I didn't put them on. But then my son is going, "But, Mom, you just bought us those shoes." You know, school had just started. So he was really frantic, because he was like "we have no shoes," but the water, it was coming so fast. I mean, we couldn't do anything.

My mom was crying and she was hysterical and her friend, the other co-worker, she was hysterical, and my mom called one of the adminis-trators, Miss Adrienne, and I mean this had to be when the eye of the storm was hitting. I have no clue how they had cell phone service in the midst of all of that. She called Miss Adrienne. She was crying, and she was like, "We're going to die in this kitchen. Please, you have to tell the Broth-ers they have to come and get us. Stuff is floating everywhere, the steam tables, the kitchen—I'm afraid it's going to collapse. We have to get out of here. We have all of these babies, and we have to get out of here." So they said, "Stay put, the Brothers are on their way."

They had to come [from] two buildings [further inland] to get us. They had to come out in the storm twice: from the building that they were in which was hurricane-equipped, to where the older Catholic priests lived when they retired, which they call the house for the Brothers. So they came from the storm shelter, to the Brothers', and then down from the Brothers' to the bottom level to get us. And by the time they got there, I mean, [the water was] up almost to my neck.

And when they got there, they had to pry the doors open, because half the glass was fallen, and this metal door was halfway on, and the pieces and nails and everything were sticking out, so they kind of cleared a path for us to get through but all the while the water and the wind are still forcing, trying to push [us the other] way. So they finally get us out, and we have to go out into the storm to get to higher ground. And going out into it the first time wasn't as bad as when we had to go from the second building to the third building. It was still heavy, heavy rain and winds, and I just didn't think that I could be pushed and forced that much by wind and rain. I just never thought that it would be that intense. So we were able to get about halfway up the stairs—the water had only made it halfway up the stairs. And everybody just started crying. The kids were hysterical, and [the Brothers] kept telling us, "Calm down, calm down, we can't stay here. This building is going to collapse too. We have to go up one more level. Everybody calm down, take some deep breaths, and then we'll get you to safety." When we left that building, the Brothers' building—it literally tumbled. The elevator: we watched it fly over us and down the street. (And later on, after the storm was over, it was like ten blocks down the road by a hardware store.)

When the elevator flew over us, we just all freaked out. Because [we're just] women and children, and we're trying to go up the stairs and over the walkway. And this walkway that we had to go through was just open. Just rails. There's nothing—no walls or pillars or anything to stop the wind or the rain. The amount of water and wind, I can't describe it. It was terrible. I mean, it was just so forceful. I had never seen anything like that before in my life. And myself, my sister, and one of our sons almost went over the rail because it was just that intense. And I'm a fairly big girl. I just did not think that I could be moved like I was a piece of lint. That's exactly how I felt. I could feel myself going to the side, and I kept trying to pull back, but it was just so strong. And I said, "Sam! I'm going over, I'm going over." And he's like, "No, you're not," and he grabbed the back of my shirt, and he slung me through the door, and then he got our son, and my sister, and he slung her through the door, he threw the basket through the door, and he got the rest of the women and kids in before he jumped in himself.

Once we were in there, in safety, the administration and the other students, they were in there [already]. When they saw us come in soaking wet and crying and hysterical, you know, everybody inside just got nervous and they were like, "Oh, my God, this building is going to crumble!" And a couple of the Hispanic students were in their own little clique because some of them spoke English and some of them didn't. And this one little boy, he was about twelve, I guess, and he was a little bitty thing. You could just see in his face how terrified he was once we came in. I really do believe they thought that *that* building was going to collapse as well.

Once we were inside and we got to safety, everybody started to calm down some. But you know, I just couldn't. I just kept crying, and [Sam] was holding me and telling me, "We're going to be okay, we're in safety now." They were very good to us, you know, once we got there. They shared the food that they had. The kitchen had already packed up, you know, a couple days' worth of sandwiches and little snacks and things like that. They brought us right into the room where they had bottled water and sandwiches and things like that. But we had no clue how long we would be there. So you had to ration out what you had. It was like, if you get a sandwich now, you'll only get a bag of chips later, you know. If you take these crackers now, you may just get a water later. So you had to kind of distinguish how hungry you are now versus how hungry you think you'll be later. With us being parents, we wanted to make sure that the kids were fed for the amount of days that we were there.

We ended up being there for like two and a half days. It was tough, with the rationing of the food, and the kids not having shoes. And I mean we were just filthy from head to toe.

Once everybody calmed down, there was another level that you can go up on, where you could stand outside. You were still covered by the building, but up towards the third level of the stairs is where all of the water stopped, so we were up here and we could stand right here and just watch everything that was going on right here, [by looking] down from the stairs. A lot of people had parked their cars up under the building, and I mean those cars and the wind and the rain, they were just beating each other up. Big Suburbans and vans, they just looked like they were fighting, just slamming against each other. TV's and a lot of the houses around the school that were torn up, you could just see all the debris floating past you in the water. At one point, I think my son said, "Mom, I think that's a turkey from the kitchen that we saw in the freezer," and it just went on past. But the rain, it just never let up. The rain and the wind. And a lot of people were upset because they were standing there looking at their cars just getting destroyed, and my mother was freaking out because she parked her car right next to the dumpster at the kitchen.

So once they told us we were free to go downstairs and try to check it out, it was hard maneuvering around: trees and debris, and you know, like three cars that are just bunched up on top of each other right here or wedged into the building right here. And I remember stepping on so many nails, just trying to get around the school so we could get over there and check on my mom's car to see if we had any kind of transportation out of there. It took us about an hour to get all the way around the school safely, you know, without getting hurt. And when my mom saw her car, it looked like it had been through the car compactor. It was like this thin. And she just broke down. She cried, and she cried. She was so upset, she was like, "I can't believe it." And it looked like [her] car got wedged between the brick building and the dumpster, and it just—I mean it was completely smashed.

At this point, we had no idea if our houses were okay, you know, how the rest of the town was. Because we were right there on the beach and you could just see the street was ripped up. Normally, you could see from one end of the beach to the other if you stand at a certain point. But [now] you couldn't even see the streets, for all of the debris and the paper and people's clothing, everything. When we were going around, one of the girls that was there with us in the kitchen, she was like, "I think that's my suitcase over there." So, we all go over there, and we help her dig it out of the mud and all kind of stuff. And the only thing she was worried about was her jewelry. She had it in the side pocket, and she dug in there and it was still in there. It was muddy, but it was in there. And the other lady, her car was upside down and smashed. So they had no way of even getting in the car to try to get any of her things. So at that point, we were told that we had to go back in, there was going to be a curfew that night, by the time it got dark.

At this point, we're trying to get in touch with family. Everybody has a cell phone, but we can't get any service. And I think there were only two people who were able to get service on cell phones; they were very generous with the phones. You had lines of people standing there trying to call family and everything. So the very first time I got through to my aunt, I was like, "Aunt Lisa, Aunt Lisa, we're okay!" And she just bust out crying, she's like, "Oh, my god! Oh, my god, are y'all okay?"

"Yeah," I said, "but I don't know about any of the rest of the town, but St. Stanislaus is destroyed." And she was like, "What do you mean, it's destroyed?" I was like, "The building is still standing, but it's completely gutted. I have never seen anything like that in my life." The cell phone service kept kind of coming in and out, so she was asking me, "Have you all been to the house, can you all get out of there?" And I was just telling her, "I'm going to have to try to call you back because other people need to use the phone. I just wanted to let you know that we're okay, all of the kids are fine, me and mom are fine. I'll call you back as soon as I can." So she was on pins and needles, you know, waiting to hear from me again.

And later on that night, we were able to come down: if you were an adult, it was on you whether you went down and explored at night or whatever. But you know, they made sure all of the children that were there stayed inside. So we came out, and I was able to get a signal out to her, and I was able to talk to her for about an hour that time. And I was telling her, "I really don't think that anything in this town is left because just looking at St. Stanislaus where we are, I just don't see how it could happen." So she was just like, "what do you mean it's gone? My job is gone?" And I was like, "Your job is gone. Uncle Harold's job is gone"—that's her husband—"Mama's job is gone. You know, that kitchen collapsed literally two minutes after we got out of it. And I just thank god that we did."

But afterwards, when they let up the ban so people could go and check out their houses, we walked. We left the kids with my mom's friend, and we walked from St. Stanislaus to my aunt's house. My mom was just so destroyed she didn't know what to do. She didn't know which way to go. She was like, "Should I go to my house first?" And I said, "Well, Aunt Lisa left the keys to the old car there. We need to go to her house first," because my car had floated out to the ocean. My mom's car was beat up. So, I said, "We need to get to her house first, to see if there's a vehicle there that can be salvaged. And then we can come back and get everybody else."

So when we got there, the key was where she told me it was, and I got in there, and it cranked right up. And I just could not believe it because everybody else's cars were either flooded out or banged up, you know, really bad. Once we knew that we at least had a car to go back and get everybody else, we went inside the house. And, my grandfather's house didn't get any water or anything on the inside. The whole inside of the house was still intact, like we left it. So we went back, and we got everybody from St. Stanislaus, and it was just like another thirty minutes, because walking you could step over the debris, or go around it, or map out another route. But driving: there were really no streets that were clear. You know, and you had to watch out for the debris because there was nails and glass and everything, everywhere. So we would go down this street and get halfway down, and there's a big tree, or half the street is uprooted, so we would have to turn around and find another route back to the house. So once we got back to the house, we're like, "Okay, we have to get a game plan. We have to get clothes for the kids, and shoes for the kids," and you know they were starving because, three days, with maybe a sandwich in the morning and a bag of chips at night: we had to get food. So we went to my mom's house, to my uncle's house, and to my grandmother's house. That was my mom's first time seeing her house, and she just broke down because she lived in a townhouse apartment, and the whole bottom floor was destroyed. Halfway up the stairs was wet. But the other half, everything upstairs, was okay.

And then we went to my uncle's, and my grandma's, and both of their houses were just totally destroyed. My grandmother's ceiling in her living room and in her bedroom had caved in, over her bed and over the sofa, the two places that she sleeps the most. And my uncle's house: you could see the water all the way up on the ceiling. So there was nothing salvageable in his house or my grandmother's house. Other than the food that was in the freezer because before they left, we went and duct-taped the refrigerators so we could keep the food for as long as it was going to stay fresh. So we emptied out all of the freezers, and we went back to my aunt's house.

At this point, everybody in the neighborhood is just devastated, because that's like something that you see on TV. You know, you don't expect it to be in Bay St. Louis. You see that all the time in Florida. You don't expect for it to happen in your own backyard.

The whole town was, you know: "If you got this, I got that." So we checked the shed, got lighter fluid and as much charcoal as we could, and we just lit the pit. My mom basically fed our whole neighborhood. Because we had a lot of food. But we didn't have a lot of charcoal or lighter fluid. So, you know, like cousins behind us were like, "I got the charcoal," and "I got the lighter fluid." We basically traded, and borrowed, you know, for about three days. But it was just hard, with the kids, with no electricity, no running water. And then when the water did start to come, it was only in little spurts, and it wasn't for drinking; it was strictly for bathing or wash-ing your hands or things of that nature. So it was really tough on the kids, especially being used to having everything at your disposal and then the next minute: no water and no lights. That's devastating.

We were like that for about a week and a half. Cousins and people would just come by to see if we needed this, or if we had that. It was an exchange thing. We got a flat from one of the nails that were in the street. And my cousin was like, "Well, I'm hungry. If y'all got some food, I got a tire on the spare truck, in the back, y'all can get the tire and just give me a plate of food." So it was basically like that, but gas, you know—there was none. There was about a half a tank in the car when we got it, but just try-ing to get back and forth from that house to this house and making sure we had everything, that gas was gone. And my poor fiancé, he siphoned gas out of the old cars that was in my aunt's yard, the parking lot, wherever— you know what I mean. If there was [an] abandoned car there, somebody was syphoning gas out of it. So we were able to get a whole other full tank of gas. He was woozy, he was out of it. I kept saying, "Why don't you just stop and rest a minute." And he's like, "No, give me some water," and he'd swish his mouth out with water and spit it out, he's like, "Okay, let's keep going. We got to get gas 'cause we are getting out of here."

And so he got that car full, and we went back to the house, and the next morning we just packed up as much as we could, and a friend of his who had a truck—him and his girlfriend wanted to come to Houston, but they didn't know how to get here. So we said, "Well, we have too many people for this car anyway. If we can put some people, you know, and some things on your truck, then y'all can follow us."

So one of my sons was on the back of the truck, with Sam's friends, and we had clothes, and my mom barbecued for a week so we had plenty of meat and bread and things like that, so we packed up whatever we could and we told people in town, family, that we were leaving, just keep a eye on the house. We would try to come back if we could. And we got on the road that morning as soon as it was daylight, and we left. And a couple hours into the drive we needed gas again, so we stopped in a town right outside of Baton Rouge. And they had gas but they had just ran out. So we were like, okay, what are we going to do?

And this police officer was coming out of the store, and Sam's friend asked him, you know, "Do you know anywhere to get gas around here." And so he's like, "Well, there's this little convenience store around the corner." So he's giving us directions; he said, "Not too many people know they have gas there." We were like, "We don't know what he's talking about." And another man was coming out the store and he was like, "Do you all know what he's talking about, how to get there?" And we said, "No." He said, "Follow me, I'm going that way." So when we got there, we were like the third person in line for gas, and that was amazing because the gas lines were hours long, you know. We got gas there and we drove more, and we made another stop. And we came in the store: it was a truck stop. And everybody was going to use the bathroom and cool off for a minute and everything.

(And my grandmother, my father's mother, lives across the street from where my grandfather's house is. But her whole house collapsed while my uncle and his girlfriend were in the bathroom. So all of the insulation from that house was all over my aunt's house and all over the car. But we got out of there in that car. You could tell, we had just been through hell.)

So when we came in the store, we sat down, and my mom started talking to this older man that was sitting there and he said, "Man, y'all look like y'all been through hell." And she said, "Well, we fought Katrina, and we won—but we had to get out of there." And there was another gentleman sitting behind me and my son, and my son got up to go to the bathroom, and he asked my son, he said, "Hey man, y'all were just in that storm?" And my son said, "Yeah, and it was bad." And he said, "Are you hungry?" And my son said, "You know, a little bit." And he said, "Well, take your mom and go up there and get you something to eat." And so I turned around and I said, "We appreciate it, but, you know, there's nine of us." And he was like, "I don't care how many of you all it is. Everybody go up there and get something to eat. Come sit down. It's all on me. Get as much as you want, get something to drink, get something to go. You all sit down, take a deep breath, enjoy your food." And he was like, "I really wish I could do more." He's like, "You know, I have daughters myself, and if this were to happen to them, I would hope someone would be kind to them and feed them and make sure that they were going to be all right on the road." So he did that for us, and we got back on the road, and by this time we were an hour outside of Houston, and we needed more gas.

So we found a little gas station that was off the road, and the minute we were getting out, [there] was a pastor for the church that was down the street, his wife, and his two daughters. And when we pulled up to the gas tanks—it's just written all over your face, you know, when you've gone through something like this. So they come up to the car and they were like, "Were y'all in the storm? Are you okay?"

And we were like, "Yes, we were in the storm." So they were asking us about it, because they said, "We were so terrified that it was going to come here. It was so close to hitting Houston before it turned and hit New Orleans and Mississippi," and things like that. "Pull your cars up. Pull the car and the truck up. Gas up. We'll pay for it and everything." And it was like forty-five bucks for the car and like fifty-five dollars for the truck. They gassed us up. They took us in the store. They bought the kids snacks. They bought drinks. They were like, "Does anybody need any cigarettes?" You know, "Everything you need, get it. And we'll cover it." They did that, plus they gave us money, when we were getting ready to leave.

So we were blessed all the way from Mississippi here to Houston, and once we got here it was just like, "Thank God." Because we just got on the road, basically, with a wing and a prayer, praying that the car was going to make it. Praying that we would have enough cash for gas for the car and the truck, and making sure that the kids were comfortable, coming from what they've come from, trying to get them to safety. So once we got here, you know, it was just like, "Thank God," because we really did not think that we would make it.

Angela's family possessed deep roots in Houston's "Frenchtown," a neighborhood that was largely settled by Louisiana Creoles after the

Great Mississippi Flood of 1927, which caused the overnight displacement of nearly 1,000,000 people, more than any American weather disaster in history, except Katrina. When Angela first came to Houston, her family stayed briefly with Frank Broussard, a Frenchtown native whose father had helped rescue Louisianans from their rooftops in 1927. She and her family then occupied an apartment within a mile of Frank's house for the following two years.

By 2007, Bay St. Louis was rebounding, and Angela and Sam were able to find work there and move their family back to the Mississippi Gulf Coast. Both Angela and Sam now work in the healthcare industry, and they pass daily through the landscape that had been so suddenly reduced to ruins on the morning that Katrina struck.

SIDNEY HARRIS

"On the strength of my little nephew, I started getting a little strong"

If a contest were held to name the worst possible job for a New Orleanian trapped in the city by Katrina, there would be many serious contenders, but few would outscore prison deputy. Even before the hurricane, the Orleans Parish Prison was a rough place to work. Perpetual overcrowding lowered the morale of prisoners and guards alike and contributed to a state of constant tension. But on the morning of August 29, 2005, when Katrina's waters filled its first floor, the prison became a deathtrap, and it was left to a handful of guards to lead hundreds of disoriented, enraged, terrified prisoners to the only high ground available: a highway overpass, where they would suffer for days in searing heat, forced to fend for themselves to find food, water, and other bare necessities.

The unenviable prize of Katrina prison guard fell to, among others, Sidney Harris, who was just twenty-four years of age at the time. He is one of the few "official" responders who appear in this collection. Sidney spent the night in the Orleans Parish Prison to do a task, which he performed with remarkable dedication. Indeed, like the civilians whose stories are central to this book, he considerably outperformed the official standard. As

Sidney and his fellow officers faced the worst that Katrina had to offer, their commanders and reinforcements were not to be found. Each deputy was essentially on his or her own to try to forge the human bonds that would ensure survival. In Sidney's case, as in so many others, the powerful bonds of family continued to function as all else failed. Ironically, he had brought his nephew to the prison to ensure the boy's safety, but thereby cast him into one of the most dangerous corners of a city where danger was painfully easy to find. Sidney modestly admits the feelings of fear that assaulted him during the crisis, but he beat them back in order to be strong for his kin. In the end, he effectively enlisted his nephew as a deputy at a time when many of the official deputies were throwing down their badges and fleeing the bridge. Again and again, Sidney overrides his nephew's pleas to seek safety; he gives up their places in the evacuation line to prisoners, the elderly, and the injured. But when Sidney offers the boy a choice between staying with him and a ride to safety, the boy stays and tells his uncle, "You lucky I love you." Sidney simultaneously faces off seven hundred prisoners, cares for numerous people in distress, and inducts his nephew into manhood.

Fellow survivor Darlene Poole recorded Sidney's story on February 1, 2006. Born in 1980 in the Ninth Ward of New Orleans, Sidney lived in a house that his father had occupied since 1950, surrounded by sibs: eight brothers and nine sisters as well as extended family. He begins his narrative with memories of his neighborhood.

It was all right. I mean, some people might say that it was a bad neighborhood, but the block I stayed on was quiet. And the blocks surrounding probably was a little bad, but they had people that mostly got along, and we just didn't have nobody come around and ruin it for us: [folks from] the younger generations living on the other blocks. See, my block was mostly older people; that's why I used to have to go on other blocks to see my friends, or we would meet up at the park and play basketball or football.

I lived in the Ninth Ward, on Bartholomew Street, off of Claiborne. Yeah, most of [my family] lived in the Lower Ninth Ward—in eastern New Orleans. It was laid back, you know. Well, I'm going to tell you, the crime really this year here, 2005, the crime rate it started picking up. And you know it was more drugs in the community, but it was younger people too. They had younger generations: like on my block a lot of the older people moved or died off, but a lot of the younger people too. The few we did have, they was gone too so that led us, the ones who was left, to go another block. And it was, it was violent, you know, but a lot of people got along, though. But it was, I guess you could say, turf wars.

[I lived in Ninth Ward] all my life, since—well, my dad been there since 1950. He actually bought our house, like, three times. And we rebuilding right now, so he plan on staying back there; I been there for twenty years, but he been there since like the fifties.

Well, during Hurricane Katrina, I had to work. So what I was trying to do that day was make sure my mama and them left town. But my dad, he didn't want to go so he stayed in our house in the Ninth Ward. I worked at the New Orleans sheriff's office, criminal sheriff's office. The day started off for me; it was cloudy, a normal day. But you expected a hurricane. What we did that day was, we came in to work early, about four o'clock that evening, and what we had to do: we could bring our family members with us, to come into the prison, and we keep on the third floor and we had to do our regular post, be on our tiers.

The first day it was okay and the hurricane came sometime in the middle of the night. You know, I actually slept overnight when the hurricane came through. But when I woke up the power was out and I came downstairs because my shift was over, but when I came downstairs the water wasn't really in our *building yet*, it was just like right on the outside and like ankle high. But when you stepped out there, you actually looked to the street, you saw cars floating and you saw the stop signs just covered under water. I mean you just really saw water. I mean you really stuck in a building. You didn't have nowhere to go.

I went back upstairs, and I was hanging with my nephew because I brought him with me. He wanted to stay with me through the hurricane and we all just chilled out and stuff. Because most of us worked the night shift, we was on the third floor, you know, while we was off and everything.

So, after that the night was coming and I went back downstairs; we had roll call and I went downstairs. We did our roll call. I went up and came back down, and when I came back down I actually slipped on the *stairs* because they was so wet and slippery and the power was out, so it was *hot*—and stairs was wet.

After that, we had to put garbage bags on our feet and everything because by that time about—I say, about seven o'clock—the water was like knee high. The water was just rising and during that time all I could think about was my mama and them. You know, in prison you hear rumors, so you just was hearing rumors about what areas was flooded and how it was out there and what happened here, what happened there. But at the same time, the main thing I was worried about was my daddy, because they told me that the Ninth Ward was totally flooded, and I know he stayed home. And it was trying to deal with these inmates and still try to worry about your family *too*. And as the time went on, it was getting darker, you know. You had one or two flashlights, but we talking about a prison building that holds seven-hundred-plus inmates. And you talking about the deputies: it was only like, I might say forty at the most, deputies. That's not enough deputies to control that facility and, like I said, the water—I went back downstairs and the water was thigh-length.

So it's like a scary feeling, knowing that the water's just getting higher and you don't know actually how high it's going to get. And you go back upstairs, you got to deal with inmates that's hungry, but you got to give them a excuse or try to prolong it because we trying to get them *food*, because the food they had is floating in the water downstairs. And they getting agitated, they starting to get riled up. And what made it worse was, the water got waist-high.

So we had to move the inmates from off the first floor onto the third floor. So when we did that—I mean by that time when we was moving them—I mean I actually was standing in the water for about two hours. And it was just like feces water, you know, and gasoline, diesel, all kind of stuff. And I mean we bringing them up there to the third floor so now we talking: on the tier it's four dorms and in each dorm they have thirty-nine inmates so now you doubling it and you have [seventy-eight] inmates in each dorm. With no air, no food, no water. So you kind of figure in your head something bound to happen.

And by us being understaffed at the time, it was only actually one person to a tier. So, you have no weapon, you on a tier by yourself. It's dark, and you just have inmates surrounding you trying to break the glass. And you just thinking in your head and praying that none of them break the glass. Because you can't fight them off. Times when I felt like they was going to break the glass, I'll walk off the tier. You know.

And we had this force [like a SWAT team], SID, that's the name of them. They came in with machine guns, assault rifles, and they was actually coming in one dorm on each tier, and they're shooting like a bean bag into the first person, you know, the closest person to the door, the closest inmate to the door. They'll shoot a bean bag into his chest. And make the rest of them get on the floor, put their face on the sweaty floor, you know, curse them out. Whatever, but you know some of them deserve it, some of them don't. They was really cutting up, you know, and they didn't really understand. It was like a big misunderstanding. They didn't know what was going down outside the dorm. And they thought we was eating, they thought we was drinking water, they thought everything was all good. But *we* didn't have water, food, or nothing either, for them three days we was in the jail.

Now, all right, it was like this went on for three days and the water had got to the second floor, in the jail. So by that time I actually, I say by the third day now I was off and I just had this feeling like, you know, I just didn't really care to even try to fight no more. I just laid down and was like whatever going to happen is going to be, you know, and the minute *I did that*—you know, it was hot and we had little mats we laid on the ground. It was rioting. People was getting shot. You was just hearing gunfire, you know, screams, everything.

And you just was scared. I was just sitting down thinking about all that, and the floor was just *wet*; so all your sheets was wet, you just felt uncomfortable. And as soon as I just gave up, really like, like I really don't care no more, that's when [more deputies] came in and was like it's time to get the inmates out, so we was happy.

We started getting the inmates out and when we was bringing them down—we had to bring them down, like I said, dorm by dorm, because you couldn't really let them out all together, you know, because they was already rioting. That took a whole day. And for that whole day, I stood in that water with AIDS needles, the needles that the AIDS inmates use, and feces from the outside sewers, and from the inside sewers. You know, so it stink. It was just crazy, because after all that rioting and stuff, every inmate that passed me up, when they came down into that water, some of them was scared to even get in it. So it was like these same inmates, I was starting to be afraid of, I guess because there was so many of them. I was starting to help them, because at the same time, it was my job, but I wouldn't have wanted to leave nobody behind either. And they all was apologizing, you know, and saying how they's sorry, and they didn't know what was going on. They saw their food, they meat, and they bread floating in the water, you know, and now they know why they wasn't getting no food and stuff.

But some of the other deputies had chips on their shoulder because it's like the inmates was handling us so bad, cursing us out, you know, talking about us, and we all adults. We have to accept it because it's our job, but we don't take well to it, and it's like they wanted our help out of there. So some deputies didn't help. Some did. Some walked away, you know. And just tried to get out theyself. And by that time, like I say, it took a whole day, and me and a couple of more deputies was like the last ones to get out of the jail. Besides, like my captain, now he dead. He had a heart attack right after the hurricane.

And a couple other deputies: one of our majors, he had a heart attack that night, two of our girls had asthma attacks, one of our male deputies broke down, you know, plus we trying to hold our composure, trying to keep our composure through all that. And it was unbearable. I just never really imagined myself being in that situation, so I didn't know how I was going to deal with it. But I think I did pretty good.

We was wondering why they never came got us. And actually, honest, they never would have came, but they had to get the inmates out. And once they got the inmates out of the jails, they brought them to the Broad Street "bridge," the overpass. And they left us in the jails. So they had some men riding on the boats, and some of the female deputies and stuff was begging them to come get us, showing them our badges: we deputies.

And we was just standing in water. And it just smelled like diesel, you know, and it was scary, because they had people still smoking, knowing this was water and gas, diesel, and all this here. And they throwing these cigarette butts, you know. There was all kind of little stuff like that going.

And once we got on the bridge we found out that some of our other deputies was caught in other buildings, you know, stuck: having to shoot inmates, and it was hard because some of them on a personal level, outside the job, you know, was close friends. I know I had a few of them and it's like all the ones I was close to was stuck in our building, H-O-D [House of Detention]. And that's where a lot of the gunfire was at.

My nephew, he was helping me out a lot, and I had to try to be strong for him. And one of my deputies—you know, one of my friend deputies, his wife and his sister [were among] the family members. And my nephew, while he was up there, he got to know them, befriended them, so he was like, "We need to keep them by us." And when he told me who they was, I was like, "All right."

Once we got on the bridge, it was no water, no food. It was so *hot*. It was so hot on the bridge. They had ants biting us at night. You had to lay on concrete, try to sleep and get you some rest because you been up for like four days now. Try to get you some rest, but how can you sleep? You got like about six thousand inmates on the bridge next to you with civilians on the bridge and your family members? Not knowing what they going to *do*. Another hurting part about it was, they left a lot of inmates in there: like in [prison building] Templeman 3, the whole first floor drowned. They tried to cover it up for the longest. But you couldn't cover that up, you know. That's over a hundred inmates, you know, that died.

I mean now you could picture all these inmates. And now they tired. They passing out, they got female inmates, you know, they all getting rowdy on the bridge. We got to move all the civilians; but you got to move all the civilians on the whole opposite side of the bridge because the inmates starting to get riled up.

People passing out; nurses quitting because it's too stressful, and [across from the bridge in an unevacuated prison building] you see other inmates burning sheets, t-shirts, whatever they can, screaming out of the cells, out of the windows trying to get the police and all the deputies' attention.

They wanting to get out, and two whole days while them inmates was on that bridge [no one tried to] get them dudes. And like I said, the saddest part about that was when they *stopped*, when the dude *stopped*, 'cause for two days strong he was burning stuff out the window, trying to get their attention, *screaming*; I'm talking about at the top of his lungs. And it was a lot of them, and when they *stopped* you couldn't think nothing but the *worst*. And then you had some to the point of trying to jump out the window. They broke a window, squeezing out a window, *jumping*. They was jumping, but what [the prisoners on the bridge] didn't know was they had a like SID and all them was shooting them down, with their little beanbags and stuff and they was dropping into the water—but us being deputies, we couldn't say that's what was going on—and everybody thought they was just jumping. And a lot of them dudes didn't make it. It's not funny, but a lot of them dudes died when they hit that water. You know, jumping from that high up.

You know, it was a lot of stuff going on that just made it kind of hard. Man, one time I really kind of broke down because I was just thinking about my mom and them, my dad and them. I had like a bum battery left [on my cell phone] and I called my brother, and he was just crying. He was like, "Everybody been looking for you." We didn't know. We been seeing it on the news and seeing everything but they didn't know what happened, and it was a big relief to them *and* to me. But we still didn't know what the turn-out on my daddy was.

I knew my mom was all right then, you know. And I knew my sisters and them was all right. I didn't know—my friend, Patrick, I told him, "Leave." But he kept being stubborn because he stayed for the last storm. He said *he* wasn't going to go. So I didn't know if *he* had left. Or whatever. So I mean there was so many people I was worried about, and I didn't even think to check my answering machine, so I turned my phone off.

And so we were on the bridge, and when the inmates was about to start rioting on the bridge they gave us shotguns. But it was like twenty of us with shotguns, you know, and all them inmates. And these guys are at the point where they was like, "You could shoot some of us, but you can't shoot all of us."

And they was *ready*. And, man, when they did *that*—pshoo—it was like the Angola [State Prison] and Hunt's [Hunt Correctional Center]: all the deputies came just in time. Because they stood up, all the inmates just stood up and they was getting ready for *war*. And we was cocked and ready. And as soon as they was about to make their move, and Angola and Hunt's—all those deputies come up there with the firepower and all the men we needed to discipline the inmates. So that turned out good, you know, I guess the Lord had heard a lot of our prayers. And they finally got that organized.

But they still had so many people on the bridge with no water, and you had no food. So basically it was a mind thing. If you could get it up there mentally, you know, you would have been all right.

So I think on the strength of my little nephew, I started getting a little strong, you know, because he kind of broke down and was like, "Man, why can't we just go home?" Because a lot of deputies had *quit* and walked off. But on the strength of him, I just found it somewhere in me. I just wasn't scared no more. Like, I was like, we going to make it. I just told him, "All right, we're going to make it, we're going to be all right." So my little nephew, he was seventeen, but he smokes cigarettes. I made sure he had cigarettes. They had looters that was selling cigarettes. They had people, going, breaking into Kentwood [Spring Water facility] right there, getting water. You know, I always keep money on me. They was selling water, *high*. I was buying it. I didn't even want it, you know. Like, I think I might buy a bottle of water for myself, and get him a big old gallon. And my deputy friend: I get his wife and his daughter, and his little kids, you know, a gallon of water. And if somebody was coming selling chips or something like that, I was getting that, so I wasn't really worrying about me, because actually from Katrina, I lost like twenty pounds. Just being out there on that bridge for three or four days, I had lost like ten pounds. Because I ain't eating.

The sun was just killing me and the oil and the diesel was still in our skin. So it was burning us and we just was so funky, you couldn't even stand to smell yourself. You know, I was wanting to smack myself because, I'm like, "Man, you really"—I hated that smell, and it's like, you walking around people, but once you realize that them people been in that same water you been, and that they smell the same way, it was all right. You know?

So we had this one deputy. He had just came. He wasn't a deputy this long, and he was in the military, and to me, I feel like he did one of the most heroic things, and ever since then, like I told this dude, "Man, I love you for that," you know, and that's my dog to this day.

[It came to a point that] they had no more water. We had some more deputies, females, passing out. You know? And SID and Angola, Hunt's: all the water they was getting, they was keeping it for themselves, hiding it, you know. So this man jumped from the bridge, from the Broad [Street] bridge, he jumped into the water, swim all the way to Templeman 1 and 2, which is about two long blocks. And he swam in that water, you know, and the water was high. It was high. He swam in it—that dude swam *in* the building. He went in Templeman. And he got one of the old garbage can barrels, filled it up with water bottles, and treaded back with it. And I'm like, "Thank God, this dude went military. He did this by his self, and he came back."

When he came back, they was trying to crowd him: the ones who already had water, and was trying to grab him. And he was like, *"No-o."* Like, "No. It's for our people now," you know? "You all holding your own water." So we finally got some more water and that's when they came with more Kentwood water. But this time the dude was giving it away.

And we was down to like ten deputies, because some threw their badges, you know, on the ground, walked away. Or whatever. They got down to the other bridge and they walked away and so we was just on there trying to figure out what was going to be the next move.

And it was *nighttime*. Oh, man, there were some dudes were listening to the radio in the deputy car, in the sheriff's car. And all we heard was sheriff saying that he didn't call none of his deputies to come in to work, that we *volunteered*; you know, he not responsible for their actions. He didn't want to pay us. And it just made a lot of people mad. And it was hurting me, because it was like, you got this job, man, you doing all this for these people, and they *human*, so it's in you to help them, but it's like, as far as your job, you don't really want to be a part of it 'cause your boss is really throwing you to the wolves.

And he told us, we got to fend for ourselves. And for you to just sit up there and say that we had to fend for ourselves. So you leave us on the bridge. And what made it even worse, the next day, he came and they's some deputies had got to the news people and stuff, and this man got dressed out there, put on some shorts and some water boots, and made it seem like he been out there, and did an interview on the news. But what happened was, some of the deputies went to throwing stuff at him, so it kind of messed the news segment up. It never got played on the news.

You heard about the deputies, you know, throwing the stuff at him or whatever, cursing him out. So he came back, and when he came back he had bodyguards and stuff. [The deputies] was trying to rush him and stuff and he was telling everybody that he going to stay here as long as we here, he going to be here and he going to make sure we get a way out.

Finally buses arrived to carry people off the overpass. They took a bus-
load of deputies. And they was like, "Well, we were going to start getting
people." But it was messed up because they was like, "All we want is the
deputies and their family." And you had old women out there, and it was
like for some reason you had a lot of old, obese people out there with dia-
betes and illnesses so it was like it made it even worse.

[Some agency] brought a whole bunch of sandwiches and stuff, and in
order for [people] to get it, they had to get down into the other bridge. So
it was to the point where they were like, "We ain't even taking the deputies'
family, we just want the deputies." Now, who in they right mind, going to
leave their family behind? So, me myself—as long as you had something
on representing you was a sheriff deputy—I gave my nephew a sheriff
jacket with a badge on it, so he got on the boat, we made it down.

You know, everybody ate; I even ate, I ate, I think, a sandwich, and
that *was it.*

It got dark. [The other deputies] had took all the lights that they had
the night before; they had all the lights down there when the inmates was
down there. And it was just pitch black. And it was like me and this other
dude, [this deputy]. He kind of took charge. He was like one of the dudes
that always was like *goofy*. Nobody took him seriously. But I swear, that day
this dude took charge. For real, like a grown-up man, he took charge. And
he handled the situation, he organized everything. He told us like what we
need to do. And we was able to control all them people down there, all the
civilians. All the inmates was gone. Long gone. They left us, and we was able
to control the civilians. And we didn't want nobody else to come and mess
that up for us. We was hearing about all the shootings at helicopters, and
stuff at the Superdome, and we was afraid them people might come down
there and start shooting so we all had our guns and stuff. We was ready.

Fortunately, nobody ever came. Well, they had some that came, but
they wasn't looking for trouble, so we took them in. And they had this one
dude. He had a bus, and he running it from the Ninth Ward, RTA bus, and
on this bus, this dude had so many clothes, and like chips, and candy, cold
drinks, you know. He had everything you wanted on this bus. And the
main two things I want he had: soap, you know, and he had a toothbrush,
toothpaste, and he had different shirts and stuff.

Man, I took a bath out there, for real. Changed them clothes, brushed
my teeth. They had so much bottled water, you couldn't even drink it. You
know, after they came and dumped all that. You couldn't even drink all
that water. And I was just using it, just taking a bath, I'm like scrubbing

for real. And it made you feel just a little better. But you still was stuck out there, so it only made us feel a little better, but you smelt better.

After that, I see, I forgot about my phone. For real. And I turned it on, so I called my brother and he was like, "Where you at? I'm calling to CNN." So my brother was trying to call them. Then my nephew's daddy called: you know, he in the air force and he *high rank*.

And he had called, and we told him what was going on, and like—ten minutes, here come a helicopter. So it was difficult because everybody was trying to run to the helicopter, and we was like, "No." You know, we going to organize, we going to let the old people go first, the old, sick people. Then we going to let the ladies and the children go. You know, the older men, or whatever, and the younger men—the young men was going to stay there and hold it down.

But they had some dude actually out there trying to hit women. You know, like they awful, like they punks. They was trying to beat up on women and stuff 'cause they really wanted to go, but we wasn't going to let you get on the helicopter till we feel like it's your turn. And this dude, they had one dude slap his mama so hard out there because she told him to wait. And he like really slapped her hard. Punched her. And that's when it hit me: like, this hurricane making people do some stupid stuff.

And [my nephew's] daddy called back, and was like, "The helicopter get there yet?" And I said like, "Yeah." I said, "That was *you* who called that helicopter?" He was like, "Yeah." Damn. So I went and told the [helicopter pilot] who I was. He was like, "All right." He was like, "All right. We going to come back. And we just going to be taking a full load." Like ten, twelve; however many they could take, they were going to keep coming back.

But for some reason, he took the first load and he didn't come back, all the way till that night. And by that time, they done had some people that went, broke into the Kentwood [water company], and took the Kentwood trucks, so they still had a bunch of people out there. And he finally came back that night. And he brought like four or five loads. And he say he was tired. He said, "Man, I'm tired, wore out. I been flying all day." You know, he was like, "I'm going to have to come back tomorrow." He think you could, you know, hold it to tomorrow.

I'm like, "Yeah." So my little nephew just broke down like, "Why we can't go?" Like he didn't understand that I had to do my job. Like he felt like they was messing over me. So why should I do what I'm doing? I'm like, well, I've still got my badge. That's my *job*. And, you know, he knew his daddy called for the helicopter—but at the same time, you ain't the only one that got to be saved. But I told him, I said, "If you want, they flying to the airport, you could go there where they got food, water, you know, medical, and you can wait on me."

He was like, "No, I ain't leaving."

"All right," I say, "well stay and help me then." And he stayed and helped me. We got everybody on that plane the next day. They brought two [helicopters], and then we asked them to go get our deputies out of the building. Then we got our deputies out of them buildings, and we was the *last ones* to leave off the bridge.

[The pilot] was like, "You know, you go get one more load; when we come back we go get the rest of you all." And he was like, "You and your nephew, you all getting on this last ride." [They rounded up more people for the last flight. There were] so many that all of us couldn't fit on. I said, "Well, look, take them." My nephew got mad at me again. I was like, "Man, just bear with me, man."

He was like, "Man, you lucky I love you."

You know, I was like, "Yeah, I'm *glad you do*."

So, [the pilot,] he was like, "Well, all right, I'm [going to] make this one more." He came back and it was like five of us and two more dudes like just walked up and they was like, "Y'all want go to the airport, you know, go." They hopped on and a dude and his girl came and we got a whole load again. But, we got on and that was a wrap. I finally got to the airport.

And we checked in and everything. We went to San Antonio. And it was like you couldn't find nobody. I didn't see none of the deputies. I ran into [just one of them], but that was my last time I saw him. I wish I could find out where he at, but, you know, things happen. I know he went to San Antonio 'cause that's the same place I went. And I was still worried about my daddy. We found everybody except my daddy and my uncle.

And my sister came and got me from the airport, and when she came got me, we were funky in the car. She took us to Wal-Mart. We walked in to Wal-Mart funky—one of them people was like, "Man." She went and took us to get some clothes and everything. Went back to the hotel, took a bath about four hours, you know, and still worrying about my daddy. Calling my mama, mama and them, couldn't get in touch with them. I finally charged my phone. Listening to my phone [messages]. My sister and them was just calling and they kept calling like, it was crazy 'cause I was so happy that we survived. It was like my sister just left like five messages and on each message, she kept getting sadder and sadder, and on the last one she was just crying. And that was like heart touching, because me and my sister never really did get along, and it's like all in her voice, I could hear how much she loved me. Like even though we just never get along, she was crying because she didn't know where I was and she just wanted me to come home, so I was ready to see them. And come to find out, they was in Mississippi somewhere. And they was in Mississippi, and by that time I was in Woodlands, Texas. I had left San Antonio.

Only thing run across your mind was like, damn, I don't know who made it, like my friends, I don't know if I'm ever going to see them, you know. Dang. This girl. You know. All kind of stuff. You just thought you was going to never know nobody no more.

And one night we was just in the hotel and a lady called and was like, "Well, your daddy here in the shelter." So, my sister just jumped up and was like, "I'm going to get daddy." She went—*bang*—and got him. She went got my daddy. He didn't want come from out the shelter.

My daddy was like, "I'm staying here until I get all the assistance I need." So he was like all the way in College Station, Texas; Bryan, College Station, that's like a hundred miles from Houston. So, she called me, she was like, "You think you want to talk to Dad, because he don't want to come." So the next day I went down there and we all went down there. We saw him. I saw him and I just *punched him.* I was like, "Man, you *stupid* like for staying." I said, "I bet you ain't going to stay no more."

He was like, "*Hell no*, I ain't go stay." He say, it could be a Category 1, he *leaving.* And whatever, and he showed me the pictures and everything, man. He took pictures. Like I got pictures of how high the water was on our block and our neighborhood. And stuff. And he walked from our street, Bartholomew, and Claiborne [about two and one-half miles] all the way to St. Bernard Avenue and St. Claude. I'm like, "Dang, you did all that?" And I was like, "You deserve that 'cause you should have left. You had the chance to leave." You know.

And he was like, "You talk to your mom and them?" And I'm like, "Yeah, I talked to them," you know, and I called my mom and let her talk to him. It was like a family reunion, and stuff. And we just sat down and talked the whole night. You know, everybody was asleep, but the people just let us talk all night. We finally left. He still didn't want to go because he wanted to make sure he get all his assistance, like with FEMA and Red Cross and all that.

So like two days later he had called me and was like, "I want you to come over here, sleep over here tonight. And in the morning you go with these people; they said they going to go down there to Mississippi and get your mama and them." And he said, "I want you to drive my truck back out here."

I'm like, "For real?" You know. Man, I was like, "All right." So we left and got my mama and them. They spent about a hour hugging me. My nieces, nephews, my sister, and we came back to Bryan, College Station, and when we came back, we had a brand-new house. Like it was a nice house. My sister had a nice house, you know. And them people, they showed so much love out there, it was ridiculous [laughing]. Like, you wanted for nothing. You didn't have to cook. I mean, you wasn't eating fast food or nothing. They was actually cooking. You know. They would buy you clothes, and they was like it just didn't matter, you know.

So I finally got settled down out there. Now, a couple of months, about three months ago, I went back to the city. I remember when I first went back. And I'm like, "Man!" You saw it on the news, because the whole time after the hurricane, I was just like everybody else, just sitting in front of the TV, looking at CNN, looking at the news to see if they were going to show your neighborhood, or see who missing and stuff. And they were showing it, but the TV just didn't really show what it's really like. It was messed up and for real.

It was messed up, and I mean. I still decided to stay, and I been down there for like the last three months, and it is damn near livable now. I mean, a lot of people have moved back. And it's crazy, I mean, the crime is down, I guess, because most violent ones never came back, but I had the same fun down there that I had before. You know. And I think the Lord blessed me, because some friends I had in my life, and didn't know how to get rid of, He got rid of them for me. And the ones I wanted to keep, still there. You know. And that basically bring me here now. So I mean it was a long, long little journey, but I mean, *shee*, I'm here now to tell the story.

Darleen Poole, the interviewer, asked Sidney: "How did you feel, finally getting on the helicopter?"

Ooh, I felt relieved. Actually, I think part of it, why I didn't get on before a lot of people, was like, *dang*, I ain't never rode on no helicopter. I loved riding on airplanes, but I'm like, a helicopter, you know, I ain't really too sure about that. So when it came time, like you either going to stay on this bridge, or you in this water, you and these little sandwich bags, or you going to civilization? I'm like, man. So I finally manned up and it was a relief. And I was looking at the city. Like, man, it was just like big old puddles. I was relieved, but at the same time I just couldn't get over that sadness, because some people, I just didn't know where they was at. I was happy to get off that bridge. But like I say, it was bittersweet, 'cause you didn't know what your next move was going to be or where your next dollar was going to come from. That's how I felt.

As Sidney's story relates, he returned to New Orleans as soon as he could. He returned to work at the Orleans Parish Prison, again proving his courage and endurance. On June 2, 2008, at his New Orleans home, Sidney once more sat to record an interview with a fellow survivor, Dallas McNamara.

VINCENT TROTTER

"All I knew was, I had to get home"

Vincent Trotter was born in New Orleans's Charity Hospital in September 1973. Though he has nine half-siblings, he was the only child between his father, who held a variety of jobs, and his mother, a truck driver. He spent his childhood in the Mid-City and Uptown neighborhoods of New Orleans, before moving across the Mississippi River to Algiers. Like Sidney Harris (the narrator of the previous interview), Vincent became a deputy sheriff for the Orleans Parish Prison, and he was on duty on Sunday, August 28, 2005, as Hurricane Katrina closed in on the city.

Vincent's prison narrative differs remarkably from Sidney's. The two run parallel in presenting scenes of remarkable deprivation and hardship, but Vincent emphasizes the extreme cruelty of the elements rather than the dangers posed by the inmates that appear prominently in Sidney's story. And where Sidney finds strength and redemption in caring for his nephew, Vincent finds a saving grace in small acts of kindness exchanged between guards and prisoners. The guards and the inmates reach a status of equality that underlines their common humanity.

Vincent Trotter, 2008, at the Broad Street overpass, New Orleans. Three years earlier, Vincent was one of a handful of Orleans Parish Prison deputies guarding hundreds of inmates trapped on the overpass in the wake of Hurricane Katrina. Photo by Dallas McNamara.

When recorded, Vincent was a trainee in the Surviving Katrina and Rita in Houston project. On March 20, 2006, the first day of his training, each of the survivors shared his or her storm story with a fellow trainee. His co-worker Dione Morgan expressed the sentiment of the group at large in saying, "I'm in awe of Vincent's story." Thus Vincent was chosen to narrate the first recorded story before the entire group. Looking back, I believe that the power of Vincent's narrative lies in its unlikely combination of horrific conditions with tiny acts of goodness, mortal danger with comic relief, all conveyed eloquently and calmly by an unassuming, self-described "man of few words."

David Taylor, folklife specialist of the American Folklife Center, was the interviewer.

When I was in elementary school, believe it or not, I wanted to be a chemist. My mom bought me my first microscope. Well, actually she bought me a microscope because she refused to buy me a chemistry set. She didn't want me blowing up things around the house. But, you know, being a kid—she bought me that microscope. I thought of everything under the sun that I could put up under that microscope to look at. So I had a really interesting childhood, you know; I would go out to the country sometimes and we'd think of things to blow up. We'd put gasoline and kerosene and oil in a jar and pitch rocks at it to see if it was going to explode. But, we were kids, you know.

As I got older, I was in my senior year of high school, had absolutely no idea what I wanted to do because, actually, I had planned to join the military. My dad was in the army. So I wanted to join the army, be a soldier like my dad, but I loved being in the band. I knew the military had a band, so that's what I wanted to do. I went down to the recruiter's office and they asked about my medical history and once I told them, you know, my medical condition, they told me I couldn't join the military because if something happened to me, they would have to take care of me for the rest of my life. And I was like, "Okay," but I still wasn't accepting that answer because after I left the army recruiter's office, I go over to the marine recruiter's office. Six months after that, after the marine recruiters told me no, I go over to the air force base. I'm really trying to get into the military because it is all I knew I wanted to do. Because I hadn't considered going to college, you know, because I didn't know what I wanted to be. All I knew is I liked playing that saxophone.

[A former high school band director] offered me a scholarship to [University of] Arkansas, Pine Bluff. After a semester there, I returned back to New Orleans because actually I got robbed and I felt I had never run across this kind of behavior in New Orleans, oddly, and it takes me to go away [to] get robbed. So, I'm like, "If I can get robbed in the country, I'm going to go back to the city." I went back and I started to attend Southern University in New Orleans, where I studied music education for three and a half years. You know, after that three and a half years I injured my back and it got hard for me to go to school so I ended up sitting out of school. Along the way, I ended up having a son. So that put school on the back burner. So I just started working jobs here and there, you know, to provide for a family.

I was working for a company called St. Charles Contractors. We got laid off after three and a half years of employment there. So, I had a talk with my uncle and he said, "Why don't you go be a deputy sheriff?" And at the time I was thinking, "I don't want to be a deputy sheriff, they don't make no money." You know, so what. I needed a job, so I went anyway. Got the job, you know, working in jails.

First day on the job, I'm walking in and the inmates knew the new recruits 'cause we all wore these white shirts as opposed to the regular deputy uniforms. And you walk in there and they show you how to do roll call and they tell you, "Okay, you press this button to open that door. You press this button to open that door." And you're just sitting in this box with two hundred inmates surrounding you. And you sitting there like, "Oh, Lord, what have I gotten myself into? These guys get out of here, they're going to kill me." But you couldn't let the inmates know you were scared so you just went with the flow.

They had thirty-two hundred inmates in that one particular facility. On a shift, you would have twelve [officers] on a good day. On a day when we were shorthanded, you would have anywhere from six to eight, which meant some officers would have to handle two sides on a floor.

I had one instance where an inmate told me he was having chest pains. And me, being a watchman, I have to take care of it. I can't just ignore him and say, "Okay whatever, your chest hurts. Go lay down." You know, if he is having chest pains, first thing we're thinking is he might be having a heart attack, so we got to get him to medical. So I called downstairs to tell the control desk that I got inmate so-and-so that needed to go down and see medical. In turn, the control officer would talk it over with the supervisor. And the supervisor called back up to me and said, "Okay, bring him down." When I opened the door, ten inmates walked out behind him. Now, the control officer can see everything that is going on on my floor, so to avoid a potential break-out situation, there is a door that slides—shuts every-thing down. So, I'm locked in there with those ten inmates. And that was a real scary situation. Now like I said, I wouldn't let the inmates know I was scared of them. I'm standing on the module going—and it's odd because I'm a soft-spoken individual—but I'm standing there screaming at the top of my lungs, "All of y'all lockdown. Lockdown," you know. Do what you got to do. You trying to intimidate them and they're refusing to move. So, by this time I'm standing there screaming "*Lockdown*," but I'm pressing that button, hitting the panic button, in time to get somebody up here. They aren't doing what I'm telling them to do. And, eventually, you know, four or five guys came up to try to diffuse the situation. Which, in all actuality, they didn't want to do anything [to me]. They had been complaining ear-lier because the air wasn't circulating properly in their cell, and they were trying to get out to get some fresh air. I knew this but, you know, I had to follow procedure, so I did.

Every time we get a hurricane, as law enforcement officers, we know we have to report into work anyway so we're watching them [on the news]. But on this particular instance, you know, they made the announcement the day before that we would have to come in to work, bring whatever we needed, and be prepared to stay in case the hurricane hit. So you know, I'm thinking in the back of my mind, "I'm not going to work. I'm calling in sick." But I didn't want to lose my job, so I went. You know, took my little backpack, my extra change of clothes, another pair of shoes because I didn't want to wear those combat boots all day, and went in to work.

I wasn't really scared to go to work because I am thinking, "Okay, we're going to go to work and we're going to come home, just like before." But, right before I left home, they shut the city down. The only reason I was able to go to work is because I had my badge. My badge would get me across the [GNO] bridge to go to work. And I looked, after I had packed up all my clothes, you know, got dressed for work, getting ready to leave, I stopped for a second and I looked back at the door because my dad was at the house, and he just looked at me; he said, "I know, son." Because my dad was a jailer also prior to me working there, and he knew that I didn't want to go but I had to go. And, you know, aside from getting into all the mushy stuff that men don't like to talk about, he just looked at me and said, "I know, son."

So, we go to work. It starts storming, and, you know, you're in the jails. You figure, okay, it's a little rain, no problem. The wind is blowing hard, no problem. We're in the jails; the jails are made of brick. I want to see the big, bad wolf blow this house down. But, after being there and still not knowing what it looked like on the outside: the water started to rise. So we knew we had to move inmates from the first floor to higher places within the facility without causing overcrowding and things of that sort. So, you know, that caused problems because you had to put some inmates in unsecured spots, in back areas of the facility that didn't have locks on the door, so we just put them all up there.

After the storm passed, the water had receded some and we knew that we had to get the inmates out. Now, me, I hadn't been outside, so I didn't know exactly how deep the water was. Eventually, we finally got the order from the major—all deputies downstairs to the first floor. So I'm thinking, "Okay." You're walking down the stairs and, you know, if you ever been baptized, you know what cold water is like. So, you walk and you trying to prepare yourself for stepping in this water and nothing can prepare you for it. You step into this water and you just—suck it in and go on and get in the water. You figure you're going to get used to it eventually. I stand five foot, four inches; the water was at least four and a half feet deep because the water was up to my chest. And I am standing in this water, and you could see everything floating by in this water from rats, to bread, to diesel from a transistor that had exploded. You could smell the oil in the water, but it was what we had to do to get them out of there. So after we, you know, lined up the deputies that were in that facility to where they could have each cell come out and be escorted through, where we could sort of like barricade them, that is what we did.

We herded them out of there. For lack of a better term, we herded them out of the jails to safety; we had to actually walk them over to another facility where the boats could actually get in and take them to what was known as the "Broad Bridge" [a section of Broad Street], which overpassed the interstate.

After the prisoners were evacuated from the building, they moved us to the same bridge with the prisoners where we slept for three days. You know, guarding, in shifts. We guarded the inmates there on the bridge until they brought in buses to take them out. And that was rough because, mind you, we hadn't eaten after the little food we had packed to bring to work with us had run out, and now we are stuck up on this bridge with nothing to eat.

Now this was the odd thing; people were starting to loot and walking around with ice coolers and grocery baskets of food but when they come to the bridge and they realized that we were law enforcement, they wouldn't even give us anything to eat. Which in turn, ironically, turned us into criminals because we were, I'd say, fifty yards from the Ozone Water Company, and you could see the trucks sitting in the water but they were not completely submerged. So we would swim over to the Ozone Water Company, break in the trucks, take their water, bring it back to the bridge just so we could have something to drink, if nothing else.

Another thing that got me through was an inmate, that had been up on my tier, had looted one of the neighborhood stores and all he had in his basket were Little Debbie cupcakes and liquor. In my state of mind, I knew one thing: I was hungry and I was thirsty. And the other thing I knew was that liquor was going to calm my nerves at least for a little. So, he said "Capt [for "Captain"], I got something for you. You look like you going through a rough time, I'm going to hook you up." He gave me a can of King Cobra, and a bottle of Hypnotiq [liqueur], and about ten Little Debbie cupcakes. I took them and stuffed them in my jacket pocket, stuffed the King Cobra in my inside pocket, and the Henessey in the other pocket. I went back over to my lieutenant, cause we were all smokers. We're running short on cigarettes, everybody's nerves getting bad. I said, "Capt, I got something for you." I pulled that one jacket open. He said, "Man where you get—man, where you get it from? Give me some."

That pretty much got us through, but after the three days were over with was when I decided I couldn't take it anymore, and the inmates were going over the side of the bridge and I asked one of the guys, the officers that had come in to take the inmates out, "Am I allowed to climb over that scaffold?" And he told me, "You got a badge, you're allowed to do anything you want to do." Okay. So I talked to my ranking officer; I said, "Since you're the only person I see that's in charge, I am letting you know that I am about to go. I'll see you when I see you." And I walked from that bridge to my house in Algiers. Didn't know if I had a house to go to, I just knew I couldn't stay on that bridge.

Vincent's March 20 interview ended long before his story was over. The next day, two of Vincent's fellow trainees, Nicole Eugene (who also shares her story in this book) and Johnna Reiss, took up the thread of his narrative, which concludes below. Vincent leaves the prison, seeking his home in Algiers, a New Orleans suburb directly across the Mississippi from downtown. No longer a man with a badge, he finds that the only people who block his path are official responders. The real sources of help are friends, family, strangers, and church groups.

All I knew was, I had to get home. Whichever obstacle I had to take to get to my house, I was willing to take it. And I knew that the bridge would take me on a direct path to Algiers. So I just started walking, you know, and was bound—or should I say determined?—not to let anything turn me back. I figured I had my badge in my hand, and I was walking.

I left the bridge, I would say it was about five o'clock. And when I got home, it was dark, so it had to have been like eight. You know, it took me, I'd say a good two and a half hours to walk home. That walk was of course long, and a bit excruciating because I had already developed—I don't know if it was boils or corns or whatever, from my feet being inside of the boots, aside from being in the floodwater. So, you know, my feet were really hurting. I tried taking off my boots and walking, but that just made it worse, so I put them back on and just kept walking. While I was on the bridge, walking home, I ran across a middle-aged man. And he was walking across the bridge too, so I'm like, cool, I got somebody to walk with, see. And he was walking a bit slow and was slowing me down, With my feet hurting, I'm sort of like in a hurry, I'm ready to go. But, you know, he was somebody to talk to, so I just slowed down to his pace and we kept walking. About a half hour to forty-five minutes after we started walking, a convoy came by. It was a SUV with a five-man boat hooked to the back of it. And they were picking up people that were walking. And they stated that they only had room for one more person. And I figured since the guy that was walking with me was having a harder time walking, that it would be better if he went than I. So he got into the truck with the other guys, and I kept walking. By this time it's starting to get dark. I'm just approaching the GNO bridge, the Mississippi River bridge. I don't know if you've ever been on that bridge, but if you're walking, there are gaps in the bridge. And if you look down while you're walking, you can actually see water below you. So I just kept my head up straight, and kept walking. And, like I said, it was dark, and oddly, I took a wrong turn. Because when it's a bit different, it's dark out there, you can't see where you're going. You sort of lose your sense of direction. And I took the wrong exit. So when I got down to the bottom, I was like "Oh, my goodness, where am I?" So I had to really think about it. So what I ended up doing was walking back up the bridge, and coming back down on the other exit ramp that I knew would take me towards my house. Because I didn't want to take a chance of walking across an empty field not knowing whether that area was flooded or anything and end up, you know, falling in a sinkhole or something like that. So I decided to take the bridge and walk back a route that I knew was safer.

As I get down to the bottom of the bridge, I can remember being able to see the light fixtures. Although it was dark, you could still see the light fixtures because they did cast sort of a shadow in the moonlight. And I knew that was the street I needed to turn down, which was Shirley Drive. I walked. As I'm walking up Shirley Drive, because my feet were hurting, I'm trying to think of the shortcut, you know, because there's a street that you can turn, to get to the street I lived on, that would make the distance seem a little shorter. And you couldn't see street signs. That's just how dark it was outside. You know, I'm standing right next to the street sign and still couldn't read the street sign, so I'm like "Oh, my goodness, my feet are hurting."

I got to this one street, which I thought was Lawrence, the street I should have turned on, and I decide to take that left. Walk down the street and could only get so far because there was a fallen tree. And the tree was so big that I couldn't climb over it. So I decided to turn around and go back. Now that was the confusing part, because when I turned around and went back to the street I was on, I immediately lost my sense of direction. I didn't know whether to go left or go right. Luckily I took the right turn, and walked three blocks down to the street I stayed on.

When I arrived at my house, my neighbor was standing in the middle of the street, and he begin to question me. He's like, "Who are you?" And I'm like, "Mike, I'm Vincent." "I don't know if you're Vincent." And he's standing there with a shotgun in his hand, now, because he's guarding the houses in the neighborhood from looters. And I'm going, "Vincent, I'm Tony's cousin, I'm Tony's cousin." Tony was my cousin that lived in the house before me. And he said, "All right, go ahead." So I go up to the front door, can't get the front door open. So I'm thinking, you know, I know how to break in my house. So I walk around the back. Window's locked, so I couldn't get in there. So I go to the side window, and I broke it, so I can get in. And I went inside.

First thing I did of course was get out of those boots because my feet were killing me. Still couldn't see anything in the house, couldn't find my slippers, so I decide I'm just going to lay in this bed and try to go to sleep. I slept for a while, woke up, still dark. You know, I go outside, because it was strangely hot inside of the house. Mind you, I stayed in a brick house and they tend to hold the heat, as also when it's cold outside they hold the cold air. But this particular day it was hot, so it held the heat inside of the house. So I go outside and sit in the garage with the door open, to try to get a cool breeze, and eventually, you know, I get tired again so I go back inside, try to take another nap. That time I slept till daybreak. Once day broke, I decide, "Okay, let's see if I got hot water." Because you know, mind you, I had been on this bridge for three days, I smell like—Lord knows. I need to try to get cleaned up. Luckily I had hot water. The gas was still working. So I took a shower and changed my clothes.

And that's when I started to look for things to eat in the house. I knew I couldn't go in the refrigerator because the power had been out so long. Then I remembered the MRE's [military-issue "Meals Ready to Eat"] that my cousin kept stored in the storage room in the back. So I went and found some MREs, since there was gas I was able to, you know, take the MREs out of the box and I actually cooked them in a pot. After that, you know, it was pretty much just waiting. I tried the phone, phone didn't work. I couldn't dial out, so I figured that was a lost cause. But there was a dial tone, that was the crazy part about it. I couldn't dial out but there was a dial tone.

While I was sitting outside in the yard again, my neighbor passed up the street. And because I smoke, he knew I was rationing cigarettes. I'm going to lose it if I run out of cigarettes, so he said, "Man, you smoke, don't you?" He said, "You smoke Marlboros?" I said, "Well, right now, I can't discriminate." So he gave me two boxes of Marlboros, and I was good. He said, "You got something to drink?" And I'm like, "I got a couple of bottles of water in there left." And he said, "Well, you drink liquor?" And I'm like, "Yeah, cool," so he gave me a bottle of Seagram's Seven. And once the water ran out, the Seagram's Seven—I would take a capful of it and drink it, just trying to stay hydrated. Because by now it was hot. It's ninety-something degrees. And with the standing water I guess that just made it worse.

And after that I decided, okay, I'm going to walk back to the bridge I left. I got to the interstate and there was some cops standing there. And I just kept walking. And one of them told me that I couldn't walk. And because my feet hurt so bad, I really didn't bother to pull out my badge, I just told him okay and I turned around and went back home. So I'm sitting at home, and on my way home that time, I passed another neighbor about four blocks from my house. He was a blessing in disguise because he said, "Hey man, what's going on?" And I'm like, you know, "I just got off from work. Went home, took me a shower. I was trying to walk back but couldn't go back." And he was like, "Well, you got something to eat?" And you know, normally, you don't trust a stranger, but an instance like this? I'm like, "No, man, I don't have anything to eat, everything in my refrigerator gone bad." He's like, "Well, I got some food in my refrigerator that's still good. You want some?" And I'm like, "Sure," you know, "yeah, cool." And so he gave me some hot dogs, he gave me a can of chili, and some hot dog buns. And I figured, okay, this'll at least last me for a day, maybe a day and a half because I could figure out a way to try to keep the hot dogs cool so they wouldn't go bad. And I ate those. And of course he gave me another pack of cigarettes. So I'm really doing good.

The following morning, I was sitting out on the porch again, and my neighbor that stayed two houses over from me invited me over because he found some shrimp in the freezer, that he was boiling. And we're all sitting out on his porch, and he had a generator, so I was like, I'm in heaven because he had a fan plugged up to the generator, we all sitting on the porch, you know, cooling back, drinking cold, cold drink—because he had ice. And while we're all sitting out on the porch waiting for the shrimp to boil, my other neighbor rides up the street, messing with me: "Man, what you doing here?" And I'm like, "I'm here." And he say, "Well, I'm—." So that immediately made me ask him, "Well, where are you headed?" And he said, "Well, I'm going back to the house to get some stuff, then I'm going to Baton Rouge."

Light goes off in my head: Baton Rouge. And that meant I could at least get to somebody that I knew. And, you know, possibly they have power and everything else. So I said, "Would you drop me off in Gonzales?" because I knew my ex-wife's mom stayed in Gonzales. And he said, "Yeah, I'll take you to Gonzales." Fortunately he dropped me off in Gonzales, but it was about a mile away from where I actually wanted to go, so I had to walk some more. So here I was walking. The strange part there was, when I got in the truck with him I had my sandals on because my feet were hurting. And I knew I couldn't walk that distance in my sandals, reach in the small bag that I had packed, and I had a pair of tennis shoes, but they were mis-matched. It was a left shoe that was mine, and a right shoe that was from my ex-wife, which meant one shoe was smaller than the other. So I put them on anyway and started walking.

And, now, a smoker's worst nightmare is to have cigarettes in your pocket and you don't have a lighter. So I'm walking. I'm needing a cigarette, but I'm toughing it out. And I finally cross this daiquiri shop. I wanted to find out exactly how far I had to walk because I knew Burnside was in Gonzales but I didn't know exactly how far it was for my destination. So I stopped in there, and I asked him how far I had to go. And he said, "Oh, it's right—you're not too far away from it, once you get to the Wal-Mart, you're there." And when I told him that I had been walking, and why I was walking, he was like, "Oh, man, you serious?" And I'm like, "Yeah, man, you know, I'm stranded. I'm just trying to get to where I'm going." He couldn't leave at the time because he was pretty much running the daiquiri shop, but any guy working in a daiquiri shop is going to give you what he can give you, so he gave me a daiquiri. Which in the heat, cooled you down. You know, it had a little alcohol in it, but not enough to make me hot. So, I thanked him for that and I kept on walking. And about a half hour later, I reached my destination. My ex-wife was at the Wal-Mart, and we walked over to her mom's house.

Her mom didn't have enough room for the both of us. You know, so we were trying to figure out where we would go from there. Luckily, I had a yellow card in my hand with some phone numbers that I had wrote down before I left the house. And it had my friend's phone number on it, so I called my friend and asked her if she could come get us from Gonzales, which was about a fifteen-minute drive from where she lived in LaPlace. So she agreed to come get us. She already had a house full of people but she still agreed to come get us. So she drove to Gonzales, picked us up, and took us back to her house. And we slept at her house for two days. We slept in her computer room on the floor.

I decided to call my sister. You know, she was glad to hear from me, wanted to know where I was. I'm like, "I'm in LaPlace. Where are you?" She said, "I'm in Atlanta. But we're on our way to Houston." So I'm like, I've driven the highways some years prior, I knew that she would have to come that way and take a slight detour to come get me. So I asked her if she would come pick me up in LaPlace. So she agreed, she picked us up, and brought us to Houston. Mind you, I still didn't know where we were going to stay when we got to Houston. And even when she told me that we were going to this church of my cousin's, I still thought we would be sleeping inside of a one-story dwelling with a whole bunch of other people. Because here I am, I felt I was homeless, didn't have anywhere to go.

But when I got to our destination, which was the Shrine of the Black Madonna in Houston, I was surprised because it was actually like an apartment complex. Actually, we slept in a spare bedroom that my cousin had that night, and the following morning, there was an apartment right next door to hers, that belonged to a friend of hers and that she was able to use. She called him and told him the situation, that we were evacuees and wanted to know if we could use that apartment, which was right next door to hers so I was still, you know, fine with it. And he said yes, so we pretty much used his apartment for a place of residence until later on when we got all our paperwork squared away and they gave us our own apartment. And I've been here in Houston ever since.

The Shrine of the Black Madonna is a church that's pretty much— I want to say nationwide, but it's not exactly nationwide. There are ten shrines, where at this time I can't recall all ten of them, but the first one started in Detroit, Michigan. And they also have a plot of land in South Carolina called Beulah Land, which is a pretty large plot of land. I can't remember the actual square footage of it right now. But, you know, it's a big church family that lives communally. And they practice what's called Black Christian Nationalism.

When I arrived at the Shrine, and saw that it was an actual place of living, I felt comfortable. The people there, they fed us, they helped us seek medical attention. They really cared for us, you know, which in my state of mind at the time was a big help to me. Because I was psychologically messed up, I was infected from being in the water for such a long period of time. So, you know, them getting me the proper medical attention and being able to see a doctor and a psychologist, you know, really helped out a whole lot.

Since I've been here in Houston, a lot of folks ask me if I plan to ever return to New Orleans. As of right now, I feel that I'm in limbo. Because when I first got to Houston, I was like, I'm going to make Houston my home, I'm not ever going back to New Orleans. But because of the job market in Houston—there are many jobs here, it's just that you need a lot of qualifications to get those jobs—I may look into other venues as far as employment, which may draw me back to Louisiana. I'm just not sure of it. The only thing that I'm worried about in returning to Louisiana is that if I'm living in New Orleans, the city isn't fully rebuilt yet, so I wouldn't actually have a place to stay and call my own when I got back. So other than that, you know, I'm just going with the flow.

Vincent stayed in Houston, living in the quarters of the Shrine of the Black Madonna until 2008. During that time, he helped his stepfather return to New Orleans and enjoyed the company of his mother and son, both of whom live in Houston. Since returning to New Orleans, he has been spending most of his time with his father's family.

GLENDA JONES STEVENSON HARRIS

"The miracles that I saw"

Glenda Harris's life revolved around the Lower Ninth Ward, one of the neighborhoods most ravished by Hurricane Katrina. The "Lower Nine," as it is known to insiders, is one of the newer sections of one of America's oldest cities. Although a poor neighborhood when measured in terms of residents' income, the Lower Nine possessed a relatively high rate of homeownership. Many extended families settled in clusters, in separate houses sitting within sight of one another.

The Lower Nine is indeed low in elevation and for that reason has tended to suffer from heavy rains, let alone hurricanes. Flooding is a continual theme in neighborhood stories. In 1965, the devastation caused by Hurricane Betsy was concentrated in the Lower Nine. The levees broke during that storm and residents, including Glenda's relatives, were convinced that the government had intentionally dynamited the levees to divert flood-waters from the French Quarter, thus destroying the Lower Nine for the sake of saving the richer, downtown neighborhoods. Official sources have never found evidence to prove that the levees were "blown" in 1965, but many lifelong residents of the Lower Nine have their own reasons, memories,

Glenda Harris, at a rally in support of child Katrina survivors, Houston City Hall, 2007.
Photos by Dallas McNamara.

testimony, and evidence to support their convictions. In earlier years, it was a well-documented and not uncommon practice for residents on one bank of a river to dynamite the levees on the opposite bank in order to spare their own land at their neighbors' expense. In 1927, during the Great Mississippi Flood—a disaster that displaced about 1,000,000 people from their homes in the American South—the federal government did indeed dynamite the levees south of New Orleans to spare the city. This event is well remembered

in New Orleans. Even before Katrina made landfall, stories were circulat-
ing through the Lower Nine that some were planning to "blow" the levees
again, "like they did in '27," or "like they did in Betsy."

As Glenda Harris grew older, she witnessed the decline of the Lower
Nine in the face of drugs, crime, and poverty. She determined to dedicate
herself to reversing that decline: one year prior to Katrina's landfall, she
became the ward's first advocacy director. Among her many self-assigned
tasks was to study and strategize how to evacuate the Lower Nine in case of
a hurricane. Glenda knew that another hurricane would bear down on her
neighborhood, though she did not expect to use her training so soon.

Glenda was a member of the first training session mounted by the Sur-
viving Katrina and Rita in Houston project. The project began its work with
inadequate recording equipment. Folklife specialists from the American
Folklife Center were co-teaching the sessions, and after hearing Glenda tell
her story, they recommended that it be re-recorded on broadcast-quality
equipment so that it could be shared with a wider audience. Therefore,
Guha Shankar of the American Folklife Center recorded the following
interview on January 26, 2006; project codirector Carl Lindahl asked the
few questions; Glenda told her story with little prompting.

Well, I was born in New Orleans, Louisiana. I'm the eldest of eight
children. I was raised in New Orleans, [in] the very community that I lived
in at the time of the disaster. In 1965, my grandmother built a house the
month after [Hurricane] Betsy hit in the same Lower Ninth Ward area. I
was raised in that area, went to private school my first few years of education, and then went to public school. I finished public school and spent
most of my life there, went on to college, raised my family in the very same
community, the Lower Ninth Ward—which is in the eastern portion of
New Orleans.

That community is predominately African American, predominately
low-income homeowners and working-class people. It has changed a
whole lot since I was a kid. We had neighborhoods that were close, and
I saw that community transcend to a community that was just left abandoned for vagrants. But I still stayed there and tried to do all I can to revi-
talize in that community.

When we were children growing up—in the four-block neighborhood
where I lived—everyone I knew in my four-block neighborhood were
homeowners and they were working people: from Miss Brown, who was
a cook's aid at the area public school, to Mr. Butcher, who worked as a
laborer in the sugar refinery. They were all from our neighborhood. And

when we were children, when we played in the blocks, Reverend Spears, who was down the street, or Miss Brown, or Mr. Butcher: if they saw us do behavioral acts that was inappropriate, they would chastise us with their wisdom, and then would send us down the street to our parents, and before we got down the street to our parents, they knew what we had did.

And it was a community effort to raise, a truest effort of a "village [to] raise a child," because I remember the words of wisdom and correction that Reverend Spears gave me, as important as I can remember the words of wisdom that my grandmother gave me, that helped to mold the person that I am today. Now, like other young people, I didn't see that as a child, but now I know the importance of the things that they said to me.

It was that village raising a child that kept me there. Unfortunately, most of the people that were of my class, that graduated in the seventies—we were the baby boomers, born in the fifties—most of us were able to get better educations, get better jobs, to go off to college. And unfortunately, instead of us staying there within the community to improve the community, we evacuated the community and went to the suburb areas. And I think everyone has a right to buy where they want to buy or purchase, but we abandoned those areas and we didn't come back and participate in the schools to give our children in that community a hero to look at: a doctor or lawyer or nurse rather than the drug dealer on the corner becoming their hero, or the young man who might have committed a burglary becoming their hero. So we abandoned our community.

And all that was in me was something that my mother and my grandmother taught me: that [of those] to [whom] much is given, much is required. Those words are scriptural words that come out of the Bible. And I've always felt that sense of honestness. And even those of my fellow students who left my community, I kind of encouraged them to come back, even if you can't live there, to come back and share at the public school, to come back and be a part of a community project to make a difference in that community, because that was the community that raised us. And it didn't do too bad by us. So let us do something to make something positive for another child.

The earlier years of my professional life: I left high school with the privilege of graduating from the high school program. And so I became a nurse and most of my working years as a professional I worked in hospitals outside of our area. We didn't have a hospital in the Lower Ninth Ward. So I worked at Charity Hospital, the major institutions, [and] the smaller hospitals. So, my earlier years of working, I didn't work within my community. Later, as I decided to go off to college (I worked and finished in accounting with a finance and law background), I decided to work for government. And so I worked for City Hall.

You tell people you work at City Hall, and everyone you see is a neighbor down the street. "Well, we got a problem. They got a pot hole in the middle of the street, and we've called and called and no one's responded." And there was a big gap between government way uptown and the local communities. And I thought it was just in Lower Nine, but when I went to meetings in other areas, in Carrollton and on the West Bank in Algiers, which is west of the area I live in, I found people complained about the same problems. So it was important to me to start participating in efforts in my community to improve it.

As time went along I assisted one of the local gentlemen, the local ministers who ran for state representative and I helped him with running for office. I worked in his campaign. He offered me three times and I didn't want to accept the job. I wanted to just be through with it once he was elected. He wanted me. He thought I had the heart for the people of the community. He said I had my pulse on the community. And he asked me to work. So I went to work for him. So for the first time in my life, I was able to come back and work in the community that I loved and lived in for so long.

I'm still a nurse everywhere I go, so health issues are important. The needs of children (that was my first area of outreach with my church) are important. The needs of elderly are so critically important to me; it often bothers me that elderly people make a decision every month if they're going to buy their medicines or they're going to eat. So those issues are personal to me. So whether I'm in the Lower Ninth Ward, or if I'm in Carrollton, of if I'm at a City Hall council meeting, those issues come out of my mouth, and people know that when they see me.

I had the real fortune to work when the next [state senator from the Lower Ninth Ward] was elected, Senator Anne Duplessis. She appointed me as an advocacy director. The new governor, Kathleen Blanco, decided that we needed to make [government accessible]. We talked about it so much during the campaign that we needed to make government accessible to the community, so the governor decided to make a pilot project and put advocacy centers in the community. Our advocacy center was the first in the state of Louisiana. And we had just completed a year, right before the storm hit. And we were successful in accomplishing tasks of [pooling] the resources of government and an information bank and a library, and making resources readily available to the constituents of that community. The governor and the senator were very well pleased.

I started working with projects within the local community. And I just been appointed to the American Red Cross board of Brother's Keeper that dealt with hurricane evacuation, and there's a long story about that, that started back from January of last year. And we were talking even with the Mayor's Council on Aging that we would have an appropriate evacuation plan to evacuate the seniors, and that was a concern for me.

When [Hurricane] Ivan happened, almost two or three years ago, eighteen thousand body bags were brought in by the National Guard, because even if the appropriate evacuation would have taken place in New Orleans, these many elderly, these many people that were not able to be readily transported, were assumed to have been lost. And so it was important to me as we talked about the Brother's Keeper's program, which was the mentoring of a New Orleans ministry, with a ministry outside of the shoreline [thus out of hurricane storm-surge range], with transportation for elderly and those who didn't have transportation to get into a safe harbor. And so that's why we worked so hard with this campaign. And I couldn't walk away from that burden of dealing with that: that any life loss was the wrong life loss. And so if it took forty hours out of my one day, it was worth not losing a life.

Carl Lindahl: When Katrina happened you must have thought a great deal about your experience earlier on.

Oh, I did. I said, "Lord, this is why I couldn't stop thinking about this." This is why I couldn't stop dealing with this. I couldn't understand why was it such a burden for me that it wasn't important to that many people. I encouraged the mayor, because I knew Mayor Nagin, and I started encouraging him, so he started getting [help] to get involved with setting up contracts with Amtrak and with the New Orleans Steamship Association, to [seek] other transportation means: that we couldn't just sit on this, that we had to operate.

So my office had been watching the storm tracks [of Katrina] from when it first was projected that it was going to go to Florida, ten days out. And so that Friday, I kind of instructed my staff, "We're not going to do anything we had scheduled. I want everybody to get on the phone and call the elderly people in this community." Because we're a close-knit community. "You know the families, you know what's going on. Anybody needs to go to the grocery store to get water, anybody needs any assistance to get medicine, extra medicines, anybody needs to get that, that's what we're going to do today."

And so we did that. My administrative assistant assisted us in that. Everyone that was in our office, she got on the Internet and got all of us hotels in safe zones outside of New Orleans while we worked hard on it. So that Friday I spent my day knocking on doors, making sure you have water, talking to Miss Ellen, talking to Miss Sue: "Have you called your daughters? Have you called your son? When are you going to leave from out of this community—because your sons and daughters live in suburbs away—when are they going to come and get you? Do you need some help to get to them?" You know, and we did that. And we went into the community. We went into the area pharmacies. Both—out of the three area pharmacies in our area and asked Majestics, and asked H and W, and asked Walgreens to give them extra medicines, so if they're on the highway they will have enough to last them and sustain them.

And so we spent our Friday doing that. And by Saturday, I started preparing my two young daughters, who both are young mothers, that we would be leaving out of town, evacuating Saturday. So that's exactly how we addressed it. And so on Saturday I just went kind of into evacuation mode. Once I had felt that I took enough time to go to the senior citizens center on Friday and dedicated my time to seeing those people that I could see about, and my other four staff members, that we had done all that we could do for the community, and I conveyed to the senator and to the area representative and to the council person what we had gotten accomplished—then it was time for me to take care of my family.

On Saturday I went into my own personal family evacuation mode, and after I prepared, I called both of my daughters, really late that Friday night and told them to get ready for Saturday—we were going to be leaving Saturday. And I did that primarily because both of them are young mothers and I did not want the risk of them trying to scramble at the last moment with young babies, trying to evacuate the city, and having the lack of transportation that they have. So we prepared Saturday. I packed Saturday morning, and for some reason inside of me, I locked the front gate to my home—my wrought-iron gate, and the back gate—which I normally never did, and said something that old ministers say when you put a body in the ground. I said, "Lord, into thy hand I commend the spirit of this house. And only You will keep it standing if You decide that it's going to stand. And only You will do whatever You have to do with it."

And I put my luggage in the back of my car, and the other papers and documents that I needed, and I left my home and never went back. That day, I checked with my daughters. They were preparing and getting ready. I told them to be ready for about three o'clock that day. All that day I rode around and saw family members. "Are you leaving? Are you going? Have you prepared? Do you have a way out?" And for some reason, there was a cousin that I had, who lived all the way uptown on Carrollton. I hadn't seen this girl in five years. Her mother and I were close. Her mother was deceased. And something inside me told me to go and see Debra and see about her. And I went up to go see about her. She said, "Girl, no indeed. I'm not leaving going anywhere. I'm going to stay here and ride this out. You all rode the roads for [Hurricane] Ivan and nothing happened. I'm not going anywhere." And I sat there trying to convince her. "But I'm glad to see you, girl. I hadn't seen you in so long." She said, "I know you're my cousin. I know you love me, but I'm not going nowhere." I tried to convince her. I offered to pay for her to be transported out. I offered to bring her out. I offered to rent her a car to get her out. And she wouldn't leave. So I went back home to my local family. Most of my immediate family lives in the neighborhood where I am. And we decided that we were going to leave that afternoon. My aunt was waiting for her son to get off from work. And she sat there, my elder aunt, who's my mother's only living sister left, saying, "Well, I don't know what I'm going to with your uncle Jessie." And my uncle Jessie's seventy-nine years old, but he's a bilateral amputee and he's had a stroke and only has the use of one arm. And I told her, if you'll excuse the French, "What the hell you mean what we going to do with Jessie? When we throw Jessie in the car he can't come walk back out. I'm not worried about what Jessie said." And she said, "What were you telling Jessie when you were back there talking to him? 'Hey, Jessie, how you doing? What's going on?' You didn't tell him we were leaving. You didn't try to convince him."

"I'm not going to try to convince Jessie, because me and Brian going to pick Jessie up, because he's bedridden, and we're going to put him in the back of the car comfortably, and we're going to go where we have to go. Jessie can't take care of himself and so we're going to have to make decisions so that he will be safe and he will live. Because if a storm happens you're not going to be able to get Jessie out by yourself."

So at about midnight, my cousin decided—we all got together by my aunt's house and you would think it was Mardi Gras. There must have been about forty cars. We thought it was going to be eight cars. There must have been about forty cars outside. We were blocking up all the street where my aunt lived at. We all getting together to leave. Everybody with their sandwiches and the cold drinks for the kids and the luggage. We all thought when we left that night the storm was going to hit, it might be two or three days we'll be gone. There might be some damage to the community, but we'll be able to come back and repair it and restore it. None of us expected what happened, that happened. But in my spirit I kept feeling like one day it's going to happen to New Orleans, because New Orleans had been spared three times the year before, when it kept hitting Florida. One day it was going to happen. But I still wasn't thinking it was going to be that day.

So at about midnight we left. It wound up being about eight cars at midnight, and then three to four cars left later. My brother and them left later. Most of my immediate family left. The only immediate family members that I left in New Orleans was my youngest daughter, who was a manager at one of the area hotels; my sister, who was really fighting with the elder cousin who raised her 'cause she didn't want to leave, and so they were putting off leaving till Sunday morning. And I kept trying to encourage them to go, but they said they'll wait. So we left that Saturday night, and the only time we had any traffic jams was with [what] the state and local officials call the contraflow, and I need to explain that. The contraflow is when all of the interstates that exit the city turns outward, eastward out of the city. There is no traffic that comes in the city. It's called contraflow, so the outgoing and ingoing lanes go one direction.

And so while we were there in Metairie, at the point of contraflow, we might have been in the line, in a little traffic for about fifteen minutes, but after that there was no traffic in the midnight hour on those roads. And I have to slow my cousin down, because he was the lead, and I told him, "Brian, I haven't slept all day, I've been around." He said, "Nobody told you to be a Paul Revere all around town, running and rallying everybody up." He said, "So you should have slept. You know we had to drive tonight." And I said, "I didn't know when we were leaving."

And so we stopped in Baton Rouge. And then, when again I told him I had to stop in Lake Charles, he said, "We not going to do all this stopping." But the traffic was moving really well, and all the kids were comfortable. They weren't angels, but they were comfortable. They knew we were going to safe harbor. Because for our children, most of them thought, "Well, we're going to be able to go to Astroworld when we get to Houston." They're not thinking about the hurricane or the affects of the disaster we were facing. All along the road, we all listening to the radio, trying to hear what's going on in New Orleans, concerned but saying our immediate primary intention at that point was to get everybody to safe harbor.

Well, about a quarter of eight that morning we arrived in Houston at the hotels that we had reserved. We got everybody in their rooms, got everybody safe, and then when we got in the rooms we started calling. And I wanted to call to make sure my brother left and my sister left. Well, the sister who thought she would be leaving on Sunday morning did wind up leaving that Saturday night about two or three o'clock in the morning and she went to one of the area hotels. Well, she was only there a minute, because when she started hearing more and more about the storm coming to the Gulf and New Orleans was going to be hit, her and her husband decided that, "Well, we must move on." And he had family in Mississippi, so they decided to go to Mississippi rather than come to Texas. And my daughter, who was the only one, my youngest daughter, who was left there—she was in the car with them.

Now, grant you, I was concerned about leaving her, but I had her two younger children, and my words were to her, "You can make a decision to stay for your job, but they can't make that decision," and she didn't argue with me because she knew I meant it, that I wasn't going to let them be a fatality in a storm [when] they didn't have a right to choose if they would stay or if they would leave. And so I was comfortable that my two grandbabies were there with me and they were safe, and that their mother had gotten out safely. When I talked to them last, they were above I-12 in Mississippi on their way to Natchez, Mississippi, which was a pretty safe area according to where they said the storm surge was going to be.

So by the next morning—all night that night on Sunday, and all day that day, we all sat by the TV, everyone waiting to see what would happen. And when we saw that Monday, after the storm surge had passed New Orleans, that once again a barge, or what was alleged that was a dynamiting of the levee, that led to the flooding of our community, many of my cousins and my other family members were angry. Because there was much rumor and much paranoia that that's what happened in [Hurricane] Betsy. And that's why there was flooding in Lower Nine to all those homeowners because the local levee was dynamited so that they could relieve the water pressure off the other part of the city. So they felt angry about it, because [in 1965] they lost their homes and they lost everything that they had.

Later, the news [reported] that the 17th Street Canal later was damaged, and the area in Metairie and Lakeview was damaged, so it started relieving them, but I tried to share with them in truth, anyone who had a loss was not good for any of us, because we shouldn't rally or say that it's now fair that they have lost some property, because anyone who's had a loss is all of us who had a loss. I'm sure that there were people who were damaged by the levee breaking in Lower Nine as there were people who were damaged in Metairie, so it's still families affected. They say, "Go ahead, Glenda, you Miss Goody Two-Shoes, you always got to find a positive role." I said, "Well, God's going to take care of us, so I'm not worried about it."

Right after that, we had located all of our family members, everyone was safe, and I thank God we didn't have any fatalities. Our next thing was what do we do now about our survival. The news reports have said our whole area's flooded, so there's no home for us to go back to, so we got to start looking, to start looking at least for some temporary shelter until the water pressure is relieved in New Orleans and we can go back in those areas.

I was blessed in that my eldest daughter, who was there with me, with her two children: one of the local churches who came by to assist us. The mentor that was assigned to her from that church knew about a job with a company that deals with local telemarketing services. And the telephone company immediately hired her. That was the Tuesday after the storm. So once I knew she had employment, I was going to assist her with getting an apartment, because living in hotels was very expensive. Now, grant you, during that time, we were blessed and we were fortunate [for] every opportunity of resources that Houstonians offered to us—churches and nonprofit organizations—I was very pleased.

People were very helpful. I went to the grocery store and people were telling me, "Look, you know, if you need some food, my church is giving out food. If you need some clothing—." And when they would see me with my small grandbabies it was amazing. I had people walk up to me and give me twenty-dollar bills. I was in a grocery store line in Kroger's and a lady said, "Let me pay for everything in your basket." Bought the babies milk. When they got all their milk, they bought their Pampers. Bought everything they needed and I was saying, "No, I'm all right," and they'd say, "No, we have to do something."

There were people in the VA Hospital. I went there to get my uncle some other medicines. A lady was there letting people use her cell phone because people's cell phones were not working from New Orleans. She just stood in the lobby: "Look, I got to do something." Sitting there with tears in her eyes. "I got to do something. Take my cell phone. You need to call somebody? Call or do anything that you need to do. Don't worry about if it's long distance or whoever you need to call."

So everyone felt that there was something that they had to do for you. And so I was so blessed by it and I said: "God, you know, this is just a miracle." Everyone who I've talked to since this tragedy's happened asked me, "Well, Glenda, what was so great about Houston, that people went to Houston?" I share with them that I think the greatest thing about

Houston, Texas, for us as a matter of evacuees was that before the federal government or any governmental agency could say anything, the people out of their hearts in Houston reached out their arms and reached out their hands and reached out their heart to say, "I understand. If it's not but by the grace of God it could have been us rather than you all. So we're grateful and we're going to do all we can to help you."

I've witnessed in my lifetime some things. I always saw people in Louisiana show love, because we're folkish people. But I never—it was amazing to me to see whole families: I saw a young couple out of Spring Tabernacle Church take another young couple that I referred to them and bought them every room and piece of furniture that they needed. And I know that had to be very expensive, but because they had to do something—. It was amazing to me. I stood in the middle of Gallery Furniture store crying. And no one, I guess, could understand, but I realize now that I don't cry about what I lost. I cry about the miracles that I saw. Because when we get all the houses and land that we have to get, our legacies ought to be about how we touch the lives of people, how we make a difference. Because that's our truest legacy. Because when we're buried in a grave in the ground, we can't take a house with us, we can't take a car, but what we can take with us is the lives of people that we touched and how we've made a difference.

And when a lady came to me to say, "Well, let me do something for you, Glenda," I told her I was able to get my furniture and get the things that I needed, but I knew that young couple didn't have a way and they didn't have any finances to do it. And later on that day, another minister called me who knew about my past, said, "Glenda, I know you're working with some families there in Houston. Let me do something to help them. Do you have a place to stay? I want to find out." I say, "Well, I'm all right, Pastor, I'm all right." He say, "Well, rather than me taking by furniture for a family, let me pay the rent for two families." And so I saw the blessings in the word of God come true, that when you give just to the least of these, He will double the offering. I saw that over and over and over again.

I could stay all night telling you about miracles that happened. I started thanking God that God started keeping my family safe. My grandson who has sickle cell never had a crisis: immediately when I brought him to Texas Children's Hospital, they said anything he needed, they would provide. I had so much food that people had given me. My daughter said, "Mama, don't bring no more food, somebody [laughing] else must need some food. Don't go get anything else." And that's how God have blessed us. And I said, "God, look at You." I said, "in the midst of where we only left New Orleans with three days of clothing, You have given us more than what we've needed. Look at, look at you, God, that everyone's safe. We didn't have to go back to bury anyone. We might have lost houses and land, but we have our lives to rebuild again."

And that was the thing that was important to me, as God started moving me throughout Houston when I went to the Reliant Center, when I went to George Brown, and I found people that had been through the shelter process at the Superdome, who were angry, who were upset. I was able to direct them to resources that helped them and even brought some of them to the facilities that helped them. It made a difference for me, it gave me something to do more than just to think about what I had lost. And every day became the next day of assignment. I left my house in the morning, left the hotel (I call it my house) in the morning at eight or nine o'clock and I didn't get back till five o'clock in the evening, like I was on a regular job.

But it helped me and it healed me to know that God would provide wherever I was. And that's what was important to me. Since this has all happened, I thank God that all of my family members are in their own apartments, they've accessed all the resources that they needed.

I lost my whole home. My home. I've been back to the area. My home was down the street, and I thank God that God had given me some wisdom, that I had the appropriate insurance, and I believe that was the hand of God too, because it allowed me to be free, because I was able to work with my insurance very easily; it allowed me to be free to help other people who were having problems with their insurance company, or who didn't have insurance, to assist in with applying for FEMA, or knowing where to go to get assistance that they needed. I was so grateful to see the Disaster Recovery Center open, because it was like I had a regular taxicab bringing people into the Disaster Recovery Center. I remember one time, the lady I met at Spring Tabernacle Church said that their church were going to help a few families. And I started bringing people to the church, and she said, "Well, Glenda, I just got a question: how many people did you tell, that we were doing assistance?" I say, "Well, you know, I got a big mouth, so I tell everybody when I find something good, and I find people who have a heart." She said, "Well, you know, Pastor really appreciates it, but I don't need nobody else to tell, because Sister Glenda tell everybody. Everybody come through the door, 'Sister Glenda told me that you all were helping people here,'" and they were so loving, and they were so helpful, it really was amazing to me.

And now that we're past the point that everybody has their own apartment, all the kids are in school, everybody's in good health, and my great-uncle and my aunt have their medicines and everybody's kind of situated, our goal and function right now as a family is to look at our long-term goals, where are we going to get [our] home. The community that we lived in Lower Nine has been projected not [to] be redeveloped. I love Houston, I love the people of Houston. They've done a wonderful job. But I know the assignment that God has for me, for all that I've done here, He has prepared me to go back to rebuild that city. And I don't know if I'm going to be there a lifetime. I don't know if I'll be returning to Houston, but I know that my responsibility is to go back and build New Orleans back again. Because for all of its problems of high crime, for all of its problems of poverty, for all of its problems of political corruption, for all of its problems of a failing school system, it was still the city that people cared [about]. It was still a city that people who loved, loved hard. And I believe that New Orleans has a place in history, and it's a place in history more than that the worst disaster America has ever faced. I think it's a place in history where the best and the brightest of musicians have come, the best and the brightest of cooks and chefs have come, the best and the brightest of people in entertainment have come, the best and the brightest have been developed. We have the major universities—Tulane University, Loyola, and UNO, LSU Medical Center—that put out the best and the brightest minds this country has ever had, and I think if we start focusing on the positive of what New Orleans has to offer, and we start focusing on the best that New Orleans has to offer, then we can rebuild that city. And, you know, and I love Houston, and anything that I can to contribute to this city, I'll do. I think that my family for the most part, most of the younger people in my family, my young daughters have found great opportunities here, and want to stay here in Houston. And I applaud that. I applaud them wanting to move forward and be progressive.

But most of us who are middle-aged homeowners, because of our love and our growing up in the city, want to eventually return, so we'll be returning to help in the rebuilding of that city. My only hope is that I have a great-aunt that's about eighty-nine years old, and I'm watching her deteriorate; she keeps telling me she's fine, but I'm watching her spiritually deteriorate because she's doing like Dorothy in *The Wizard of Oz*, clicking her heels, saying, "I want to go home. There's no place like home." And I'm trying to do all I can to just rebuild the house. If I can't build but two bedrooms, to build a room that I can get her as close to New Orleans as I can. Because I believe that she ought to be home. And if home for her is New Orleans, that's where I want to be, and if that's all I got to give her, then that's what I want to do. So, that's my story.

Carl: Well, it's an amazing story. That takes my breath away. I wanted to ask you a little bit, about your aunt. At age eighty-nine, does she remember when they blew the levee in 1927?

Vividly. Vividly. In 1965 was Betsy. In September of 1965. My aunt lived very close to the area where the levee was broke. And her words always was that my great-uncle, her husband, who was living then, decided to stay back when the rest of the family left, and he affirmed to her, to his deathbed, that him and several other men in the community—heard the blasting of that levee.

And so she was very upset that there was damage to the levee [during Katrina]. And there is a question in the minds of many people from that community. The rumor was that it was dynamiting of the levee [that caused the levees to break], but there was no evidence I saw up there. What I saw when I went to visit the community again (because I've had an opportunity to go back) was that there was a barge that broke into the levee. And the barge is still there. This is five months later. The barge was there last weekend when I was there. It's still there. And my concern is the federal authorities had notice of a seventy-two-hour evacuation of that community. What was a barge doing in a harbor navigational canal when that whole area should have been cleared? If there was mandatory evacuation for that city, what was a barge doing in that canal? Knowing the history of that community, that levees were right there, and that we were facing a storm surge and a hundred-and-seventy-five-mile east winds, what was a barge doing there?

And that's what makes the whole matter suspect for everyone, you know. And so I just wish that somebody could answer that question for me. For me, as a homeowner, a taxpayer of that community, because when you remove my rights and, and my choice for a property that I developed and I invested in. I could have lived anywhere in the City of New Orleans, I could have lived anywhere in the country. But the Lower Ninth Ward was my choice. It was my choice. And I did the best to keep my property up, to keep it clean, I paid my taxes, I did what I could do to contribute to invest in that community. And someone decided beyond God, with a natural disaster, to take away my choice.

Like I said, I can't prove it. And probably if that barge hadn't been there, I wouldn't even question it, because I really didn't. I heard the rumors about dynamiting, but I rode that levee, I even walked the west side of the levee, where they say the dynamiting was. There wasn't any damage to that levee. I didn't see any damage, but I did see that barge there that did damage to the levee. And the reason why I suspect that's what happened is the area where the barge was: the homes in that particular area—my sister had a home in that area—it was like her house was completely shattered. It was like a bullet hit those homes. You couldn't see houses for almost four or five blocks in there. So it really made me feel that the water really came in where that barge came in. And that the other part was just a rumor, because I didn't see anything about any dynamiting. And we walked that levee. I walked it from the West Side, from [Delaware] Street—that's where my office was—all the way to North Claiborne where the barge was, and I didn't see any other breaks, but in that area where the barge was.

I went back [to New Orleans] before it was really allowed to be occupied, because of the capacity of my office. I had a connection with that project with the American Red Cross. I had a connection with the National Guardsmen, they were our partners in that community—so I knew the sergeant master who was over the project. He had one of those commercial vehicles, and there were still about two feet of water in the Ninth Ward when they escorted me down to see the community. And that was under the capacity of my office that I went down as, as a program director—they called me the executive director for the Advocacy Center. So that I can come back and share with others exactly what I saw.

And I took some pictures, you know. The first time I went there, it must have been about two weeks. And the water had gotten down to about two or three feet, and they put me in this big truck, and I had to have special gear on, and they rode me throughout the community in the areas and streets that they could access. And that was my first seeing of it.

Glenda was a full-time community advocate long before Katrina hit. Her e-mail address identified her, tellingly, as "GlendaReadyToServe." Thus, it surprised none who knew her that, at the first available opportunity, she became a responder for Houston-area evacuees less fortunate than herself. Within six months of her interview she became the Katrina specialist for the Children's Defense Fund. She used the interviewing skills she had honed with Surviving Katrina and Rita in Houston to conduct and publish a series of interviews of child Katrina survivors.

For several years, Glenda divided her time between New Orleans and Houston. She helped those who moved back to the city at the same time that she tended to those who remained in exile. Because, by her estimates, 80 percent of the population of the Lower Ninth Ward was still in Houston as late as 2008, she had a great deal of work to do in Houston. By 2009, a large number of the Houston exiles were back in New Orleans, and Glenda was spending most of her time there, engaged in disaster response and serving as a lay minister with New Orleans's Ebenezer Baptist Church religious work. She passed away on February 2, 2010, at age fifty-two.

CHARLES A. DARENSBOURG

"If you do not give, you do not receive"

Almost to a person, the older survivors of Hurricane Katrina tend to center their stories on the times and events that transpired before, rather than during, the disaster. No matter how much they may have suffered in the midst of the storm and flooding, their greatest sense of loss surrounds the homes and neighborhoods that no longer exist. Thus, Charles A. Darensbourg's narrative—recorded on March 23, 2006, when he was seventy-four—is, more than anything else, a celebration of the life that he has shared with his wife, in the house and neighborhood that they occupied together for half a century before Katrina destroyed it. His interview is also a tribute to the city that he deeply loves and to the people of that city.

Mr. Darensbourg speaks slowly, precisely, and philosophically, in tones that suggest that, because the place that he has loved so long now exists only in his words, he feels he must make those words sturdy enough to do justice to that place, to rebuild his neighborhood for his listeners, to allow them to see it with their minds' eyes. His first few sentences immediately evoke the scale of his loss. He invokes the fifty years that he and his wife, Jackie, put into planning for their "twilight years," and the savor with which

Charles Darensbourg and his wife, Jackie, at their home in Spring, Texas, 2007. Photo by
Dallas McNamara.

*they experienced every day that they spent in New Orleans. A listener who
has not met Mr. Darensbourg may expect that sorrow will soon overwhelm
him. When he says, "Jackie and I will not start out all over again," we might
expect him to sob. But he does not. He continues to tell the story of a good
life, a story too important to ruin with remorse.*

*That story embraces a major movement in civil rights history. The
home that the Darensbourgs occupied for half a century was one of the
first built in Pontchartrain Park, one of the earliest southern communities designed for middle- and upper-income African Americans. Charles
moved in within a year of the first home sales in Pontchartrain Park and he
participated in the integration of the local Catholic church.*

*When Charles narrates his experience with hurricanes, it is telling that
his first story finds good even in the force of nature that destroyed his home:
in the midst of the storm his father taught the lesson that, "Mother Nature
was a thing of fury, but a thing of beauty," too.*

My name is Charles A. Darensbourg. Before Katrina I was retired.
My wife and I had settled down for our twilight years. During our more
productive years we prepared ourselves for such a time.

Our house was comfortable. It was not a large house as compared
to houses of today but it was a convenient house that we bought in 1955.

We enjoyed our home. Our children were grown and married. Our obligations were met and we were comfortable. We enjoyed an evening sitting on our easy chairs and looking at television. We enjoyed going to the numerous festivals around the area. At the festivals we enjoyed the food and the music. There was always music. We enjoyed the classical music, the popular music, country, jazz, Cajun, and zydeco. We enjoyed the dancing and we enjoyed the atmosphere and of course, in summers, the cool breeze.

On many Sunday afternoons, we would go to City Park where there was always music and food and time to relax and there we would spend the day. Sometimes we'd go to the French Quarter and stay at the tent and listen to music for hours on end. In the French Quarter we'd visit the Flea Market. We'd go to the Moon Walk, sit down, watch the lazy Mississippi flow by and the traffic on the waters. We would go to the River Walk and shop around even though sometimes we didn't buy anything.

Our house, it was purchased in 1955. When this was done there was only a few blocks: one street in Pontchartrain Park near the lakefront. There were model houses but no houses built to be bought and we selected our house from the model houses. We were shown a map of where Pontchartrain Park would be built. It was to be built in a horseshoe shape around the golf course and there would be parks and recreation centers. As the houses were built a few blocks at the time, the streets were made to accommodate these houses. And then the streets were made a few more blocks. And the houses were built starting on the left side of the golf course and proceeded on to the far end of the golf course and around the other side. Our house was on one of the first to be built. After the—Pontchartrain Park was completed, it was home for various classes of people—middle class, more working people, upper middle class, professional people, and we all got along very well together. There was carpenters, bricklayers, mailmen, doctors, lawyers, business executives, people who owned their own business—and we became one.

We attended St. Gabriel Church. At first, St. Gabriel's church was held in the school's cafeteria because the church itself had not been built. When we first came, in subtle ways we were not welcome because we were *Colored* people—at that time this is what we were called, *Coloreds*. And we went to the old church which we had attended before: Corpus Christi. We enjoyed Mass there. And after about a year or two, I told my wife, Jackie, I said, "We enjoy going to Corpus Christi but St. Gabriel *is* our church. We *will* attend St. Gabriel whether anybody else like it or not because that is our *church*." We attended St. Gabriel's church and soon we put together enough money to build the church. And the priest said one day, "The church is completed, but the pews are not there. They are not made yet. The church is air conditioned." And he asked us to take our time to bring pews from the cafeteria to the church so we can attend Mass in the church. And these pews would be used until the new pews would be made. The people had gotten together and moved these pews in one day. By this time the white race and the black race had become almost one— not quite yet—but they were getting there and they came close enough to work together for a common cause. As a few years went on, the relationship became closer and closer until before Katrina we all were one in a congregation. The few who would not be led to a communal Mass, left— did not come back, but they were few.

Pontchartrain Park was the first substantial subdivision built in the United States predominantly for black people. Even though white people were also welcome to buy if they wished to do so. At first only one white family bought a house in Pontchartrain Park. When Pontchartrain Park was built, the section where our house was, was swampland and wilderness. It had to be cleared away for the houses to be built and streets to be built. There was a village on the other end of what is now Pontchartrain Park that consisted of people who yearned to be free—they did not want to get a house in the city—they wanted to be in a village where they would have the freedom to do as they pleased. And they built their houses. They had gardens, raised chickens, pigs, and cows. Some of them took their produce to the French Market to be sold. They had jobs in different parts of the city. And they'd commute back and forth to their village which was in the city, within the city limits but on the outskirts because at that time the city had not built all the way across going toward Mississippi.

My wife and I were married in 1951; I was in the military for two years. When I got out of the service, I was living on Laharpe Street with my wife and her grandmother and we needed to buy a house. We shopped around for a house—and we decided that here is Pontchartrain Park about to be built and this would be an ideal location because it would be a residential community out of the business district, in the city, but away from the business district—and we wanted to be peaceful. And that's why we bought in Pontchartrain Park. And so many people like us felt the same way and purchased houses. And Pontchartrain Park *was* quiet. It was *peaceful* and it was *beautiful*—with the parks, the golf course. And the golf course was itself built like a park with its lagoon and trees. I *loved* the trees.

During World War II, Higgins Shipyard built the torpedo boats, and the torpedo boats were made because they needed something to fire the torpedoes other than submarines, that could go in between the ships and predominately the Japanese ships. They were fast, and they were built by Higgins because Higgins used to build speedboats and pleasure boats, and they were so fast they would—they could be used and although they were small they were seaworthy and could be carried on, aboard the ship and lowered and they would ride in between the Japanese ships and launch their torpedoes and the heavy artillery and large guns on the Japanese ships could not turn and face the water. And the torpedo boats had this freedom by being fast, maneuverable, and they launched a lot of torpedoes, and one of the torpedo boats, PT-109, was commanded by President Kennedy. That's where he was wounded.

And I would like to say also about the shipyard of Higgins, because I was a welder there, and they were still making the landing crafts, even though World War II was over—they were still making landing crafts and I worked on a number of those.

When A. J. Higgins started having a hard time finding contracts, he decided that he was going to sell the company. We didn't know it at the time. He didn't tell us, but we could see that he stopped painting the gantry cranes, the warehouses that used to be stocked with light bulbs and so forth started to diminish, and we could tell something was coming about, so I started looking for other work. And I put my name on the list to go in the post office. And by the time Higgins sold out to Equitable Equipment Company, I had already gone and started work at the post office, and I became a postman.

At first I was bored, because everything in the post office is repetitious. And I had been accustomed to using my hands to weld, to make things, and to do things with my hands. I was using my hands to deliver mail, but it was nothing constructive and I was bored, until I got on route, and I began to know the people, and it was a delightful thing to have the same patrons over and over. And I had the same route for over twenty years. At least twenty-four years I had the same route, the same people. I saw children being born and grow up. I had children follow me down the streets while I delivered mail. And I used to tell them, I said, "Don't get in front of me, because I've got to walk. And I don't want to trip on you. Walk beside me. And when we get to the corner, hold my hand." I'd point to the street, and if their parents agreed, we would cross the street. And if they did not, well then, they would go back home. And of course the parents would watch. And these children grew up and had children, and their children began to follow me down the street.

One day someone asked me, "Why is it there's always children around you? They follow you down the street. When you sit down and eat your lunch in your truck, children always around you. What is it about you that children want to be around you?"

"I said, I don't know. Perhaps it's because I love children so much, and they can see it."

And incidentally, last night my wife and I called one of my patrons from Lakeview where my old route was, and we were glad to talk to each other. The family is well. Not living in New Orleans anymore—their house was just completely destroyed. And I told them that our house was destroyed, and the water came up to the ceiling. The house is still standing, but it's unlivable because of the mold, and everything in the house destroyed, except two pieces of furniture which was still standing—when they were handled, they just fell apart.

And she said the same was with her house. It was completely destroyed, even though it was still standing. I said, "What about the rest of Lakeview?" She said, "All of Lakeview is gone. It was all destroyed because of, it was all under water," just as Pontchartrain Park, all was destroyed, because it all was underwater.

[Lakeview] was a white community, during the time [that I worked there]. Since then a few African Americans has moved in.

And one time I substituted—a carrier asked me, "How do you like this route, with all of those old people? Most of the people on this route is old." I told him that old people are some of the most delightful people on earth. It takes a while for them to get used to you, but once they get accustomed to you, and they learn to like you, they love you, and you get along very well with those old people. And I love to be around old people.

When I look at the city of New Orleans since the storm, I say this is something of biblical proportions. It was like reading the Old Testament. More than an imagination of today, because before Katrina I just could not imagine New Orleans looking in such a way.

The first hurricane I can remember was when I was a child. A hurricane came, and my little sister began to cry. And Daddy picked up my little sister, went to the back door, and opened the back door. And he said, "See, this is nothing to be afraid of. It's just a hard wind." He said, "Now look. You see Mother Nature at work. See the, the trees bending back and forth, and look up to the sky. There are birds still trying to fly." Those that were flying west flew freely. The ones flying east were flying backwards because they were trying to fly against the wind, and the wind was blowing them backwards. And she became interested in the birds, and Mother Nature. And she saw that Mother Nature was a thing of fury, but a thing of beauty.

That was when I was a child in St. Charles Parish.

The major hurricane that we experienced in the Orleans Parish was Betsy [1965]. We had more than that came through, but that's the one I remember distinctly, because it was a major hurricane, and the water came up to our step—our house was on a slab, so that was only one step. And it came up to the step and stopped. Did not come through the floor of the house.

There was no light for maybe about two weeks. But we ate quite well because we had gas. But no lights: the electricity of the city, it was out, and everything in the freezer would have spoiled. And we ate steak and eggs for breakfast every day, and we had enough steak and eggs to share with the neighbors, and the neighbors shared with us what they had, because it was going to spoil anyway, so we really ate good.

I was in New Orleans for Camille [1969], but Camille went through the Mississippi Gulf Coast. And at first it was a threat to us, but the media just convinced me that it was just not going to hit New Orleans, and we were convinced that it wasn't pointed our way. And it went, it went through the Mississippi Gulf Coast and the Mississippi Gulf Coast was definitely devastated because up until Katrina that was the worst storm that had come up the Gulf of Mexico in our time.

It did not take us long at all to decide about Katrina, because to my opinion, Katrina was obvious. Before Katrina became a Category 5, before it got into the central Gulf of Mexico, I had a bad feeling about this one. I said, "This one—I have a bad feeling." And when it got into the central Gulf of Mexico where the water was really warm, it became a Category 5 and in my whole life I had never seen a storm so dense. And I told Jackie, I said, "We've got to go, even if it doesn't hit the city of New Orleans, we've got to go because it's so dense." Normally you see the feeder bands come closer and closer to the, to the center, and near the center it was a solid mass of fury. On this storm, it covered the whole Gulf of Mexico with a solid mass of fury. It looked like a complete darkness, and only on the outskirts—so many miles away—would you see the feeder bands. There was no separation in any part of the Gulf of Mexico at that time. I said, this is dense, and it's going to push tidal waves into the shore of the United States that we had never seen before. I could see that. We saw it coming.

We didn't think it was necessary for us to take our car. Because as usual, we evacuated for hurricanes and would come back. We took about four days of clothes and we didn't safeguard our pictures or our trea-sures—things that we wanted to keep for the rest of our lives, we didn't safeguard these things. And we left them, and they were destroyed.

But one thing that I have found: ever since I can remember, you receive as you give. If you do not give, you do not receive. It may not be the same that you give that you would receive, but in the long run it comes back to you in some way or another. And the things that we shared with other people, our pictures—some of the poetry that I had written and different articles that Jackie had collected, shared with other people—after Katrina, just started to come back. Our kinfolks and our friends started sending back pictures that we shared with them. They sent back a few of the poems that I had written and some of the mementos that Jackie had given.

The only poems that I did not share with other people were the poems that I had written for Jackie on our wedding anniversaries, and we did not share them with anybody because I said I want this to be just for Jackie. And I want her to feel something special about these poems.

I did not share them with anybody, so they were completely destroyed—and we did not get them in return. The things that we shared, we got back in return. The things we did not share, we did not get back.

We wanted to leave in a hurry. We didn't want to take too much time because it was upon us and it was so huge that long before the center of the storm would have made shore, there would be destruction, and it could be seen.

We had intended to go to Longview, Texas, and we could not get a room in a motel that was smoke-free, because our grandchild has asthma. So we went to Tyler, Texas. This was not a problem because our daughter had called ahead of time before we left and made reservations. She could not get reservations in Longview so she made reservations in Tyler, so we went to Tyler, Texas. And it took maybe about sixteen hours. I don't remember exactly the number of hours.

During the time we were in the motel, we only came out of our room to eat. We looked at television all day and half the night—and we remember seeing that the hurricane had come through, and the reporter was saying that we dodged the bullet, because the hurricane had not caused as much destruction as we had expected, even though it was a lot of destruction.

And one of the reporters was standing on Canal Street. And every-thing looked so good. And the next day we saw on television where the levee had broken on the 17th Street Canal—and the water came gushing into the city. And it just covered and destroyed Lakeview and

Pontchartrain Park and so much of the city and the Lower Ninth Ward. That was terrible.

I think it was avoidable. The destruction itself was avoidable, because if the levee systems were reinforced they would not have broken. Where I delivered mail in Lakeview, the last part of my route was a street adjacent to [one of the canals]—that part of the levee was reinforced. On that same canal, the other side was not reinforced. It was as high, the levee itself was as solid, but it was not reinforced. None of the levee that was reinforced broke. The 17th Street Canal had levees, but they were not reinforced, and that's where the levee broke. On the others side of the 17th Street Canal, there was a street, and the street was raised, that helped to reinforce the levee that did not break. The 17th Street divides the Jefferson Parish from the Orleans Parish, and the lake did not go into Jefferson Parish as far as I know.

After spending a week in a hotel, and six weeks with relatives, Charles and Jackie Darensbourg, their daughter Lisa, and Lisa's family rented a big house in Spring, Texas, where they now live.

I think it is a wonderful area. The climate is similar to Orleans Parish. I like that. The people are a wonderful people, similar to the people of the Orleans Parish, which is unusual because I am prejudiced about the people of Orleans Parish, they all wonderful people. I loved it so much, and that's one of the things I really loved about the Orleans Parish. The people was so pure.

The people in general, I mean—because during Katrina I had made a statement a number of times, that I was in Korea during the winter of 1952. And I was in the combat zone. And I say, "The combat zone brings out the best of people, and it brings out the worst in people." I saw the same thing happen in Katrina. It brought out the best of people and it brought out the worst of people. The hoodlums who took advantage of the situation to commit crime showed me the worst of people.

The people—the family who took us in was the best of people. Our neighbors here are the best of people. We had lost our car [in Katrina]. We have to go to the doctor, so we had to go to therapy—and the Friendship Center pick us up. They're wonderful. We came to a community where they provided transportation for us to get to the doctor, and to therapy. It's wonderful. Everybody we've met have been so good to us.

Jackie and I will not start out all over again. Twenty years ago, perhaps, I would say, "Oh, my goodness, boy, this is an opportunity. This is a challenge." We'd be all excited about going back, and to build again, and say, "we'll make a new life again." But at this stage, we will not start all over again. We are very fortunate to have our children say we are welcome to be with them.

When I was a child, my daddy asked me, what do I want to be when I grow up. I said I wanted to be whatever the opportunities provide. I will take my choice. But most of all, I want to find peace and contentment. In the Orleans Parish I found peace and contentment. I was living with my uncle in Orleans Parish when I got married. And Jackie and I are married for fifty-four years. And for these fifty-four years I found peace and contentment. As it is with most Orleanians, the people of the Orleans Parish work hard. Work long hours. Work diligently. That includes the working man, the skilled man, the professional man, and the professional women—and when I say man, I say it in the Bible way of speaking, as "man, woman, and child." That's what I like about New Orleans. Not only the location, but it is the people. And I found so much peace in City Park at home, and seated on our recliner chairs, looking at television, and I could just reach across and touch Jackie's hand. And the feel of her hand made me feel so good. And just the knowledge that she was there. Even when we had stopped speaking during the program, in a silent way we felt each other's presence.

I would like to mention that for fifty-four years of our marriage Jackie and I had prepared for today. We wanted to be comfortable in our twilight years. I had a house built that would be suitable to us and our children—when our children grew, we started to make it into what I would consider to be a retirement center. I had planted flower gardens and things that I could do, because I knew that when a person retire, sometimes they get to be bored. I don't ever want to be bored. I said, "Well, this is something I can do. If it is no more than two hours a day, I could work in the yard, and perhaps another day for four hours, and keep the yard neat, grass cut, shrubberies trim, trees trim—and I did plant a number of trees.

And in 1981, I suffered a severe heart attack. When I went to the hospital that Sunday night, the examination showed a mild heart attack. And on Monday I felt well, and on Tuesday I was still in the hospital when I suffered my severe heart attack with a pretty bad infarction. And the doctor explained to me that it was too late to do bypass surgery, because that part of my arteries had already died, and that part of the heart that it served had already died. And the flesh of the heart and the brain are the only two part of the body that cannot rebuild itself, but scar tissue would be built around that area and it would become solid enough to keep the heart from being like a balloon. And that did happen. I was recovering from the severe heart attack when I developed an arrhythmia problem. My heart would skip about six beats. It would race over three hundred times a minute and just stop. And they would shock me with the defibrillator on my chest and bring me back. In four days I blacked out eight times, and they brought me back eight times. In those days—of 1981—the defibrillator implant had not been invented. I was in the hospital from January, through all of February, and into March. This, this left me with a condition that I had to look into, and take it easy. I had to slow it down. And some of my preparation for my future changed, because they said that I would not be able to do as much as I was before, when I retired. So I started to do away with some of those flower gardens. And over the years, I cut it down more and more.

And then Jackie started having problems with her legs, and they was the referral pains from her back. So now most of those flower gardens are gone—I had a garden around the back of the fence, the side fence, and across the back, and on one side of the fence I planted tomatoes against the fence and staked them, and in front of the tomatoes, I had bush beans, and the snap beans were enjoyable. We had so many that we gave to the neighbors, and we cooked some and froze them. And I had four flowerbeds on the four corners of the back yard, and we had a fig tree. We had orange trees, lemon trees, and a grapefruit tree. When I suffered my heart attack and I was recovering—I was home almost a year before I could go back to work—I told my son, "I'm going to do the things that I want to do. I could move a mountain—if I had the time to do it—with a teaspoon." And he laughed. But this is the truth. I said, "Most likely, I'll never cut a tree down again," because I used to tinker with things like that. If somebody needed a tree cut down, I'd cut it down for them, just for the heck of it. This grapefruit tree had grown much higher than I thought it would because I would not have put it so close to the fence. It was too close to the neighbors' house. I had intended it to be the normal size of a grapefruit tree, but this thing grew huge. The neighbors' houses was a two-story building and it grew higher than the second story over, across that house. And I cut it down, which I thought I'd never be able to do again. When I put out the garbage can, there was always two garbage cans filled with a part of that tree. I just cut a little bit down, and I filled the garbage can, and it took me two years to cut down that tree.

So like the mountain and the teaspoon, I had the time to do it, piece by piece, without hurting myself. And I did not even buy a chainsaw. I bought a bow saw to cut down the trunk, and a little bit at a time, I cut that piece by piece, with that bow saw. I had the time. I was retired. And I cut down that tree. And you—when I finished, you could not tell the tree was there. And the neighbor said, "I can't understand how you did that, because it took two, two years, but I don't see how you did it." But I did.

Jackie and I were married fifty-four years ago, and for fifty-four years she has been my sweetheart. And she *is* my sweetheart.

Charles concluded his narrative with an account of his former Pont-chartrain Park neighbors.

The neighbor on one side of our house, when we were inside the house, the neighbor to the right, she left with her children. And she experienced about the same problem with everybody else who evacuated, but she evacuated in time. On the left of our house, not facing the house, but from inside of our house, it is the two-story building that I just mentioned where that tree was; [the owner, Robert] decided to evacuate with his family. His son brought his wife and children to Robert's house and said, "Daddy, I'm going to stay upstairs with my family, even though you're going with Mother, we're going to stay upstairs. This is a two-story house, we'll be safe."

And Robert said, "You must have not been looking at the television and seeing the same thing that I see, because we're leaving, and you've got to leave. You cannot stay here."

He said, "Daddy, I am determined. I will stay here." And Robert said, "I cannot physically take you with me, but I will not leave your wife and children here. I will take them with me. They're coming with me. Now, you're welcome to come along, but I will not leave your wife and your children here."

And Robert took them with his wife and they left. The son stayed in the house. And the water rose up to the ceiling of the first floor, and as the water was rising, he realized there was no place to go. There was no electricity. He said he realized that if he had stayed on that second floor, he probably would have died on that second floor. So he went up to the roof, and he was rescued from the roof.

We have come in contact with a number of our neighbors and friends from Pontchartrain Park, most by telephone, and we have learned about a number of our neighbors who died. At the corner of our house, this old man would not leave. I call him an old man, but he was about my age—to his son, he was an old man. He would not leave, and he died. In the next block from our house, one of my co-workers would not leave; he and his wife died in that house. Around the corner from us, another family died because they would not leave. And another occasion where a son tried to get his father to leave—he would not leave. And after the water began to rise, the son left. He said, "I'm going, because my family has already evacuated; I'm going with them." He could not get his father to leave, so his father died.

My wife was talking to someone else last week, and she said that someone in the neighborhood had gotten into the attic when the water had risen to the ceiling. They suffocated and died in the attic, because there was no way for them to get oxygen. Someone else called and said that in another part of the city a barge had settled on top of five houses, and she didn't realize how large a barge was, because when she see barges in the water, they're loaded down, and most of them is under water, but to see it sitting on top of five houses, she realized how large it was. And she realized how deep the water must have been for this barge to wind up on top of five houses and settle there.

Charles and his wife, Jackie, are still living in the northern suburbs of Houston.

CARL LINDAHL

Epilogue
A Street Named Desire

Heroic Endurance

The common heroic response of these eleven Katrina survivors was, simply, to save each other and thereby themselves. Among the many acts of rescue recited by Marie Barney, Josef Brown, Charles Darensbourg, Nicole Eugene, Dorothy Griffin, Glenda Harris, Sidney Harris, Chantell Jones, Shari Smothers, Angela Trahan, and Vincent Trotter, there are few that would answer to the stereotypical, action-movie definition of heroism. True, Henry Armstrong does dive into poison floodwaters to save a stranger's baby, Angela Trahan's fiancé pulls his charges to safety from a building that is literally being blown to bits around them, Josef Brown breaks into a house to save his mother and aunt from drowning, and Sidney Harris guards hundreds of prisoners on an overpass, standing them off by shear force of courage until reinforcements arrive.

Yet, throughout these accounts, the acts of heroism most often committed and witnessed by these narrators are simple and seemingly tiny

Second liners in Houston, Texas, mark the fifth anniversary of
Hurricane Katrina, August 29, 2010. Photo by Carl Lindahl.

gestures through which the rescuer and the rescued demonstrate their
common humanity. Chantell Jones gives away her tiny cache of food to
strangers' children, an inmate gives a Little Debbie cupcake to his hungry
jailer Vincent Trotter, Vincent gives up his ride to dry land to someone he
has never met before, Glenda Harris is surrounded by strangers in stores
telling her they "have to do something" and offering her everything they
have, just as other strangers step forward and, unasked, provide food,
money, and gas to Angela Trahan's caravan as it struggles toward Houston
on "a wing and a prayer."

Sometimes these acts of rescue are inspired ideas that arise suddenly
and instinctually in the press of cataclysmic events. Watching his fellow
New Orleanians from a perch on an overpass, Henry Armstrong remarks
on the desperate inventiveness that enabled them to keep their heads
above the floodwaters: "I've seen some flotation devices that you would
not believe. I mean we got some geniuses in our race who don't even know
it. I mean, you'd be surprised: empty barrels, telephone posts that's fallen
down—they'd ride them, you know. There's things that before then you
would never have even thought they had use for."

Sometimes the rescuing gestures came, ironically, from earlier experiences in crime, newly adapted to respond to life-threatening situations.
Henry's ability to hotwire cars was what inspired him to commandeer a
water truck and drive it to a thirsty crowd on the overpass.

Yet, most often, the act of heroism that saves rescuer and rescued
alike is not so much an action as a state of being: a heroic endurance

grounded in respect for all human life, a transforming endurance that can turn anyone into a hero. I would argue that there is something inherent in disasters that causes people to rise above the pettiness that tends to dog us all at other times. Henry would agree, for he remarks that "Katrina brought the best out of even the worst of us." Every one of these eleven narratives displays common people exchanging gestures of uncommon grace and goodness.

The older survivors teach us something about the redemptive capacity of transforming endurance. Marie Barney, Charles Darensbourg, and Dorothy Griffin do not report themselves to have committed any heroic acts. In reading their narratives, we might, at first glance, view the narrators not even as actors, but as victims who have been acted upon. In her storm story, Marie Barney often depicts herself as helpless. But as her goddaughter, Shari Smothers, notes, throughout Marie's "story of the losses suffered before the storm and after it, she found humor in her experiences: at times it seemed that she laughed almost in defiance of the difficulties those experiences presented." Marie's transforming endurance is most evident in her ability to laugh.

Charles Darensbourg's transforming endurance rests largely in his steady persistence, as exemplified in his story of the grapefruit tree: after his heart attack, he tells his son, "I could move a mountain—if I had the time to do it—with a teaspoon." He undertakes to cut down a large tree. Charles's son laughs, and Charles himself does not at first believe that he can do it. But, cutting a little bit every day, over a period of two years, he finally makes every vestige of the tree disappear.

In their demonstrations of endurance Marie and Charles show both humility and a deep awareness of their vulnerability. Yet neither trait obscures the power of their love for their spouses and families; rather, their vulnerabilities simply underscore their commitment to family and to fellow human beings.

Essential to the transforming endurance of all of the survivors, old and young, is a recognition that their strength comes to them through others. In reading their narratives, you may feel inclined to see each narrator as the hero, but each narrator, her- or himself, situates heroism in the acts or identity of others. Sidney Harris may fit anyone's definition of a hero, but it was his bond with his nephew that made him overcome his fear and find strength. Henry Armstrong also openly admits his fear, and also finds his strength in the ties that bind him to others: "I knew that they all would be depending on me and I couldn't let them down because

I was Daddy, I was Papa. And everybody knew that Papa would get them through." Thus, the rescuers repeatedly give the rescued the credit for the rescue.

The narrators also express repeated, palpable gratitude for all of the goodness shown to them by others. In reading her narrative, we may identify Glenda Harris as the very definition of the good Samaritan. Yet Glenda herself is reduced to tears by the generosity of others: "I realize now that I don't cry about what I lost. I cry about the miracles that I saw"; those "miracles" were acts of human charity. Similarly, Angela Trahan could have ended her narrative by foregrounding the life-saving exploits of her fiancé, Sam, but her closing words instead express her gratitude to those strangers who provided food, gas, and encouraging words during her family's long drive to Houston.

Such deep expressions of thanks for the smallest gifts are all the more moving because they come from people who know, profoundly, how to give. Once given help, they never forget. Even when given help, or while nearly helpless themselves in the midst of Katrina's fury, they helped others, often saving family, friends, and total strangers, just as friends, family, and strangers have helped to save them.

Although Charles Darensbourg lost the home where he and his wife, Jackie, had lived for five decades, he also learned in the course of Katrina that one receives only what one gives away:

But one thing that I have found: ever since I can remember, you receive as you give. If you do not give, you do not receive. It may not be the same that you give that you would receive, but in the long run it comes back to you in some way or another. And the things that we shared with other people, our pictures—some of the poetry that I had written and different articles that Jackie had collected, shared with other people—after Katrina, just started to come back. Our kinfolks and our friends started sending back pictures that we shared with them. They sent back a few of the poems that I had written and some of the mementos that Jackie had given.

The only poems that I did not share with other people were the poems that I had written for Jackie on our wedding anniversaries, and we did not share them with anybody because I said I want this to be just for Jackie. And I want her to feel something special about these poems. I did not share them with anybody, so they were completely destroyed—and we did not get them in return. The things that we shared, we got back in return. The things we did not share, we did not get back.

Charles offers the key to endurance, the secret to survival: give everything you have. No one will receive any more than what he or she gives away.

The Paradise Built in Hell

Charles Darensbourg had lived in New Orleans more than half a century before Hurricane Katrina forced him to relocate to Houston, Texas. I would understate his case to say that Charles loved his New Orleans neighbors:

> The people of Orleans Parish, they all wonderful people. I loved it so much, and that's one of the things I really loved about the Orleans Parish. The people was so pure.

But apparently not *all* of the people, for Charles continues:

> The people *in general*, I mean—because during Katrina I had made a statement a number of times, that I was in Korea during the winter of 1952. And I was in the combat zone. And I say, "The combat zone brings out the best of people, and it brings out the worst in people." I saw the same thing happen in Katrina. It brought out the best of people and it brought out the worst of people. The hoodlums who took advantage of the situation to commit crime showed me the worst of people.

The worst people seem always to be the headliners in disasters like Korea and Katrina, and even when they don't exist they cast an impenetrable shadow over the pure people that Charles Darensbourg knows best. When nature shuts down the power—beginning with electricity, but extending to encompass the communication and transportation networks that sustain the power to police—disaster reports inevitably discover the worst of people. Those who live outside the boundaries of the chaos create a chaos of their own through a legendary script that turns people into animals. When nature undoes the props of civilization, human nature descends to its lowest common denominator. We would all be good people, if only, like the grandmother in Flannery O'Connor's "A Good Man Is Hard to Find," there were "somebody there to shoot [us] every minute" of our lives. But without that law-and-order gun to our heads, we become subhuman.

So goes the script. But the people that Charles actually encountered in the course of the disaster were anything but subhuman:

the family who took us in was the best of people. Our neighbors here are the best of people . . . . They're wonderful. . . . Everybody we've met have been so good to us.

In his daily life in New Orleans, and during his evacuation to and exile in Houston, Charles Darensbourg *saw* only goodness, but from a distance he seems to have *heard* a great deal about its opposite. In a recorded interview nearly ninety minutes long, he spends more than twenty minutes describing and praising the good acts that he witnessed and from which he benefited, but "The hoodlums who took advantage of the situation to commit crime"—those eleven words are all he has to say in the course of the entire interview about the worst of people.

If everyone that Charles Darensbourg met was the model of goodness to him, where did he encounter the "hoodlums?" Not one in person; it seems that every one of them was introduced to him through the media and its allied legendary scripts.

The script of criminal minorities possesses a staggering power. A few news items, repeated endlessly, whether verified or not, come close to trumping lifetimes of experience. Under the influence of this rumor complex, Charles and the other narrators whose stories appear in this book bestow on "the worst of people" a weight that counterbalances all of the unalloyed good that they actually experienced. Chantell Jones witnessed terrible things in the Convention Center; yet, clearly, the truth was not bad enough, for even in the midst of horrors that she could see, she heard rumors of horrors that never happened: the "euthanizing" of patients at Baptist Hospital and murders at the Convention Center, both stories of human brutality that were later proved false. Similarly, Sidney Harris didn't need the help of rumors to imagine a terrible situation. He was already in one. But poison floodwaters, lack of food and water, prisoners on the verge of rioting, and people in grave need of medical attention were not trouble enough. Even in the midst of these afflictions, Sidney was also afflicted by one of the most grotesque rumors that swept the world in the wake of Katrina: the claim, since shown baseless, that survivors were shooting at helicopters: "We was hearing about all the shootings at helicopters, and stuff at the Superdome, and we was afraid them people might come down there and start shooting so we all had our guns and stuff. We was ready." Charles, Chantell, and Sidney didn't need baseless rumors to make their situations horrific, but all three were in fact exposed to such rumors.

If such legendry could influence even these heroic survivors, we do not have to imagine what it did to the rest of us. As news of Katrina's

devastation of New Orleans spread, it seems that most outsiders immediately assumed the worst: that most of those who had stayed behind in
the city to face the storm remained only for the worst reasons: to steal, to
loot, to prey upon the helpless, and to commit acts of nihilistic savagery
so extreme as to defy any attempt to assign a motive. Shooting at rescue
helicopters? Just to make matters worse?

The legendry of urban chaos stretches back for centuries and its pat-
terns have been studied at some length in recent years. Rebecca Solnit's
research establishes such rumor complexes at work as early as the 1906
San Francisco earthquake (Solnit 2009); Carl Smith's *Urban Disorder and
the Shape of Belief* goes further back, to the 1871 Chicago fire (Smith 1997).

In 2006, I identified this general tendency as the David Effect—the
flipside of a phenomenon that Gary Alan Fine has labeled "The Goliath
Effect." Fine's Goliath Effect posits that legends that assert corporate neg-
ligence and crime will migrate up the food chain and ultimately attach
themselves to the largest corporations. For example, the rat rumored to be
stuck in a soda bottle will most likely be found not in an RC bottle or even
a Pepsi bottle, but in a Coke bottle.

I think we tend to find comfort in the notion of the Goliath Effect,
because it suggests that we favor the underdogs and give them the benefit of the doubt. The David Effect, however, suggests less pleasant things
about us. When chaos breaks out in a disaster-stricken city, the fingers of
blame tend to point toward the very bottom: the poorest, the most marginalized people, the people who least conform with the self-image of the
ruling powers.

Yet the survivor storm stories that appear in this book belie the David
Effect. They prove the existence of the opposite phenomenon, a remarkable and positive effect that is far too often overlooked. I speak of what
Rebecca Solnit calls the *Paradise Built in Hell*, to name *The Extraordinary
Communities That Arise in Disaster*. Her recent book of that title is a spec-
tacular corrective to our obsession with legends of post-disaster cruelty,
violence, evil, and neglect.

In spite of the predominance of horror legends in the media and in
our memories, on-the-ground documentation, and especially the narratives of the survivors themselves, has produced an altogether different
view of the motives and actions of the citizens who were trapped in New
Orleans by Katrina. On the outside, government officials, the press, and
the broader public assumed the worst, circulated negative legendry, and
sacrificed rescue efforts to "law-and-order" initiatives. Over the past century such negative legendry has contributed to the loss of thousands of

innocent lives. In New Orleans, only two days had passed after Katrina's landfall when Mayor Ray Nagin decided to suspend life-saving efforts and redirected the energy of the police to containing looting. At that time tens of thousands of people were still trapped in the city without the barest necessities, and many of them were in extremis—needing immediate treatment—which did not come—to stay alive.

Meanwhile, Solnit reminds us, on the inside, survivors, with no or too little outside help, went about the business of saving each other with repeated acts of selflessness and sacrifice. Solnit shows that disaster victims, so far from descending into bestial savagery, do the opposite: they become *better* than they are: selfless, generous, and heroic at levels they have seldom if ever reached before. They become so good that they create perfect communities, refuges of decency, paradises built in hell. As Henry Armstrong states, "Katrina brought out the best of even the worst of us." Henry and his fellow survivors know exactly what Solnit is talking about.

Solnit has finally named a thing that many of us know from our own experience. I had noticed it in my earliest contact with Katrina survivors, in the George R. Brown Convention Center, where the first man who shared his story with me spoke with profound modesty of the almost superhumanly difficult acts through which he risked his life daily to keep seven elderly people alive. Everyone who narrated to me told a story of becoming better than they were—but without a hint of bragging, because they were as humbly astonished by the sheer goodness of their fellow survivors and themselves as I was. I had also noticed the sense of joy—even euphoria—people experience, when for the first time in their lives they find themselves members of groups in which everyone treats all others equally and well. When I co-founded Surviving Katrina and Rita in Houston to record disaster survivors, the very first narrator whom we recorded expressed this sense of a surprising, newfound social utopia. Angela Trahan, who had lived most of her life in the racially divided community of Bay St. Louis, Mississippi, saw that town reach heights of decency as remarkable as the extremes of destruction that the hurricane had wrought:

That was one time our town really, really as a community came together, And everybody chipped in together. A couple people with trucks basically ran a shuttle for people who didn't have a way to get their supplies. Several times in the day no matter where you were you had somebody stopping by saying, "Hey, do y'all have ice, do y'all have water, do y'all need this, do y'all need that?" By that time, of course, people are on survival mode. (SKR-CL-SR02)

All of the survivor narrators whose words appear here seem to share Charles Darensbourg's conviction that the road to healing, the road to survival, runs through generosity: one gets only what one gives.

The essential, selfless generosity of Katrina's survivors must always be borne in mind, because the hurricane has become the center of a fierce national debate over how generous Americans can afford to be. Many have used the baseless rumors of criminal survivors as an excuse for abandoning the survivors. Yet when we look closely at the ways in which citizens have responded to the survivors, we find occasion for hope.

In 2008, a survey conducted by Rice University sociologist Steven Klineberg recorded two important findings concerning Houstonians' response to Hurricane Katrina—one distressing, the other a cause for optimism. When asked if the influx of Katrina evacuees had been a good thing or a bad thing for the city, only 7 percent of the respondents said that it had been a good thing. But, on the other hand, when asked what Houstonians should do if another such disaster drove survivors into their city, the overwhelming majority answered that the city should offer as much help as, or even more than, had been given to Katrina's evacuees. Regardless of what they feel the survivors have been, or have not been, given, Houstonians remain eager to give to those who need. In their own way, the Texas responders, too, adhere to Charles Darensbourg's rule that one gets no more than one gives.

Having received the gift of knowing and working closely with Houston's Katrina communities, I am grateful for their gifts. As their words express, these are not only people who received from Houstonians the life-sustaining gifts that they most needed, but also people who gave, and who continue to give, selflessly to others in need. These are precisely the sort of neighbors that any of us would wish to have.

A Street Named Desire

I introduced the survivor narrators with a brief description of the human tide that overran Houston in the wake of Hurricane Katrina:

> In early September 2005, with New Orleans under water, as hundreds of buses emptied the Superdome into the Astrodome and the Ernest N. Morial Convention Center into the George R. Brown Convention Center, Houston's population grew by as many as 250,000 while New Orleans's dwindled to a few thousand. With stunning swiftness, Houston had become New Orleans West.

"New Orleans West" as a synonym for the newly transformed Houston was a phrase that occurred to me when I first visited the shelters and witnessed some of the immediate effects of the massive, overnight migration. But I did not hear a single survivor utter those words until August 29, 2010, five years to the day after Katrina's landfall.

The survivors did not merely utter, "New Orleans West," they shouted it in chorus while dancing down a busy Houston street in the most remarkable act of festive reclamation I have ever witnessed. The idea was to observe Katrina's anniversary with a "second line" on Richmond Avenue, just west of Houston's downtown, in the trendy Galleria neighborhood.

A second line in the Galleria? Most of us outsiders were deeply skeptical. The second line is the most New Orleanian of New Orleans celebrations: an unofficial, processional dance that parallels the "main line," an official event, say, a parade or a funeral. Second liners follow a brass band, alternately dancing and strutting, and often twirling parasols or waving handkerchiefs as they step in time to the music. The second line was born as an unofficial improvisation and, true to its name, it has kept that loose, make-it-up-as-you-go quality throughout its long history, which stretches back to the African cultures of the ancestors of today's dancers.

Nothing seems more New Orleans and less Houston than the second line. I have good friends who regularly drive the 350 miles from Houston to New Orleans to witness second lines, but who would not think of crossing the street to attend one in Houston. They, and I, simply could not imagine such a celebration unfolding in this city. But I had made promises to people who had gone through much with me: the interviewers and interviewees of the Surviving Katrina and Rita in Houston project. The fifth-anniversary second line was an event I could not miss, even if I grew queasy anticipating how grotesque it might be.

The staging area for Houston's second line was as unpromising as I'd expected. The group assembled in the parking lot of a video game bar called Dave & Busters and was to process a little more than half a mile from there to a hip-hop bar, the Rocca. The Houston police, with no experience of second lines, had cordoned off one lane of a six-lane street, Richmond Avenue, as the path for the dancers. They seemed to assume that second line meant "straight line."

But the dancers somehow pulled it off. Over the previous five years, they had proved their transforming endurance, their will to survive—and not simply to continue breathing, but to live in grace and interconnectedness with their fellow survivors. The Hustlers Brass Band formed the core of the procession. This was an archetypal post-Katrina creation, a pick up band born in Houston, comprising great displaced New Orleans musicians playing alongside an equal number of Houston converts.

The dancing mass spread out, bursting the bounds of its assigned, one-lane route and overrunning all the westbound lanes of Richmond Avenue. In small circles radiating outward from the core, people began their own improvised shows, forming rings around frenzied dancers taking turns in the center. Second liners strutted and danced with each other as they watched their special stars dance alone. In the midst of the procession, survivors would spot fellow survivors, some of whom they hadn't seen in five years, and begin to hug and dance with re-found friends.

One man in the midst of the press followed the band with a street sign he'd pulled from a post in New Orleans: DESIRE PKWY. He held that sign aloft defiantly, as if to rename Richmond Avenue, DESIRE—the perfect label for the new place that the second liners were fashioning with their dance steps.

Taking the street sign as their charter, upward of a thousand dancers re-created New Orleans in the center of Houston. As the dancers began to realize how thoroughly their desires were transforming their world, they became transformed themselves. They chanted, in echoing unison, "New Orleans West! New Orleans West! New Orleans West!" They had crafted that term into something much more than I had first meant by it. They renamed a place where they had been dumped as a place that they had molded to their own best hopes with their feet and shouts and music.

The event had billed itself as a thank you to Houston, but in fact there were almost no Houstonians taking part. Two friends and I were, I believe, the only pre-Katrina Houstonians on the route, and I was the only white male within sight. So people were extra sweet to us. They kept asking us if we were having fun. We were having a good deal more than fun, but it was easy to say yes.

At the end of the line we hung out with a family—mother and daughter—who'd been interviewed by our first trainees, in January of 2006. They had been seriously afflicted by numerous hardships back then. But they were strong and happy now. Nearly every survivor in that procession had experienced some form of rebirth in the course of their post-Katrina lives in Houston, and this one evening was the communal flower of their combined rebirths.

The fifth-anniversary second line was a remarkably choric demonstration of transforming endurance, a festive twin of the narratives gathered in this book. Each of the survivors' stories accomplishes—in a quieter, solo voice—what these one thousand chanting dancers accomplished in unison on the streets of Houston. Each presents a portrait in humility, generosity, and love, a proof that in adversity we can, and do, become better—not worse—than we are. These stories compel us to listen. If we listen closely enough, they will extract from us a promise: that the next time we are forced to witness a mass disaster, we will not let rumor dissuade us from helping, and we will not seek the truth of what the survivors did from anyone but the survivors themselves. In keeping these promises, we will receive the gift of transforming endurance.

Acknowledgments

Part 2 of this book is dedicated, with gratitude, to the spirits of the more than four hundred narrators and interviewers, living and dead, who shared their stories and good will with the Surviving Katrina and Rita in Houston project. Special thanks go to the eleven survivors whose narratives constitute the soul of this section: Shari Smothers, Marie Barney, Nicole Eugene, Henry Armstrong Jr., Dorothy Griffin, Josef Brown, Chantell Jones, Angela Trahan, Sidney Harris, Vincent Trotter, the late Glenda Stevenson Jones Harris, and Charles A. Darensbourg—as well as to survivor-interviewers Phylicia Bradley (who recorded Josef's and Chantell's stories), Darlene Poole (who recorded Sidney), and Johnna Reiss (who, with Nicole Eugene, recorded Vincent); and survivor photographer Dallas McNamara (whose photos of Nicole, Henry, Josef, Angela, Vincent, Glenda, and Charles appear in these pages). Katrina survivor and folklorist Katherine Parker transcribed several of these interviews, refined the transcriptions of others, and lent her expertise to the editorial process.

Additional interview credits: David Taylor, folklife specialist at the American Folklife Center at the Library of Congress, who interviewed

Angela and Vincent; and Guha Shankar, folklife specialist, American Folklife Center at the Library of Congress, who recorded Carl Lindahl's interview of Glenda.

The editors thank the Johns Hopkins University Press and the editors of *Callaloo* for permission to print revised and updated versions of three articles from *Callaloo*'s Katrina issue, *American Tragedy: New Orleans under Water* (volume 29, number 4, 2007): Nicole Eugene, "Bridges of Katrina: Three Survivors, One Interview," pages 1507–12 (Eugene 2006, the source for her chapter of the same name in this book); Carl Lindahl, "Recording Katrina: The Survivor Duet," pages 1506–7 (Lindahl 2006b, a source for much of the chapter in this book titled "Survivor to Survivor: Two Duets"); and Carl Lindahl, "Storms of Memory: New Orleanians Surviving Katrina and Rita in Houston," pages 1526–38 (Lindahl 2006c, a source for much of the chapter titled "Transforming Endurance"). All three articles: © 2007 Charles H. Rowell, revised and reprinted with permission of The Johns Hopkins University Press.

Notes on the Surviving Katrina and Rita in Houston Interviews

The Interviewing Process. As the work of Surviving Katrina and Rita in Houston went forward, we discovered that we were not merely documenting the development of new communities: we participated in their creation. The survivor trainees entered our schools as mutual strangers, but they quickly forged bonds that transformed them into mutual helpmates and friends. Trauma specialist Mary Armsworth has observed that Pat and I, in creating a documentation project, had also unknowingly laid the foundation of a trauma prevention program. Armsworth pointed out that the great majority of people who suffer through traumatic events do in fact recover, through calling upon their inner forces of resiliency (Raphael et al. 2000). Following her lead, Pat emphasized three distinct parts of our project that constitute a three-stage recovery program: telling one's story, forming social networks, and building communities. The day-to-day work of the field schools has generated the first two building blocks. Now more conscious that the process should not end with these networks, Pat and I worked toward ways in which the project could take an active role in community building. We had experimented with several approaches by the time that the project's funds were exhausted, in December 2010. Although our last survivor training sessions took place in 2007, interviews continued into 2011, and we continue to seek means, such as this book, by which we may share survivors' stories with the world.

Transcription Style. The first drafts of most of these interviews were made by volunteers for the Surviving Katrina and Rita in Houston project. The initial drafts included all words spoken by the interviewees, even repeated words, hesitation phenomena, and false starts. Thus, if the narrator had said, "Then, you know, I went— no, she, she went to the Superdome, you know," the transcriber included all of the words.

In the texts prepared for this book, however, repeated words, hesitation phenomena, and false starts were edited out. Thus, the sentence above would be rendered "Then she went to the Superdome." Certain passages of some of the interviews were omitted from this book, either because the interviewee chose not to share them or because the editors deemed the passages too arcane for the general reader. For example, many of the interviewers spoke in great detail about New Orleans geography in ways that only longtime New Orleanians would be able to follow; in other instances, they discussed complex family relationships that were not always understandable to outsiders.

Square brackets are used to enclose words that were not spoken by the narrators; we have tried to use brackets as sparingly as possible. All words outside the square brackets are the narrators', rendered as precisely as we could from the sound recordings.

Copies of the unedited manuscripts of some of these interviews may be found online through the Houston Folklore Archive, http://folklore.uh.edu.

Notes on the individual interviews. Carl Lindahl has added commentary before and after each interview. That commentary often refers to historical and geographic details, and also to various rumors and legends that circulated at the time of the hurricane and that were later found to be distorted or completely inaccurate.

Here follow notes on each of the interviews, including source information for the commentary and further information on the narrators.

Shari L. Smothers, "A New Orleans Life: Sharing Marie Barney's Story." Marie Barney's interview is archived in the Surviving Katrina and Rita in Houston database as SKR-SS-SR10. Portions of Marie Barney's narrative may be heard on the Surviving Katrina and Rita in Houston Web site (2012: http://www.survivingkatrinaandrita .dgs-sites.com/InterviewExcerpts.php). Portions of Shari Smother's and Marie Barney's narratives were published earlier in the magazine, *Houston History* (2010): 37–38. Shari Smothers served as the archivist for the Surviving Katrina and Rita in Houston project, 2006–2007, and contributed to a study of young Katrina survivors (Lindahl et al. 2009). Some of Shari's observations on interviewing appear on an episode of the radio program *Talk of the Nation*: "Can Sharing Stories Help People Heal from Tragedy?" (NPR 2006a). http://www.npr.org/templates/story/story.php?storyId=5691131.

Nicole Eugene, "Bridges of Katrina: Three Survivors, One Interview." Nicole's story appeared earlier, along with a longer version of her interview with Henry and Dorothy, in *Callaloo* (Eugene 2006). Her interview with Henry Armstrong Jr. and Dorothy Griffin is archived in the Surviving Katrina and Rita in Houston database as SKR-NE-SR04. A brief audio excerpt of Henry's story may be heard on the Surviving Katrina and Rita in

Houston Web site: http://www.survivingkatrinaandrita.dgs-sites.com/whoweare
.php. Nicole served as archivist for the Surviving Katrina and Rita in Houston project
in 2007–2008, and in that capacity contributed to a study of young Katrina survivors
(Lindahl et al. 2009).

Josef Brown. Joseph's interview is archived in the Surviving Katrina and Rita in
Houston database as SKR-PB-SR09. His brother Cedric was also recorded for the
project (by interviewer Shari Smothers, September 4, 2006 [SKR-SS-SR14]), as was his
mother, Debra (by interviewer Larry Kraus, April 14, 2007 [SKR-LK-SR04]).

Chantell Jones. Chantell's interview is archived by the Surviving Katrina and Rita
in Houston project as SKR-PB-SR08. When Chantell became a trainee for Surviving
Katrina and Rita in Houston, she was recorded a second time, on June 19, 2007, by
fellow survivor Linda Nellum (SKR-LLN-SR01). For documentation of the verified
crimes and death toll at the Superdome, see Thevenot (2006) and Thevenot and Russell
(2005). For separation from loved ones as the most commonly reported traumatic
experience among hurricane victims, see Lindahl et al. (2009). For evidence that Katrina
survivors' first-person accounts of fellow survivors emphasize their heroism and rarely
report witnessed crimes, see Lindahl (2012).

Angela Trahan. Angela's interview is catalogued as SKR-DT-SR01. Because the
sound quality of her first interview was compromised, she was interviewed again four
days later by Carl Lindahl, on January 27, 2006 (SKR-CL-SR02, an excerpt from which
appears in the Epilogue of this book). Statistics on the intensity of Hurricane Katrina
at landfall in Bay St. Louis are available through the Web site "Hurricaneville": http://
www.hurricaneville.com/historic.html and http://www.hurricaneville.com/katrina.html.
Portions of Angela's interview may be heard on the radio program, "Oral Histories Show
Generosity in Evacuees" (NPR 2006b). A brief account of Angela's extended Frenchtown
and Mississippi families is found in Lindahl (2011).

Sidney Harris. The interview featured here is SKR-DP-SR04. A follow-up interview
of Sidney by Dallas (Alice) McNamara is SKR-AM-SR15. Accounts of the extreme
conditions in the Orleans Parish Prison include Human Rights Watch (2005). Among
the best documentary accounts is the British Broadcasting Corporation's *Prisoners of
Katrina* (BBC 2006).

Vincent Trotter. The two interviews presented here are SKR-DT-SR02, recorded
March 20, 2006, and SKR-SKR-SR01, recorded the next day. A little over two years
later, on April 2, 2008, Dallas (Alice) McNamara recorded Vincent a third time, in
New Orleans (SKR-AM-SR12). Portions of Vincent's first interview were also featured
in a traveling exhibit developed by the Field Museum of Natural History and entitled
"Nature Unleashed," which opened in Chicago in May 2008 and toured the country
until January 2012 (see atureunleashed.php). An interview of Vincent by Charles Henry
Rowell was published in *Callaloo* (Trotter 2006).

Glenda Jones Stevenson Harris. A two-minute excerpt of Glenda Harris's interview
may be heard on the Surviving Katrina and Rita in Houston Web site: (SKR 2012: http://
www.survivingkatrinaandrita.dgs-sites.com/whoweare.php). A portion of her interview
was featured in *Houston History* (2010): 38–39. Some of the stories centered on the

alleged dynamiting of the levees during hurricanes Betsy and Katrina may be found in Lindahl (2012).

Charles A. Darensbourg. Charles's interview is archived as SKR-AB-SR03. Charles's wife, Jacquelyn (Jackie), was also interviewed for the Surviving Katrina and Rita in Houston project on March 26, 2006 (SKR-AB-SR02). Audio of portions of Charles's interview may be heard on the Surviving Katrina and Rita in Houston Web site (2012: nterviewExcerpts.php). Portions of the interview were also featured in the traveling exhibit "Nature Unleashed," which opened in Chicago in May 2008 and toured the country until January 2012 (see http://www.survivingkatrinaandrita.dgs-sites .com/natureunleashed.php). Information about the history of Pontchartrain Park is available through the Greater New Orleans Data Center Web site: http://gnocdc.org/ orleans/6/31/snapshot.html (accessed January 9, 2012).

References

Baum, Dan. 2009. *Nine Lives: Death and Life in New Orleans.* New York: Spiegel and Grau.

BBC. 2006. British Broadcasting Corporation television program, *This World: Prisoners of Katrina.* August 13. Accessed through the Internet as http://topdocumentaryfilms .com/prisoners-of-katrina/, January 8, 2012.

Brinkley, Douglas. 2006. *The Great Deluge: Hurricane Katrina, New Orleans, and the Mississippi Gulf Coast.* New York: William Morrow.

Dyson, Michael Eric. 2006. *Come Hell or High Water: Hurricane Katrina and the Color of Disaster.* New York: Basic Civitas Books.

Eggers, Dave. 2009. *Zeitoun.* San Francisco: McSweeney's Books.

Eugene, Nicole. 2006. Bridges of Katrina: Three Survivors, One Interview. *Callaloo* 29 (4): 1507—12.

Fine, Gary Alan. 1985. The Goliath Effect: Corporate Dominance and Mercantile Legends. *Journal of American Folklore* 98: 63—84.

Guzmán, Mónica. 2005. Westbury High Tension Explodes into a Brawl. *Houston Chronicle*, December 8.

Horne, Jed. 2006. *Breach of Faith: Hurricane Katrina and the Near Death of a Great American City.* New York: Random House.

Houston History. 2010. Surviving Katrina and Rita in Houston. Conversations with Shari Smothers, Marie Barney, Glenda Harris, and Linda Jeffers. 7, no. 3 (Summer): 37–40.

Human Rights Watch. 2005. New Orleans: Prisoners Abandoned to Floodwaters. September 21. http://www.hrw.org/news/2005/09/21/new-orleans-prisoners -abandoned-floodwaters). Accessed January 10, 2012.

Hurricaneville. 2012. Web site with digest of information of the velocity and storm surge of Hurricane Katrina. http://www.hurricaneville.com/historic.html and http://www .hurricaneville.com/katrina.html. Accessed January 12, 2012.

Jasper, Pat, and Carl Lindahl. 2006. The Houston Survivor Project: An Introduction. *Callaloo* 29 (4): 1504–5.

Lindahl, Carl. 2004. *American Folktales from the Collections of the Library of Congress.* 2 volumes. Armonk, NY: M. E. Sharpe.

———. 2006a. The David Effect and the Right to Be Wrong. Paper presented at the annual meeting of the International Society for Contemporary Legend Research. Copenhagen. May 31.

———. 2006b. Recording Katrina: The Survivor Duet. *Callaloo* 29 (4): 1506–7.

———. 2006c. Storms of Memory: New Orleanians Surviving Katrina and Rita in Houston. *Callaloo* 29 (4): 1526–38.

———. 2011. Shapes of Tradition. *Cite* 87 (Fall 2011): 20–23.

———. 2012. Legends of Hurricane Katrina: The Right to Be Wrong, Survivor-to-Survivor Storytelling, and Healing. *Journal of American Folklore* 125 (2012): 139–76.

Lindahl, Carl, Jenna Baddeley, Sue Nash, Shari Smothers, Nicole Eugene, and Victoria McFadden. Archiving the Voices and Needs of Katrina's Children: The Uses and Importance of Stories Narrated Survivor-to-Survivor. In American Bar Association, *Children, Law, and Disasters: What We Have Learned from Katrina and the Hurricanes of 2005* (Chicago: ABA Center on Children and the Law and University of Houston, 2009): 61–111.

NPR. 2006a. *Talk of the Nation:* Can Sharing Stories Help People Heal from Tragedy? National Public Radio broadcast featuring contributions from Pat Jasper, Carl Lindahl, Glenda Jones Harris, and Shari Smothers. August 22. http://www.npr.org/ templates/story/story.php?storyId=5691131. Accessed January 15, 2012.

———. 2006b. *All Things Considered:* Oral Histories Show Generosity in Evacuees. National Public Radio Program narrated by Johnna Reiss and featuring the recorded voices of Angela Trahan and Vincent Trotter. August 25. http://www.npr.org/ templates/story/story.php?storyId=5711527. Accessed January 12, 2012.

Radcliffe, Jennifer. 2009. UH Study Finds No Katrina Effect on Grades. *Houston Chronicle.* September 12. Retrieved December 15, 2011.

Raphael, Beverley, et al. 2000. *Disaster Mental Health Response Handbook: An Educational Resource for Mental Health Professionals Involved in Disaster Management.* North Sydney, New South Wales, Australia: NSW Health.

Smith, Carl S. 1995. *Urban Disorder and the Shape of Belief: The Great Chicago Fire, the Haymarket Bomb, and the Model Town of Pullman.* Chicago: University of Chicago Press.

Solnit, Rebecca. 2009. *A Paradise Built in Hell: The Extraordinary Communities That Arise in Disaster.* New York: Viking.

———. 2010. Reconstructing the Story of the Storm: Hurricane Katrina at Five. *The Nation.* September 13. Retrieved from the Internet, December 11, 2011, at http://www.thenation.com/article/154168/reconstructing- story-storm-hurricane-katrina-five. Accessed January 13, 2012.

Surviving Katrina and Rita in Houston. 2012. Project Web site. http://www.surviving katrinaandrita.dgs-sites.com/. Accessed January 15, 3012.

Thevenot, Brian. 2006. Myth-Making in New Orleans. *American Journalism Review*, December/January. http://www.ajr.org/article.asp?id=3998. Accessed December 15, 2011.

Thevenot, Brian, and Gordon Russell. 2005. Rape. Murder. Gunfights. *Times-Picayune*, September 26, 2005. http://www.pulitzer.org/archives/7087. Accessed December 15, 2011.

Trotter, Vincent. 2006. Interview, recorded by Charles Henry Rowell. *Callaloo* 29 (4): 1334—43.

Vollen, Lola, and Chris Ying. 2008. *Voices from the Storm: The People of New Orleans on Hurricane Katrina and Its Aftermath.* San Francisco: McSweeney's Books.

Wilson, A. N. 1980. *A Life of Sir Walter Scott: The Laird of Abbotsford.* Paperback edition. London: Mandarin.

Contributors

Barry Jean Ancelet is the Granger and Debaillon/Board of Regents Endowed Professor in Francophone Studies and Folklore at University of Louisiana at Lafayette. He has published articles and books on various aspects of Louisiana's Cajun and Creole cultures and languages, including *Cajun and Creole Music Makers, Cajun Country, Cajun Music: Origins and Development,* and *Cajun and Creole Folktales.* He has also contributed to numerous documentary films, including *Against the Tide.* He is a Fellow of the American Folklore Society and the 2009 Louisiana Humanist of the Year.

Mike Davis, a contributing editor for *The Nation*, teaches in the creative writing program at the University of California, Riverside. He is the author of many books, including *Prisoners of the American Dream, City of Quartz, Ecology of Fears,* and *Planet of Slums.*

Jon Griffin Donlon and **Jocelyn H. Donlon** left Louisiana in the 1980s to complete their doctoral work. They later returned home for teaching and research. In 2001, Donlon and Donlon established their consulting business in Baton Rouge, specializing in cultural interpretation. Currently, the

Donlons divide their time between Japan and the United States. Jocelyn's book, *Swinging in Place: Porch Life in Southern Culture*, was published by the University of North Carolina Press in the fall of 2001. Jon publishes regularly on leisure, travel, and tourism.

Anthony Fontenot, a New Orleans native, is pursuing a Ph.D. in architecture at Princeton University. He has written on contemporary conditions in Berlin, Beirut, Kabul, and New Orleans.

Ernest J. Gaines is Writer-in-Residence Emeritus at University of Louisiana at Lafayette. He is the author of nine books of fiction, including *The Autobiography of Miss Jane Pittman*, *A Gathering of Old Men*, and *A Lesson before Dying* (winner of the National Book Critics Circle Award). He is a MacArthur Fellow and a Chevalier of the Order of Arts and Letters in France. He and his wife, Dianne Saulney Gaines, live in Oscar, Louisiana.

Marcia Gaudet is Professor Emerita in English at University of Louisiana at Lafayette. Her book *Carville: Remembering Leprosy in America* was awarded the 2005 Chicago Folklore Prize. Her books include *Tales from the Levee* (1984) and *Mardi Gras, Gumbo and Zydeco* (2003). She has also published widely on Ernest J. Gaines, including *Porch Talk with Ernest Gaines* (1990) and *This Louisiana Thing That Drives Me: The Legacy of Ernest J. Gaines* (2009). She is a Fellow of the American Folklore Society.

Carl Lindahl is Martha Gano Houstoun Research Professor of English at University of Houston. He is a Fellow of the American Folklore Society, a Fulbright Distinguished Scholar, and a Folklore Fellow of the Finnish Academy of Sciences. His book *Swapping Stories: Folktales from Louisiana* (1997) was named the Louisiana Humanities Book of the Year by the Louisiana Endowment for the Humanities. Among his other books are *Cajun Mardi Gras Masks* (1997) and *American Folktales from the Collections of the Library of Congress* (2004). In 2005 he cofounded Surviving Katrina and Rita in Houston, the world's first project in which disaster survivors have taken the lead in documenting fellow survivors' experience of disaster.

Dave Spizale is director of KRVS, the NPR radio station at University of Louisiana at Lafayette. He is a native of New Orleans.

Note: Contributors' information for **Robert LeBlanc, François Ancelet**, and **Glen Miguez** is included in the introductions to their pieces. Information is included in Part 2 for all contributors in that section.

Index